AN ENQUIRY INTO THE NATURE OF CERTAIN NINETEENTH CENTURY PAMPHLETS

CONSTABLE'S

Bibliographia Series

Studies in Book History and Book Structure.
Edited by Michael Sadleir

Each book limited to 500 copies.

* *Out of print*

AN ENQUIRY INTO THE NATURE OF CERTAIN NINETEENTH CENTURY PAMPHLETS

by

JOHN CARTER

&

GRAHAM POLLARD

With four plates

London

CONSTABLE & CO LTD

New York

CHARLES SCRIBNER'S SONS

1934

PUBLISHED BY
Constable and Company Limited
LONDON
•
Charles Scribner's Sons
NEW YORK
•
The Macmillan Company
of Canada, Limited
TORONTO

First published in 1934

PRINTED IN GREAT BRITAIN BY R. CLAY & SONS, LIMITED, BUNGAY, SUFFOLK.

"The whole thing proves once more that, easy as it appears to be to fabricate reprints of rare books, it is in actual practice absolutely impossible to do so in such a manner that detection cannot follow the result."

Thomas J. Wise,
Bibliography of Swinburne, I. 93.

CONTENTS

PART I. DEDUCTION

PART II. RECONSTRUCTION

PART III. DOSSIERS

LIST OF PLATES

ACKNOWLEDGMENTS

For the technical analysis of the papers we are indebted to the assistance of Messrs. Cross and Bevan; for information on the historical side of the subject to Dr. C. J. J. Fox and Mr. L. G. S. Hebbs, of that firm, and to Mr. S. E. Fox, of the Technical Section of the Paper Makers' Association of Great Britain and Ireland.

For information and suggestions in matters of typography we are indebted to Mr. Alexander Shanks, of Stevens, Shanks and Sons, Ltd.; to Mr. Cecil Clay and Mr. E. H. Jolin, of Richard Clay and Sons, Ltd.; and in particular to Mr. S. Morison.

For general advice we are indebted to Mr. J. P. R. Lyell, and for sundry criticisms and suggestions to Miss J. E. Norton and Mr. Dennis Proctor.

For the loan of books, the provision of photographs and the answering of specific inquiries we are indebted to Mrs. Flora V. Livingston, of the H. E. Widener Memorial Library, Harvard University; Mr. Herbert Gorfin; Viscount Esher; the Librarians of the John H. Wrenn Library, Austin, Texas, and of the Wellesley College Library, Wellesley, Massachusetts; Mr. W. Turner Berry, of the Typographical Library, St. Bride Foundation, London; the Librarian of the Turnbull Library, Wellington, New Zealand; Mr. F. S. Ferguson; Messrs. Pickering and Chatto; Messrs. Elkin Mathews; and the officials of the

British Museum, the Bodleian Library and the University Library, Cambridge.

Finally, for criticism on a number of points raised in the course of reading the proofs, we are indebted to Mr. Richard Jennings, Mr. Dudley Massey and Mr. John Sparrow.

PART I
DEDUCTION

B

CHAPTER I

THE ORIGIN AND EARLY STAGES OF THE INVESTIGATION

DURING the past few years a vague rumour has been circulating, with a gradually increasing frequency and volume, that the privately printed first edition of Mrs. Browning's "Sonnets from the Portuguese" (*Sonnets by E. B. B.*, Reading, 1847) was not all that it pretended to be. This rumour had never, of course, got into print, and the vast majority of book collectors had no suspicion whatever of the authenticity of this highly prized poetical rarity. But in some circles suspicion definitely existed.

No one could ever offer any satisfactory evidence for it. The suggested grounds were usually quoted at second hand. Nothing had been verified. It was, in fact, extremely vague. Nevertheless, the grounds quoted seemed weighty, if they were true; and the authorities mentioned were people who were known to be usually reliable. Moreover, this book appeared to be connected with certain other pamphlet poems, of similar date, format and bibliographical status, which had a habit of turning up, in well-defined groups, in miscellaneous auction sales and in the catalogues of certain booksellers; always in fine original condition.

There was not much doubt, in fact, that there existed somewhere in the trade a remainder or cache of such pieces, which were being marketed with a discreet regard for the law of supply and demand and for the continued applicability of the words "very rare" to books which in reality did not always deserve that description. Certain sales of fairly recent date came readily to mind,[1] and a comparison of the runs of these pamphlets which occurred in each of them produced a surprisingly—or perhaps not really surprisingly—large number common to them all. It became clear that the cache contained works by Matthew Arnold, George Eliot, the Brownings, William Morris, Swinburne, Ruskin and other collected authors of the Victorian period; and although the Reading *Sonnets* has long been established in a different class, only appearing as a star piece in the sales of important collections, its general similarity to these others in everything except price kept it continually in view. It seemed to the present authors that this whole business called for investigation. Even if the origin of these books were perfectly authentic—and such "remainders," of single items at any rate,[2] have appeared from time to time—it would be useful to know the extent of the cache, so as to adjust one's estimate of the rarity of the books it contained. But, beyond this, the most cursory review of the circumstances was enough to rouse suspicions which only a more detailed inquiry could allay.

At this moment, almost by accident, the course of some entirely independent research into the bibliography of Ruskin gave a more serious turn to our speculations. We found that, as long ago as 1903, two pamphlets by Ruskin, *The Queen's Gardens*, 1864, and *The National Gallery*, 1852, had been examined

[1] For instance, Sotheby, February 17, 1919; Sotheby, February 21, 1922; Hodgson, December 6, 1928; Hodgson, June 20, 1929; Hodgson, April 6, 1930; Hodgson, March 2, 1932.

[2] E.g. *Two Poems* by E. B. and R. Browning, 1854; Tennyson, *A Welcome*, 1863; Cruikshank, *The Artist and the Author*, 1872.

by Cook and Wedderburn, the editors of the standard edition, proved to have been set up from later editions, and roundly denounced as fakes. These authorities also expressed considerable doubts as to the authenticity of *The Scythian Guest*, 1849, and *Leoni*, 1868. Scattered in small-type notes through the different volumes of the thirty-nine comprised in their great edition, these startling conclusions seem to have made no impression at all on the collecting world; probably because the collector's interest in Ruskin had already begun to diminish; and even Mr. Thomas J. Wise, the bibliographer of Ruskin, makes no reference to them under the relevant entries in the catalogue of his great collection.[1]

Now these four pamphlets figured in the group under investigation, and their spuriousness cast a very real suspicion on their companions. Previously the group had merely provoked a vague uneasiness: now, if their common provenance could be traced back beyond the immediate source of supply, if, that is to say, they could be proved to have a common origin, the verdict against some of their number would deepen the suspicion against them all. It was noted above that the auction sales in which sequences of these pamphlets appeared were almost invariably of anonymous consignments, and this promised no information. There was, however, a certain bookseller in the south of London who was known to specialise in just this type of thing, and it had not escaped the notice of the trade, at any rate, that he catalogued various pamphlets in such "mint" condition and with such regularity as indicated some sort of stock of them. The comparison of a file of his catalogues with the list we had provisionally drawn up revealed a very high proportion of common titles—so high that we felt justified in adding to the roster

[1] *Ashley Library Catalogue*, Vol. IV. pp. 179, 181, 182, 185 (1923).

of suspects any of his privately printed or "pre-first" pamphlets which were not already on it.

The next step was obviously to approach the bookseller in question with a request for information. We wanted to know three things: first, whether the list of books we had compiled had the immediately common origin we suspected; second, what that common origin was; third, whether there were any further members of the group. Mr. Herbert Gorfin readily answered our questions, and his interest and willingness to help have been invaluable to us. We were able to establish the common provenance of practically our entire list of suspects; we were able to make substantial additions to the list; best of all, we were promised the co-operation of Mr. Gorfin himself, who had been since 1898 the "wholesale agent" in the marketing, not only of the comparatively small fry, but actually till 1914 of the Reading *Sonnets* itself.

The position, then, was this. We suspected, on the grounds of their market appearance, about forty books, by the following authors: Matthew Arnold, Mrs. Browning, Robert Browning, Charles Dickens, George Eliot, Rudyard Kipling, William Morris, D. G. Rossetti, John Ruskin, R. L. Stevenson, Swinburne, Tennyson and Thackeray. Of these, the two Ruskins mentioned above were already known to be forgeries, while the two further Ruskins and the Reading *Sonnets* were under a more definite suspicion than the rest.

Of this group the Reading *Sonnets* was undoubtedly the star piece. It was the most important, both as literature and as a human document of wide sentimental appeal: it was by far the highest priced: and it was the most amply and authoritatively documented.

To establish the authenticity or otherwise of this book was therefore our first task; and on the result of this investigation depended our attitude to the others. For in the case of a book of such importance it was clearly undesirable to arouse publicly suspicions which we could not substantiate: but it was equally clear that we ought not to denounce any of the group without revealing the other books with which they were so persistently associated. So we began by testing the official story of the origin of the privately printed edition of the *Sonnets from the Portuguese*.

CHAPTER II

THE SONNETS FROM THE PORTUGUESE

MRS. BROWNING'S *Sonnets from the Portuguese* were first published to the world in the second edition of her collected *Poems* (2 volumes, Chapman & Hall, 1850), under the title which was supposed to conceal the intimate nature of the feeling which inspired them. The world, however, did not take long to realise that they were, in fact, the expression of her love for Robert Browning, written during that strange courtship in Wimpole Street which has fascinated so many subsequent writers. It is this intense human interest, as much as, probably more than, the intrinsic poetical value of the *Sonnets*, which has raised them to an eminence in the book-collecting world enjoyed by hardly any other poetry of the Victorian age.

For more than forty years after their publication, the 1850 printing of these *Sonnets* was believed, by those who take account of such things, to be the first edition. In 1894, however, Edmund Gosse told for the first time a story of their original printing, which came as a surprise even to some who had known the Brownings well. The story is now familiar—how the printing of a small private edition of the *Sonnets* had in 1847 been entrusted to the care of Mary Russell Mitford, Mrs. Browning's most intimate friend, while the newly-married pair were living at Pisa. Quite apart from the recording of " a very pretty episode of literary history," Gosse's announcement effectively dethroned the 1850 edition from its rank as the first, and set up in its stead something much more exciting to collectors. This privately printed pamphlet had been born, as it were, with a high "association" interest; its very existence had been previously unknown to the public (except for a bare mention in a note in J. H. Slater's *Early Editions*, published earlier in the same year); and it was from its nature practically certain to be a rarity, even if this was not already assured from the fact of its having eluded notice so completely, so unaccountably long.

The authorities for this story and for the history of the discovery of copies of the book itself are Edmund Gosse,[1] H. Buxton Forman[2] and Thomas J. Wise:[3] all subsequent references, in books of literary history,[4] auction catalogues and the like, derive (with varying degrees of embroidery) from these sources, and so far as we can discover there have been no independent additions whatsoever.

The importance of these accounts is such that no picking of a quotation here and there can do them justice, and we shall therefore cite all the relevant matter in full.

[1] Introduction to an edition of the *Sonnets* published by Dent in Nov. 1894. Neither Buxton Forman nor Mr. Wise, however, refers to this but to the verbatim reprint of it in *Critical Kit-Kats*, London, Heinemann, 1896.

[2] *E. B. Browning and her Scarcer Books*, Privately Printed (Ashley Library), 1896; and included in *Literary Anecdotes of the Nineteenth Century*, vol. 2, edited by Nicoll and Wise, in the same year.

[3] *A Bibliography of Elizabeth Barrett Browning*, Privately Printed, 1918; *A Browning Library*, Privately Printed, 1929.

[4] E.g. *Mary Russell Mitford*, by W. J. Roberts (1913), pp. 373, 374.

EDMUND GOSSE. Critical Kit-Kats. 1896.

p. x, from the Preface:

"What is here found, in matters of fact, regarding the sonnets of his wife and the incidents in the career of Beddoes, comes with the authority and is presented at the desire of Browning."

pp. 1–3, from the article "The Sonnets from the Portuguese."

"It was in the second or 1850 edition of the *Poems in two volumes* that the *Sonnets from the Portuguese* were first given to the public. The circumstances attending their composition have never been clearly related. Mr. Browning, however, eight years before his death, made a statement to a friend, with the understanding that at some future date, after his own decease, the story might be more widely told. The time seems to have arrived when there can be no possible indiscretion in recording a very pretty episode of literary history.

"During the months of their brief courtship, closing, as all the world knows, in the clandestine flight and romantic wedding of September 12th, 1846, neither poet showed any verses to the other. Mr. Browning, in particular, had not the smallest notion that the circumstances of their betrothal had led Miss Barrett into any artistic expression of feeling. As little did he suspect it during their honeymoon in Paris, or during their first crowded weeks in Italy. They settled, at length, in Pisa; and being quitted by Mrs. Jamieson and her niece, in a very calm and happy mood the young couple took up each his or her separate literary work.

"Their custom was, Mr. Browning said, to write alone, and not to show each other what they had written. This was a rule which he sometimes broke through, but she never. He had the habit of working in a downstairs room, where their meals were spread, while Mrs. Browning studied in a room on the floor above. One day, early in 1847, their breakfast being over, Mrs. Browning went upstairs, while her husband stood at the window watching the street till the table should be cleared. He was presently aware of someone behind him, though the servant was gone. It was Mrs. Browning, who held him by the shoulder to prevent his turning to look at her, and at the same time pushed a packet of papers into the pocket of his coat. She told him to read that and to tear it up if he did not like it; and then she fled again to her own room.

"Mr. Browning seated himself at the table and unfolded the parcel. It contained the series of sonnets which have now become so illustrious. As he read, his emotion and delight may be conceived. Before he had finished it was impossible for him to restrain himself, and, regardless of his promise, he rushed upstairs and stormed that guarded citadel. He was early conscious that these were treasures not to be kept from the world; 'I dared not reserve to myself,' he said, 'the finest sonnets written in any language since Shakespeare's.' But Mrs. Browning was very loth indeed to consent to the publication of what had been the very notes and chronicle of her betrothal. At length she was persuaded to permit her friend, Miss Mary Russell Mitford, to whom they had originally been sent in manuscript, to pass them through the press, although she absolutely declined to accede to Miss Mitford's suggestion that they should appear in one of the fashionable annuals of the day. Accordingly, a small volume was printed, entitled

Sonnets / by / E. B. B. / Reading / Not for Publication / 1847, / an octavo of 47 pages.

"When it was determined to publish the sonnets in the volumes of 1850, the question of a title arose," etc. etc.

HARRY BUXTON FORMAN. Elizabeth Barrett Browning and her scarcer books. 1896.

pp. 90–91. After discussing the *Poems* of 1850, he writes:

"those who have 'collected' the volumes merely as containing the first issue of these Sonnets have come under the necessity of reconsidering their case since the discovery of the separate private print of 1847. . . . The private print of these Sonnets is dated between the Moxon period of publication and the Chapman and Hall period, and the typography differs notably from that of Bradbury and Evans, who printed the poetess's work for both houses. The fact that it bears a Reading imprint does not necessarily imply production in Reading, as there is no printer's name, and a Reading stationer, as well as any other, might have employed a London house; but there is something of an indefinable provincial look about the thing, though certainly no reason why the printer need have been ashamed of his handiwork."

pp. 95–97.

"It has long been current that it was not till after this event [the marriage] that Browning knew of the existence of his wife's sonnets to him; and the event took place in December 1846. The bulk of the sonnets must have been written before that time, during the period when most of the writer's life was passed on the sofa from which she indited those faintly-written letters—tiny letters in a tiny hand—so eagerly desired by the autograph collector. Tradition says that one fine day Robert Browning found his wife's sonnets on the domestic table, and then read them for the first time. Tradition has usually pictured the find as a sheaf of manuscript; and tradition may by possibility be right for once; but it seems likelier on the whole that, when she had overcome her timorous delicacy and made up her mind that he should read the sonnets, she would wish him to take a readier impression of their entirety than could be gathered from what has been called her 'fairy' manuscript.[1] Such a desire would account for the existence of the Reading print, and also for its extreme scarcity. But why Reading? It was near Reading that the trusty Mary Russell Mitford lived—'our friend of Three-Mile Cross, who wears her heart upon her sleeve and shakes out its perfumes at every moment.' It is clear that if Browning's bride wished him to read her forty-three exquisite sonnets fluently, at a blow, she would not lay them on the table in manuscript; and she could not get them printed through her father; for she was unforgiven. Who, then, but Miss Mitford would she be likely to ask? And if Miss Mitford were sworn to secrecy, she would keep her oath, even though she did 'wear her heart upon her sleeve.'

"This is scarcely a matter for speculation; for Mr. Edmund Gosse * has given a circumstantial account of the whole transaction, on the authority of an unnamed friend of Browning—an account as of a solemn

* *Critical Kit-Kats* . . . 1896.

[1] It may be observed that the Mrs. George Smith MS. of the *Sonnets*, now in the British Museum, is written in a perfectly clear and fairly large hand.

secret entrusted to that friend on the understanding that it was to be divulged to the world after the poet's death. In that account Browning figures as the prime mover in getting the sonnets into print; and Miss Mitford is roundly credited with the mediumship. It is not expressly stated that Browning told the mysterious friend of Miss Mitford's part in the matter; and there are other friends of the poet to whom that part of the story is new. The fact is that in three charming pages of picturesque writing we get brought together the floating traditions of the episode, and over them is thrown the glamour of the personal acquaintance between Browning and his bright chronicler. Of course Mr. Gosse does not expect all this to be taken too seriously or literally, and it is lawful, seeing that *Critical Kit-Kats* are not history, to lean to the view that Browning first saw the sonnets in print. The point is of considerable interest, and it may be hoped that, if the whole of pages 1–3 of *Critical Kit-Kats* are really intended to rest on the authority of Browning, at least a footnote may be devoted in some future edition [1] to the record of that intention and of the mysterious friend's name."

THOMAS J. WISE. A Bibliography of Elizabeth Barrett Browning. 1918.

pp. 72–75.

"The history of the tiny volume of 1847 has already been so fully told, and the romance attaching to it so deeply appreciated, that it would be superfluous to repeat its story here in any detailed or exhaustive manner. It is sufficient to record that the sonnets were written by Elizabeth Barrett during the period of her courtship by Robert Browning, and were in

[1] *Critical Kit-Kats* was reprinted without alteration in 1902 and 1913.

the main composed while she lay upon her invalid couch in her father's house in Wimpole Street. But not until six months after her wedding-day were they shown to that husband from whose love they had directly sprung. Mr. Gosse * has recorded, upon information imparted to him by Browning eight years before his death, how in the spring of 1847, at Pisa, the bundle of manuscript was slipped by the poetess into her husband's hand. The latter, immediately conscious of their permanent value, 'dared not,' he said, 'reserve to himself the finest sonnets written in any language since Shakespeare's.' Moved by his persuasion Elizabeth consented to their preservation in print. The manuscripts were forwarded to England, and entrusted by the poetess to her nearest friend, Mary Russell Mitford, with instructions to have them reproduced in the form of a private booklet. To have herself caused them to be printed either in London or in Italy would under the circumstances have been impolitic, privacy would have been impossible. Hence the choice of Reading, Miss Mitford's home, as the place of production.

"How many copies of the little book were printed cannot be stated; no record has yet been found. At one time the book was almost unknown, but in 1886 Dr.[1] W. C. Bennett, who had been Miss Mitford's intimate friend, and who possessed a considerable quantity of her letters and other papers, disposed of some ten or twelve copies of the *Sonnets* which he had received from her hands. In one of these copies, evidently the one dedicated by Miss Mitford to her own use, was inserted a MS. of *Future and Past* of which I give a facsimile the precise size of the original. This MS. had been forwarded by Mrs. Browning

* *Critical Kit-Kats*, pp. 1–17.

---

[1] He apparently received the degree of LL.D. from the University of Tusculum in 1869.

to her friend at the time of its composition in 1850, in order that it might be added to the original forty-three and so complete the series. Miss Mitford inserted it in her copy of the booklet, and thus it remained still in her possession when, years afterwards, she gave at his request the MSS. of the remaining forty-three sonnets to Robert Browning. This copy, with the MS. sonnet inserted, I purchased from Dr. Bennett; it is one of my most valued possessions."

Mr. Wise then describes a second copy in his possession.

THOMAS J. WISE. A Browning Library. 1929.

The notes to the item in the Catalogue itself add nothing to the information given in the Bibliography. In the Introduction, however, we read:—

"Somewhere about 1885—the exact date escapes me—I became acquainted with Dr. W. C. Bennett, author of *Songs for Soldiers*, *Songs for Sailors*, *Baby May*, and other verses, and brother of Alderman John Bennett, the watchmaker of Cheapside. He had been a great friend of Mary Russell Mitford, with whom he had carried on a long and intimate correspondence. Curiously enough she confused the identity of the two brothers, as her letter quoted on p. 18 of the present Catalogue reveals. Dr. Bennett, who was an elderly bachelor,[1] and lived in rooms somewhere in Camberwell, told me of his friendship with Miss Mitford, also that he possessed copies of the privately printed *Sonnets* which he had received from

[1] Miss Mitford, in a letter of March 17, 1852, says of Bennett: "He has already four children and may have a dozen more" (*Correspondence with Boner and Ruskin*, ed. Lee, 1914, p. 207). Cf. also Miss Mitford's *Recollections* (1852), Vol. III. pp. 102, 103.

her hands. Ultimately he invited me to his home to inspect these and other literary treasures. Hence one afternoon, after 'Change, I called at the office in Queen Victoria Street where he was employed as an accountant, and accompanied him home to Camberwell. I remember that the meal awaiting us was 'high tea,' and that it consisted of hot buttered toast and sausages. After his landlady had cleared the table, letters and books were brought out, among them the much-longed-for *Sonnets*. One of the copies was in an old and broken half-calf binding, with the edges fortunately left untrimmed. But it had inserted the manuscript of the additional sonnet, *Future and Past*, which had been sent by Mrs. Browning to Miss Mitford to complete the series of forty-four. I bought the tiny booklet for £25, and carried it home rejoicing. I also purchased one of the unbound copies. It forms the nucleus of the matchless 'association volume' described at length on pages 85 to 88 of the present Catalogue. Shortly afterwards Dr. Bennett sold the remaining copies. They were bought by Harry Buxton Forman, Robert Alfred Potts, Sir Edmund Gosse, the Rev. Stopford A. Brooke, John Morgan of Aberdeen, Mr. Walter Brindley Slater, and other friends to whom I hurried the good news. Dr. Bennett received £10 for each. All were uncut and without wrappers, but traces of pale buff paper remained upon the spine of each, and told that the wrappers had once been there. The reason why the wrappers had been removed could not be explained by Dr. Bennett, who assured us that the pamphlets were in this condition when they came to him from Miss Mitford's home at Three-Mile Cross, near Reading. Some years afterwards Sir Edmund Gosse sold his copy for £50. It went, I believe, to Charles B. Foote, of New York. Stopford Brooke also sold his copy to a London bookseller for £40."

Now the story which these combined authorities unfold is at first sight a perfectly likely one. The dates fit, the motives fit, the early obscurity of the book, although not explicitly accounted for, is in keeping with its history. Edmund Gosse knew Browning; Buxton Forman and Wise are highly distinguished names in the world of bibliography. The whole thing, in short, looks perfectly water-tight and it has been accepted by scholars, bibliographers and everyone else these forty-five years, and it may seem ridiculous, even impertinent, to question it.

A second reading, however, and one is conscious of an inconsistency or two, a statement here which perhaps makes an unjustifiable presumption, a question there which has not been asked or answered. It is of small importance that Gosse and Buxton Forman give different dates for the marriage:[1] hardly more important that Gosse says the sonnets "had *originally* been sent in manuscript" to Miss Mitford, whereas Mr. Wise describes the MS. as being forwarded to her only after the decision had been taken to print them. But why should it have been so impossible to have them printed in Italy, on the spot? On the face of it this would seem both more "politic" and more "private" than commissioning some friend like Miss Mitford; and the example of Shelley, Byron and Landor might well have prompted such a course. Again, if the whole affair was so secret, why did Miss Mitford, before she died, only eight years later, give ten or twelve copies to W. C. Bennett? And how did she come to have ten or twelve copies at all?

Then who was "the mysterious friend" (as Buxton Forman calls him) from whom Gosse originally had the story?[2] His identity has never been revealed,

[1] The actual date was December 12, 1846.

[2] Cf. William Sharp's story. See below, p. 33.

but in fact on him alone rests the attribution of the story to Robert Browning himself; he is the sole element of the first hand in the whole business. It is therefore the more unfortunate that in 1918 Mr. Wise, who doubtless could have supplied this information, not only did not do so, but actually, by a slip of the pen, wrote "Mr. Gosse has recorded, upon information *imparted to him by Browning* eight years before his death, how, etc." (italics ours). This has further obscured the question by short-circuiting entirely the most important person in the chain of tradition, and fathering on Gosse statements which he himself related at second hand.

Most peculiar of all, however, is Buxton Forman's thinly veiled scepticism of Gosse's reliability and accuracy. It is clear from his earlier paragraphs that he took the book itself on trust as genuine, and there is no indication of any source of information independent of Gosse and his anonymous informant. His main concern is with his own theory, supported, it must be confessed, on rather unsatisfactory reasoning, that Browning first saw the sonnets not in MS., but in print; and this question need not detain us now. But in his final paragraphs not even his scrupulous politeness can conceal the blunt fact that he regarded Gosse's story of the circumstances under which the book had been produced as very much romanticised.

We have, then, a fairly circumstantial account by Gosse, written in 1894 and based entirely on information from an anonymous source. Buxton Forman is definitely, if pleasantly, sceptical of that source and of some points in the account itself, even though he accepts the book. Mr. Wise, on whom, as the bibliographer of Mrs. Browning, might reasonably be held to devolve the agreeable task of supporting and amplifying so romantic a story, only gives us the details of his own discovery of a cache of the books themselves in 1886, adding nothing to Gosse and ignoring Buxton Forman's criticisms altogether.

Since, therefore, the official story turns out on closer inspection to be not entirely convincing in some respects, it is only fair, to the book and to ourselves, to examine all other likely sources of first-hand information, and also to scrutinise rather more closely the history of the Reading *Sonnets* since 1894; and perhaps the simplest method of doing this will be to propound a series of questions which ought (if all that glisters really is gold) to be readily soluble after a little research in the most obvious places.

These questions fall into two groups; the first deals with the inferences to be drawn from surviving copies of the book itself, the second with the external evidence supplied by references in the correspondence, published or unpublished, of the protagonists in the story and in the works of writers about them or their books.

(1) *Are any copies recorded with presentation inscriptions from the author or her husband?*

The Reading *Sonnets* bears the words "Not for publication" on its title-page. The book was printed for private circulation in the strictest sense of the words. Gosse says that Robert Browning insisted on the printing, rather against his wife's wish: Buxton Forman believed that she had them printed in order that Browning might read them more easily. It would be a natural presumption that copies were never offered for sale, but only given away, and that only to intimate friends. Now it is an axiom of book collecting that surviving copies of a privately printed book exhibit a far higher proportion of presentation copies to the total number recorded, than a book published in the ordinary way. The Brownings were not, as some few collected authors turn out to have been, chary of inscribing copies to their friends: there are plenty of presentation copies of Robert Browning's books about, and examples from Mrs. Browning's pen survive for every one [1] of her books, from the privately printed *Battle of Marathon* (1820) onwards—there were, for instance, no fewer than three presentation copies of her *Essay on Mind* (1826) in the Browning sale of 1913. In the case of the Reading *Sonnets* one might expect, from the nature of its contents and the manner of its printing, that an unusually high percentage of surviving copies would bear inscriptions.

No single copy is recorded with an inscription either from the author or her husband; nor even with an inscription by an original recipient commemorating its gift from one of them.

Moreover, since (according to the official story) Browning was either the prime mover in the printing of the Reading *Sonnets* (Gosse's informant) or the recipient of the first copy (Buxton Forman's theory), it is a very odd thing indeed that he himself should not apparently have preserved a copy of the book at all. Yet there was none in the Browning sale (1913), which contained presentation copies of practically all both authors' works. If he possessed one, where is it? It is surprising that so precious an association volume should have disappeared from sight entirely.

(2) *Are any copies recorded with any contemporary inscriptions, dated marks of ownership, or the like—are there, that is to say, copies with a provenance independent of the Bennett cache?*

If the answer to the preceding question is extraordinary, perhaps even more extraordinary is the fact

[1] The only exception is *The Runaway Slave*, sufficient reason for which is given below, p. 170.

that no single recorded copy contains any contemporary inscription whatever. Owners do not always write their names, or the date of acquisition, in their books, but among twenty or so copies of a book of this date, which one might presume to have been treasured by its original recipients, it would not be unnatural to expect at least thirty or forty per cent. to show some mark of original ownership. It is more than unnatural to find none at all.

Even Mr. Wise's copy, accompanied as it is by a MS. of the extra sonnet and a letter on other matters from Miss Mitford to Bennett, dated 1854, has no inscription in Miss Mitford's hand, either recording her reception of it from Mrs. Browning or presenting it to Bennett. Nor does it apparently bear even Bennett's name or his authentication of its provenance.

The only other copy known which claims any early or independent provenance is the one now in the Wellesley College Library. This belonged in 1897 to W. E. A. Axon, who was at one time secretary of the Manchester Literary Club. Some time between then and 1901 it was purchased from Axon by Mr. Wise on behalf of William Harris Arnold, the well-known American collector. At the Arnold sale in 1901 it was bought by Messrs. Dodd, Mead & Co. (for 440 dollars), who sold it to W. H. Buckler. From the Buckler sale in 1907 it was bought by Professor George Herbert Palmer, who in 1911 presented it to Wellesley.

So much for such of its recent history as can be disinterred from the auction records or supplied by the Wellesley Librarian. The authority for its earlier provenance is provided by the following letter from Arnold to Mr. Dodd, of Dodd, Mead & Co., doubtless written in reply to a request for information after their purchase of it, and now preserved with the copy.

472 *West End Avenue,*
New York, May 16th, 1901.

DEAR MR. DODD—

In a letter from Mr. Thomas J. Wise dated December 8th, 1897, he speaks of an uncut copy of Mrs. Browning's Sonnets . . . "possessed by Mr. Axon. This was given by Miss Mitford (who printed it) to Charles Kingsley." Later Mr. Wise bought the Axon copy for me. When received it was in a black cloth cover which Mr. Axon had put on the book after it came into his possession. The cover was so unsightly that I removed it and had the volume bound at the Club bindery. The copy described in my Catalogue of "Books and Letters" is this Axon copy. When the book was sent to Kingsley a letter from Miss Mitford accompanied it, but unfortunately this letter was no longer in Mr. Axon's possession when I bought the book. I have since made several ineffectual attempts to secure it.

Very truly yours,
W. H. ARNOLD.

It will be seen that the Mitford–Kingsley provenance of this copy rests on Mr. Wise's report of Axon's statement in 1897; the letter which had accompanied the gift having been unfortunately lost. Axon (who died in 1913) did not, apparently, inform Mr. Wise whence he himself had obtained it, or how it passed out of the possession of the Kingsley family, whose more precious books were not dispersed until 1932.[1] In default of this information, the provenance behind 1897 falls to the ground.

There is also inserted in the Wellesley copy an

[1] At the sale of the library of Mrs. St. Leger Harrison (Lucas Malet), Charles Kingsley's daughter.

undated fragment of a letter in Miss Mitford's hand. The significant side of this fragment reads: ". . . afraid I shall mention the book, which I am sure will be beautiful wherever . . . Our kind regards to the father,—Ever, my dear friend, most faithfully yours, M. R. Mitford."

Now this fragment is a curious affair. The Librarian, to whom we are indebted for the transcript of it, informs us that there is no evidence as to who inserted it: but whoever did either thought, or wished the casual reader to think, that it was addressed to Mrs. Browning and referred to the Reading *Sonnets* itself. The first two lines lend themselves to this supposition, and that seems to be the only object in inserting a mere fragment of a letter; a whole one could have been procured without great trouble or expense if its relevance to the book were not in question. But even if the letter is addressed to Mrs. Browning—and there is absolutely no evidence that it is—it cannot belong to the year 1847. The words "Our kind regards to the father" can only refer to the husband, or perhaps to a near relation, of the recipient, and "Pen" Browning was not born until March 1849.

It is therefore clear that whether this letter was addressed to Mrs. Browning or not, it cannot possibly refer to the Reading *Sonnets*; and its relevance to our inquiry is nil.

As for other copies of the book now extant, two lists are given in Appendix I (pp. 363–368, below). The first comprises those seventeen copies which we can locate to-day; the second the nineteen which we cannot. Some of the second list may very possibly be only earlier appearances of copies included in the first, but a good many cannot be, from the dates of occurrence; and if only half of them have an independent existence, however elusive at the moment, the total is considerably above that of any previous census.

The Bennett cache accounts for " ten or twelve." Where, one wonders, did all these other copies come from—all so clean and perfect, none with a pedigree behind the 1890's?

(3) *What is the condition of the traceable surviving copies?*

In Victorian times it was the usual practice (cloth bound books aside) to bind a book of even slight value in full or half leather, particularly if its original covering was a flimsy one; and a pamphlet not thus dignified would usually be put into binders' cloth or bound up with others of its kind. It was also the usual practice of the binders to trim the book's edges. This is not to say that one may not meet with plenty of uncut copies of books of 1847, a fair number in their original boards or wrappers, a few even " stitched, uncut, as issued." Such books, however, occur three or four times in " contemporary half calf, marbled edges " for every copy in original state.

To take a very conservative estimate, therefore, we might allow for perhaps half the recorded copies of the *Sonnets* having escaped the binder's trimming—perhaps, in view of the ten or twelve copies which came from Dr. Bennett, more than half.

Scrutiny of the auction records and previous censuses and inquiry amongst the present owners, disclosed the astonishing fact that not a single copy is recorded as being in anything but a modern binding, not a single copy has its fore or lower edges trimmed. This is not to say that such do not exist; for although every copy described by its owner[1] and every copy listed

[1] Mr. Wise's Mitford–Bennett copy was, we are told, in old half calf (see above, p. 17), the edges being, by a most unusual chance, uncut; but it has been rebound.

in *Book Prices Current*, etc. conforms to this, there are other copies whose existence and location were known at one time or another, but which cannot now be traced. But where information is available, the verdict is unanimous. One of Mr. Wise's copies, one of the copies at Harvard (in the Amy Lowell collection), and two other copies whose present whereabouts are not known to us—these four copies are unbound and show the traces of wrappers mentioned by Mr. Wise [1] as being characteristic of the Bennett copies. All the rest are in modern morocco bindings by Rivière, Zaehnsdorf or the Club Bindery,—" gilt tops, other edges uncut."

This does not prove, of course, that none of these copies were in circulation in 1847, 1857, 1867 or 1877; but their condition does not in any single case provide evidence in their favour. How remarkable this negative evidence is will be appreciated by anyone with the most elementary acquaintance with the average condition ruling for books of this date and format. " Their unanimity," as Mr. Puff remarked on another occasion, " is wonderful."

(4) *What is the relation of the* 1847 *edition to the extant autograph manuscripts ?*

Lot 152 of the Browning sale in 1913 was described in the catalogue as " Auto. MS. of Forty Three Sonnets, the original MS. from which they were printed (probably in 1850) with the printer's marks." And this MS.[2] Mr. Wise says " was a transcript made when the *Poems* of 1850 were being prepared for the

[1] See above, p. 17.

[2] Two other MSS. of the *Sonnets* survive. One, which formed lot 153 at the Browning sale, consisted of twenty-seven sonnets only. " These," says Mr. Wise (*Bibliography*, p. 80), " were all that remained of the original forty-three sent to Reading in 1847, from which the booklet of that date was printed." This lot was bought by Messrs. Sabin, but we have unfortunately been unable to discover its present

press."[1] It is now in the possession of Mrs. Patrick A. Valentine, of Chicago, who has informed[2] us that the actual name of the printer does not appear anywhere on it.[3] Now Sotheby's cataloguer in 1913 must have had some reason for connecting the MS., even "probably," with the 1850 edition (he was aware of the existence of the 1847 edition, as a note to the lot shows), and that it was a good reason may be presumed from Mr. Wise's more positive statement in 1918. If, then, we may accept this for a fact, it seems reasonable to ask, why was there any need for the transcript at all? Why was not the 1850 edition set up from the 1847? A collation of the sequence of texts, 1847, 1850, 1853, 1856, 1890, reveals only five differences between 1847 and 1850: one introduction of a capital letter, three minor changes of punctuation, one restoration of two omitted words (the first *on me* in line 10 of Sonnet xxiv). There seems, therefore, no earthly reason why the 1847 text should not have been used for setting from: the *Sonnets* were now to be published, so that the need for privacy was over; and, with a few trifling exceptions, the text was a clean one. There may be some simple

---

whereabouts. It would be interesting to know the authority for Mr. Wise's positive statement. The other MS. of the complete forty-four sonnets, including *Future and Past*, was presented by R. W. Barrett Browning to Mrs. George Smith, and it is now in the British Museum. A cursory inspection of it suggests that Mr. Wise's estimate of its date and its place in the history of the text (*op. cit.*, p. 81) requires emendation at certain points; but although to a large extent it is a fair copy, several sonnets are heavily and confusingly corrected, and both this and the tightness of the back of the note-book in which it is written seem to show clearly enough that it has never been used for printer's copy. Consequently it has no direct bearing on the present problem.

[1] *Bibliography*, p. 80.

[2] For this courtesy we are indebted to the good offices of Mr. Percy Lawler of the Rosenbach Company.

[3] The printers of the 1850 edition were Bradbury and Evans.

explanation for all this. It would be interesting to know what it is.

(5) *What exactly was Dr. Bennett's qualification for the important position he occupies in the provenance of Mr. Wise's and the other copies which came from him?*

W. C. Bennett was born in 1820 and died on March 4, 1895, just four months after Gosse's announcement of the existence of the *Sonnets* of 1847, ten years before he was publicly credited with having possessed a copy,[1] and twenty-three years before Mr. Wise published the full story of his possession of the cache of copies of the book. A few details of his life and publications, beyond the facts mentioned by Mr. Wise, are found in the *Dictionary of National Biography* (Supplement, I, 168) and in a memoir by Alfred H. Miles in *The Poets and the Poetry of the Century* (1893). The important question, to us, is, how well did he know Miss Mitford? He first met her about 1847, as may be inferred from her letter to Mrs. Partridge at the end of July of that year.[2] He is mentioned on several other occasions in her published correspondence, one of these being the letter to Mrs. Ouvry referred to by Mr. Wise (see above, p. 16), in which she confuses him with his brother[3]: but of the "long and intimate correspondence" between them, no example from her side seems to be preserved in the published collections. Miss Mitford died in 1855. Bennett, then, was a friend of Miss Mitford during the last years of her life: she mentions his name a dozen times in letters to other people: she confuses him with his brother, Sir John Bennett, in 1852.

[1] *Ashley Catalogue* (the original edition), 1905, Vol. I. p. 155.

[2] Chorley (see footnote to p. 30, below), Vol. I. p. 283.

[3] "My friend Mr. Bennett, who besides being a charming poet, is an eminent watchmaker and jeweller." Cf. *Correspondence*, ed. Lee, p. 70 *n.*, for similar confusion in a letter of the same year to Mrs. Hoare.

She seems, however, to have known him well enough to give him ten or twelve copies of a book which was not hers to give; a book of which she had overseen the printing for her most intimate friend under conditions of such sacred secrecy that it escaped any reference in her own or Mrs. Browning's surviving letters, and remained, as far as can be discovered, entirely unknown to the rest of the world for forty years. Dr. Bennett is not recorded to have shown any reluctance in selling every one of these copies in 1886, and to comparative strangers at that.

(6) *Are there references to the book and its printing in the correspondence between Mrs. Browning and Miss Mitford, or elsewhere in Mrs. Browning's published letters?*

In F. G. Kenyon's edition [1] of Mrs. Browning's letters, we find that between December 31, 1843, and October 15, 1844, she refers in no less than seventeen letters to various correspondents to the publication of her *Poems*, issued by Moxon at the beginning of August, 1844. With John Kenyon, with H. S. Boyd, with Mrs. Martin, she discussed the progress and prospects of the book, in varying degrees of detail; and although no letters to Miss Mitford on the obviously enthralling topic are included in this collection, a remark in a letter to Mr. Westwood on June 28, 1844,[2] shows that she was undoubtedly being kept informed. "Miss Mitford," she writes, "says, as you do, that she never heard of so slow-footed a book."

When we turn to the period 1846–7 in search of similar references to the Reading *Sonnets*, it is a very different story. There are five letters to Miss Mit-

[1] Two vols., Smith, Elder, 1897.
[2] *Op. cit.*, Vol. I. p. 176.

ford between December 19, 1846 (just after the marriage), and December 8, 1847: there is no single reference to the *Sonnets*. The editor refers to, and quotes from, Gosse's *Critical Kit-Kats*, adding,[1] "To these sonnets there is, however, no allusion in the letters here published, which say little for some time of her own work." She does, as a matter of fact, refer to *The Runaway Slave* on February 8, 1847:[2] "In the way of writing I have not done much yet—just finished my rough sketch of an anti-slavery ballad"; but the *Sonnets*, of course, had been written before she left London.

It would be a mistake, however, to attach too much importance to the absence of any mention of the *Sonnets* from these letters, for Miss Mitford is not very strongly represented in Kenyon's selection; and when we turn to the other end of the correspondence the evidence is even less substantial. Chorley's collection[3] of Miss Mitford's letters does not contain any to Mrs. Browning, and L'Estrange,[3] though he quotes from nearly sixty to her between 1836 and 1854, many on literary topics and many mentioning her work, includes none for the years 1846 or 1847.

On February 18, 1850, however, Mrs. Browning wrote to Miss Mitford:[4] "Just before I had your letter we sent my new edition to England. I gave much time to the revision . . . the work will include the best poems of the 'Seraphim' volume, strengthened and improved as far as the circumstances admitted of. I had not the heart to leave out the wretched sonnet to yourself, for your dear sake; but I rewrote

[1] *Op. cit.*, Vol. I. p. 316.

[2] *Op. cit.*, Vol. I. p. 320.

[3] *The Life of Mary Russell Mitford, related in a selection of letters to her friends.* Five vols., 1870–72. The first three volumes were edited by A. G. L'Estrange, the last two by H. F. Chorley. Both series are ill arranged, with inadequate table of contents and no index.

[4] Kenyon, I. 436–7.

the latter half of it (for really it wasn't a sonnet at all, and 'Una and her lion' are rococo), and so placed it with my other poems of the same class. *There are some new verses also.*" Now, however offhand she might be about the other new material, is it likely that Mrs. Browning would refer with the casual brevity of the italicised sentence to that sequence of sonnets with whose secret printing she had entrusted Miss Mitford herself, only three years previously? Miss Mitford, the one person whom our authorities mention as having seen the MS., the one person who knew their history and their meaning, the one person whom there was certainly no need to try and put off the scent. *Some new verses also.*

With the exception of this extremely significant passage, it will be observed that letters between Mrs. Browning and Miss Mitford, as given in the pages of Kenyon, Chorley and L'Estrange, are comparatively few for the period which we are examining. The main bulk of the correspondence remains in MS., and Mrs. Browning's half of it is now in the famous collection of Browning material at Wellesley College, Massachusetts. These letters (there are four large volumes of them) came originally from the Browning sale in 1913 (lot 130), and one of their intermediate owners had the curiosity to examine them for reference to the *Sonnets* of 1847. He found none.

As the letters are mostly incompletely dated [1] and there is consequently a possibility of disorder in their arrangement, a really detailed search would involve reading the entire series. But the Wellesley College Librarian, to whose courteous help we are much indebted, writes: "I have gone through the correspondence, 1846–48 inclusive, without finding any

[1] For instance, a letter accompanying a presentation copy of the 1850 edition, dated merely March 22, but mentioning Chapman and Hall as the publishers, was found amongst the letters of 1847.

reference to the privately printed sonnets." Now in view of Mrs. Browning's interest in the format of her books in general, to which the letters about the 1844 volumes (mentioned above) bear witness; and in view of the circumstances under which this book in particular was being printed; one might reasonably expect, not one, but half a dozen letters at least dealing with the production of the *Sonnets*. The original request for Miss Mitford's assistance, the injunctions for secrecy, the discussion of format, the arrangements for dispatch—a hundred details crop up in having a book printed at a distance, as anyone who has undertaken it knows: and both ladies were prolific letter-writers. It is not, admittedly, impossible that all their letters referring to the Reading *Sonnets* should have perished; but seeing what a mass of their correspondence as a whole has been preserved,[1] it would be more than curious if they had. At any rate, no reference to any such letter has been quoted in connection with the book, and the fairly exhaustive inquiry into the printed and MS. collections outlined above has produced nothing but one piece of negative evidence. It seems, therefore, reasonably safe to infer that there are no such references.

(7) *Are there any other contemporary or authoritative statements, by friends of the Brownings or writers about them, bearing on the composition and publication of the Sonnets?*

When we come to examine this source of evidence, we find that there are, in fact, two alternative versions of the circumstances in which the *Sonnets* were first

[1] It is true that Mrs. Browning is known to have destroyed a number of Miss Mitford's letters which contained indiscreet references to mutual acquaintances; but this hardly seems to affect the present question; and we are not aware of any evidence that Miss Mitford destroyed any of Mrs. Browning's letters.

printed. On the one hand we have the positive story of the Reading edition, represented by Gosse, Buxton Forman and Mr. Wise; all depending ultimately on Gosse's anonymous informant. On the other hand we have a small but highly significant body of negative evidence deriving from F. J. Furnivall, Robert Browning and, indirectly, Mrs. Browning herself.

In 1890 William Sharp wrote:[1] "It was here, in Pisa, I have been told on indubitable authority,[2] that Browning first saw in manuscript those *Sonnets from the Portuguese*, which no poet of Portugal had ever written, which no man could have written, which no other woman than his wife could have composed . . . those outpourings of the most sensitive and beautiful nature he had ever met, vials of lovely thought and lovelier emotion, all stored against the coming of a golden day." And so forth. He makes no reference to the Reading edition; but as far as the place where the *Sonnets* were shown to Browning and their form at the time, he agrees with Gosse.

F. J. Furnivall, however, who had known Browning well, made the following comment on Sharp's statement in this passage.[3] "Mrs. Browning's *Sonnets* to her husband. She wrote these in London. One day she timidly hinted to Browning that she'd tried to express her feelings about him. He answered that he didn't think people should wear their hearts on their sleeves for daws to peck at, or something of the kind. This shut her up. When abroad she was one day late in putting on her bonnet to walk with him. He cald to her. Spying about, he saw a tiny

[1] *Life of Browning*, p. 147.

[2] Conceivably identical with Gosse's likewise anonymous source? See above, p. 19.

[3] *Corrections, etc.* (*For Sharp's Life of Browning*, 1890), by F. J. Furnivall, p. 3.

roll of paper on her looking-glass or table, pounst on it, and said, 'What's this?' unrolling it the while. 'Only something I wrote about you, and you frightened me from showing it to you,' said she.* And in her next edition the *Sonnets from the Portuguese* were printed.

* He told me this himself."

Now Furnivall's account, based specifically on Browning's own information, differs substantially from Gosse's as to the circumstances in which Browning first saw the *Sonnets*; and in view of the reason why Mrs. Browning had never shown them to her husband before, here stated with clarity as well as authority,[1] the picture of Browning *finding* them, rather than of her *offering* them, could not fail to impress as being more true to life than Gosse's version, even if it did not come from Browning himself. The fact that Furnivall's final sentence explicitly gives the second edition of the *Poems* as the first printing of the *Sonnets* is, admittedly, in accordance with Gosse's story of the sacred veil thrown by Browning over the whole affair. The rest, however, shows clearly enough that he had made no such secret of the more personal and even delicate details as Gosse was pleased to believe. If he told Furnivall—his friend, his bibliographer, the founder of the Society for the study of his works—so much; more, apparently, than he had ever told Gosse himself; why should he have concealed the comparatively impersonal detail of the original printing of the *Sonnets*?

That must remain, for the moment, a matter of speculation. What is established is that Furnivall, who, if anyone, might be expected to have known of the Reading *Sonnets*, was unaware of its existence as late as 1890. This would be strange enough in itself:

[1] Cf. Browning's own reference to the misunderstanding, quoted below, p. 35.

when we remember Mr. Wise's statement that ten or a dozen copies had been dispersed four years previously among such fellow enthusiasts for the Brownings' works as Buxton Forman, Mr. Wise, and Gosse himself, Furnivall's ignorance becomes even more remarkable.

(8) *Are there any references to, or bearing on, the book in Robert Browning's published correspondence ?*

We have succeeded in discovering only one such reference.[1] It occurs in a letter to Leigh Hunt, written from Bagni di Lucca, and dated Oct. 6, '57. It runs as follows:

"I should like also to tell you that I never suspected the existence of those *Sonnets from the Portuguese* till three years after they were written: they were shown to me at this very place eight years ago, in consequence of some word of mine, just as they had been suppressed thro' some mistaken word:[2] it was I who would not bear that sacrifice and thought of the subterfuge of a name."

The second half of this passage, though not very clearly expressed, agrees perfectly with Furnivall's account of the matter. It supports the theory that Browning himself insisted on their being published in 1850, and accords with the well-known story of the invention of the fictitious title. The first half is, fortunately for our present purpose, free from obscurity of any kind; and it contradicts Gosse flatly on two points. The first, of minor importance, is

[1] *Letters of Robert Browning Collected by Thomas J. Wise*, edited by Thurman L. Hood, London, Murray, 1933, p. 48. The only previous printing of this letter, so far as we can discover, is in Leigh Hunt's *Correspondence*, 1862, Vol. II, pp. 263–8, where the quoted passage was omitted; doubtless owing to respect for Browning's feelings about the "mistaken word," etc., about which he would have been particularly sensitive only a year after his wife's death.

[2] See above, p. 34.

that the *Sonnets* were shown to Browning at Bagni di Lucca, not at Pisa. The second, that they were not shown to him till 1849, two years after they were supposed to have been printed, at his insistence, at Reading. This date is established twice: "three years after they were written" in 1846; and "eight years ago" from the date of the letter, 1857.

"What becomes, then," wrote the reviewer of this book in *The Times Literary Supplement*,[1] "of the charming story, reported by Edmund Gosse . . . ? It is hard to surrender Gosse's story . . . yet it is harder still to question the authority of this letter." It seems to us practically impossible to doubt the accuracy of Browning's recollection, so positively expressed only eight years after. Instances of his forgetfulness of details in later life have been quoted, but an event of such moment as his first sight of the *Sonnets* would surely have been fixed indelibly in his mind. Moreover, the letter in which this passage occurs was a joint one from himself and his wife: she added a considerable contribution at the end, and, reading what he had written, would unquestionably have drawn attention to any error in his statement about the *Sonnets*, if error there had been.

The time and place, then, are attested doubly and explicitly by Browning, implicitly by his wife: and it therefore follows that Gosse's story, so circumstantially set in Pisa in the spring of 1847, so convincingly

[1] September 28, 1933. The reviewer also observed that it is "hard to imagine how any 'mistaken word' can have caused this suppression of the manuscript for three years!" Furnivall's report of Browning's own account of this, however, gives a satisfactory explanation of what does at first sight seem a strange proceeding. Mrs. Browning's extreme sensitiveness in such matters is well known, and that Browning also felt it to be an intensely personal and delicate point is very clear from his allusive manner in this letter. The passage of time, however, naturally allowed him to recall the circumstances without embarrassment when telling Furnivall the story.

garnished with characteristic details, must be wholly fictitious. His anonymous informant, who is the sole ultimate source for it, is discredited on the most incontrovertible authority possible; and with that story goes the Reading *Sonnets* as officially explained. But if the *Sonnets* were not printed in 1847—and it is clear from Browning's statement that they were not—when was this "Reading" edition printed? Since in its priority to 1850 lies its only *raison d'être*, why was it printed at all? If it is not what it has always been accepted as being, what is it? And what was the origin, and, even more significant, what was the purpose, of the story told to Gosse by his mysterious friend? This story is indissolubly linked with the book; and since under examination the story proves to be fictitious, the duty of investigating the book takes on an added urgency.

CHAPTER III

THE NEED FOR POSITIVE EVIDENCE

THE cumulative effect of the negative evidence relating to the Reading *Sonnets*, arrayed in the last chapter, seemed to us overwhelming. The entire absence of any particle of evidence in its favour was so remarkable as to constitute strong and immediate grounds for suspicion, and the final blow delivered by Browning's statement to Leigh Hunt, which annihilated the official story completely, reduced us to the examination of the book merely as a book, to be considered entirely apart from the now recognisably fictitious circumstances surrounding its supposed origin. If it was not what it pretended to be, what was it?

At this point, then, nothing further could be done without access to a copy of the volume itself for the purpose of applying physical tests; and it will be seen, from a glance at the census of recorded copies given in Appendix I, that there are only two or three copies in England and none of these is in public ownership. Nearly all the known copies are in America; and, although we had used in checking the collation of the text a copy of the photographic facsimile prepared by Mr. W. A. Clark in 1927, this was not sufficiently clear for the delicate business of tracing and identifying the type; and it was obviously of no use for an analysis of the paper.

We were rescued from this impasse by Mr. Stanley Morison, who was then (January, 1933) about to sail for the United States. When in New York he was kind enough to examine a copy of the Reading *Sonnets*, and on his return he explained to us which were the significant characteristics of the type in which it was printed. It is not difficult to recognise the identity of one part of one letter in different pages of text; but it requires a very considerable knowledge to be able to indicate which part of which letter will be significant in dating and identifying the particular fount of type in which it occurs. This initial and indispensable service we owe to Mr. Morison, for he suggested the importance of the "broken-backed f" and the "tilting question mark" which we shall explain at length in our typographical analysis in Chapter V.

Reviewing, then, the various methods of testing the *bona fides* of the group as a whole—including such as had already been employed on the Reading *Sonnets*—we found that the principal lines of approach resolved themselves into five. At the risk of some repetition it may be well to summarise them here.

(i) *The Paper*.

It is possible, if you put a piece of paper under a microscope, to determine the raw materials of which it is composed. It is also possible to date with some approach to accuracy (in spite of the absence of any standard work on the subject) the introduction of the various basic raw materials into the manufacture of paper. If, therefore, you find a discrepancy between the earliest possible date at which the paper of any book could have been manufactured and the date which is printed on the title-page, it is sufficiently obvious that the latter is false; and a falsely dated book, failing some satisfactory explanation, is *ipso facto* fraudulent.

(ii) *The Typography*.

If you can identify the type in which a book is

printed, it is sometimes possible by an exhaustive search through its founder's series of specimen books to discover the date at which it was first cast. It follows, then, that in some cases the same discrepancy as in the paper test may be revealed; and the same conclusion will result.

(iii) *The Collation of the Text.*

Even without the example of Cook and Wedderburn's crushing use of this method in the exposure of *The Queen's Gardens*, 1864 (set up from the revised text of 1871) and *The National Gallery*, 1852 (set up from the revised text of 1880), it was clear that collation might yield most damning results. But it was equally clear that the danger of setting up from a demonstrably later text would be fairly obvious even to a moderately intelligent fabricator of putative first editions; consequently the cases proved by this method, however effective, would be few.

(iv) *Negative evidence of the Author, Publisher or Printer.*

At first sight an author's evidence about his own work appears to be of the first importance, and it is clear that a reference in his—or anyone else's—contemporary correspondence would authenticate a book beyond all question. But absence from his correspondence does not prove that the author did not authorise it; and, even if in later life he denied having done so, it is still possible to question the accuracy of his recollection. Even without this the book may still be a correctly dated piracy, which is not the same as a forgery. The evidence of the printer or publisher may be of greater importance, because his name, unlike the author's, implies actual contact with the book itself. But few printers or publishers have preserved their records in such completeness that they can definitely affirm whether they did or did not produce any particular pamphlet. Nevertheless, the precise form of the name or the address given in the imprint may be still more significant, because no book can have been printed on premises which the printer did not then occupy, or published by a firm that was already extinct.

(v) *The Provenance and Condition of surviving Copies.*

One expects to find a fairly large proportion of books of this date in contemporary binding and with edges trimmed. One also expects, from experience of privately printed or semi-privately issued books such as all these are, a much higher proportion of presentation copies than usual. The original owner, too, often writes his name in a book. It was therefore imperative to search the auction records and other sources for copies exhibiting one or other of these hall-marks of authenticity, and, in any case where they were conspicuously absent, to make an exhaustive survey of all recorded copies.

It will be observed that of these five methods only the first three are positive. The others are negative. Now to establish a chain of negative evidence against any one of these books would be a useful preliminary measure, and it must form part of any finally completed case. But even though the cumulative effect of such evidence sometimes seems overwhelming—witness the examination of the Reading *Sonnets* in Chapter II—it suffers from the defects of all circumstantial evidence. Though productive of profound suspicion, it is never absolutely conclusive. Our object must be proof, positive and incontrovertible; and this can only be established by means of methods (i), (ii), and (iii).

CHAPTER IV

THE ANALYSIS OF THE PAPER

IN the latter part of the nineteenth century a number of new raw materials were introduced into the manufacture of paper; and, although these materials cannot be distinguished in the paper by the naked eye, the fibres of which they are composed are readily identified under the microscope. This provides a possible test of date which has not hitherto been applied to bibliographical purposes. These changes were thus summarised by an expert committee in 1898:

> "... A quantity of new fibrous raw materials have been introduced, and have taken their places in due course as indispensable staples. The more important of these, so far as concerns this country, may be noted in chronological order, thus: esparto in the period 1860–70; 'mechanical wood' or ground wood pulp in 1870–80; the wood celluloses in the period 1880–90."[1]

While this indicates the broad features of the changes, it is neither sufficiently precise nor sufficiently authoritative to justify the definite assertion that a particular paper could not have been used at a particular date. It is unfortunate that there is no really exhaustive history of the paper trade, so that it becomes necessary for us to give a somewhat detailed account of those changes upon which our deductions rest. It will not

[1] *Report of the Committee on the Deterioration of Paper.* Society for the Encouragement of Arts, Manufactures and Commerce. London, 1898, p. 1.

be sufficient to cite the dates on which the various patents were registered, because no paper at all was produced under many of them; and in other cases there was a lapse of several years between successful laboratory experiment and successful commercial production.

The original raw material used for the manufacture of paper was rags; until 1861 this was the only material used for books, and it is still exclusively used for the more expensive grades. But the supply of rags which was sufficient at the beginning of the nineteenth century did not expand with the increasing demand for paper. The discrepancy had become so serious by 1854 that *The Times* offered a premium of £1000 for the discovery of an efficient substitute: this premium was still unawarded in 1861. The scarcity of rags led to experiments in the use of straw by William Thomas at Maidstone in 1851 [1]; and, although there had been previous attempts, notably that of Matthias Koops at Neckinger Mill in 1799, Thomas was the first to market straw paper for any continuous period. The amount of straw paper made in 1860 was less than one-tenth of the total output of paper in Great Britain [2]; and what was manufactured was only used for straw boards, wrapping paper or newsprint.[3] The penny papers, such as *The Morning Star* and *The Manchester Examiner and Times*, were printed on a paper made from straw mixed with rags.[4] But even this paper was not considered satisfactory; F. A. Magnay, of Taverham Mills near Norwich, said in his evidence, "We can readily tell straw paper; it is very brittle, and very full of shoaves or specks." [5] Benjamin Brown, of Roughway Mills near Tonbridge, was asked

[1] *Report of the Select Committee of the House of Commons* (*Export Duties on Rags*) *ordered to be printed* 25 *July*, 1861, 995–6, 1024–26.

[2] *Op. cit.*, 1085–6.

[3] *Op. cit.*, 1258.

[4] *Op. cit.*, 272, 971.

[5] *Op. cit.*, 272.

in reference to a paper made from a mixture of straw and rags: "It could not be used for the paper of any book of which the copyright was of value, or the appearance of the book was of importance to the publisher?" To which he replied: "I should say certainly not."[1]

The first successful substitute to be found for rags was esparto grass, which in fibrous structure is not unlike straw. It is a long, coarse grass which grows in Spain and the north of Africa. Together with numerous other substances ranging from willow bark to nettles, it had been the subject of laboratory experiment since 1854. One of the principal inquiries of the Select Committee, whose report we have just quoted, was the possibility of finding an effective substitute for rags as a raw material for paper. Nearly every witness was questioned on this point, and an account is given of their various experiments. Among them were those of Thomas Routledge of Eynsham Mills near Oxford, who was the first papermaker to produce an efficient printing paper from esparto.[2] But it is evident that at this date, July, 1861, his experiments had only just been successful[3]; and he can hardly have put his new esparto paper on the market before the end of that year.

Routledge's process[4] consisted in boiling the esparto in a metal digester with a solution of caustic soda; and the cost of this process was materially reduced by the fall in the price of this chemical which followed the introduction of Weldon's new process for its manufacture about this date. The repeal of the Paper Duties in 1861 and the intensified scarcity of rags during the cotton famine caused by the American

[1] *Op. cit.*, 1477. [2] *Op. cit.*, 2130–36.

[3] His decisive patent was applied for on June 17, 1861 (No. 1548).

[4] English Patents 1856, No. 1816; 1860, No. 274; and the third just cited.

Civil War accelerated the adoption of esparto grass in the paper mills throughout Great Britain. The first to copy Routledge was Alexander Pirrie of Aberdeen, and many others soon followed his example. The importation of esparto, which had been one thousand tons in 1862, rose to seven thousand in the next year, and in 1865 amounted to nearly fifty thousand tons: by 1884 it was 184,682 tons, and about a quarter of a million tons are now imported annually.[1]

The next material to be introduced into the manufacture of paper, and the one that is in most general use to-day, was wood pulp. There are two methods of pulping the wood; the first, which is carried out by grinding, produces what is called "mechanical wood." As only one of the books under consideration [2] contains mechanical wood, and even then mixed with chemical wood, the process needs no further discussion. In the second method chemicals are used to disintegrate the wood and remove the superfluous matter from the cellulose which forms the pulp used in papermaking. Chemical wood is manufactured by three main processes; the soda or alkali process, the sulphite or acid process and the sulphate process. We can dismiss the sulphate process at once because it was only used to produce wrapping papers; but the other two require more detailed consideration.

The soda process was first introduced into England at Cone Mills near Lydney in Gloucestershire, where Houghton had hit on the idea by accident as early as 1856; [3] but commercial production was not attempted until ten years later, and appears to have been aban-

[1] *Forestry and Forest Products*, ed. J. H. Rattray, Edinburgh, 1885, p. 447: A. D. Spicer, *The Paper Trade*, 1907, pp. 16, 37–38 and Appendix I.

[2] Edmund Yates, *Mr. Thackeray, Mr. Yates and The Garrick Club*, 1859. Edition B, Issue Y. See p. 359.

[3] W. J. Stonhill, *The History of Wood Paper*, p. 444, in Rattray, *op. cit.*

doned after eighteen months.[1] It was not found possible at this date to construct digesters which did not lose as much as a third to a quarter of all boiling liquors; this caused the pulp to blacken, and ruined the whole charge.[2] In 1869 the soda process was taken up by Sinclair, who published an estimate in which he showed that it would be possible to make an annual profit of £13,000 on an outlay of £5350.[3] Although his figures were fantastic, he was able to produce a certain amount of paper, but the cost of bleaching it was prohibitive.[4] Even to-day, when the soda process has been much improved, the light brown colour of its pulp is in marked contrast to the creamy white of that produced by the sulphite process. Houghton's soda pulp must have needed a great deal of bleaching; and there can be no real doubt that it was only used for wrapping papers.[5] The process was not sufficiently improved to produce printing papers until after the success of the sulphite method in the early eighteen-eighties.

This sulphite or acid process was invented by Benjamin Chew Tilghmann,[6] and was first used commercially at Manayunk near Philadelphia about 1866. But Tilghmann also had trouble with his digesters, and before he had solved the problem he turned his attention to a sandblast process for toolmaking, out of which he made a fortune. The first successful exponent of the acid process was Carl Daniel Ekman, who set up a paper-mill at Bergvik in Sweden on capital supplied

[1] Erik Hagglund, *Natronzellstoff*, pp. 2, 3 in Emil Heuser *Technik und Praxis der Papierfabrikation*, Band ii, Teil 2, Berlin, 1926.

[2] C. T. Davis, *The Manufacture of Paper*, Philadelphia, 1886, p. 253.

[3] Stonhill, *loc. cit.*, p. 458.

[4] Hagglund, *loc. cit.*, p. 4.

[5] Cf. *The Stationer's Handbook*, 11th ed., 1875, p. 17; also C. F. Cross and E. J. Bevan on Dahl's process, p. 504 in Rattray, *op. cit.*

[6] English Patents, No. 2924, Nov. 9, 1866, and No. 385, Feb. 11, 1867.

by Thompson, Bonar & Co. of Dundee. The erection of this mill was begun in 1872, but it did not start production until 1874; in that year its output of pulp was 485 tons, which had risen by 1876 to over a thousand.[1] In 1883, with the backing of the same firm, Ekman started in England the Ekman Pulp and Paper Co., Ltd. While litigation about the patent was pending, this company worked the acid process secretly with one machine at Ilford Mills; but in 1886 they set up a mill with two machines at Northfleet near Gravesend in Kent.[2] The acid or sulphite process consisted in boiling the wood under pressure with magnesium bisulphite; it was carried out at much lower temperatures than the soda process, and thereby avoided trouble with the digesters; furthermore, its product was much more easily bleached.[3] Ekman was closely followed by Macdougall and Partington of Glossop with a somewhat similar process using calcium bisulphite. It was Ekman who really introduced wood-pulp into England as the staple raw material for the manufacture of paper, and the success of his product was rapid. The editor of *The Paper Trades Review* wrote of it in 1884: "The wholesale stationers are familiar with very good writing and printing papers, resembling in appearance rag papers, at nearly half their price, being sold at 4½*d*. per pound."[4] Thenceforward the proportion of wood-pulp paper used for printing has rapidly increased.

Papermaking in the United States followed a different course. The first Congress which had power

[1] See the graph of production at Bergvik given by R. Dieckmann in Ing. Heuser-Darmstadt, *Technik und Praxis der Papierfabrikation*, Band ii, Teil i, *Sulfitzellstoff*, Berlin, 1924, p. 4.

[2] *The Paper Trades Directory*, 1884 and 1887: the issues for 1883 and 1886 do not mention the Ekman concern at these mills.

[3] English Patent No. 3062, July 13, 1881. The litigation was to decide if this infringed Tilghmann's patents.

[4] W. J. Stonhill in Rattray, *op. cit.*, p. 465.

to do so imposed in 1789 an import duty of 7½ per cent. on all paper.[1] In 1832 the duty on sized paper was 17 cents a pound, and on unsized ten cents a pound. This was equivalent to 130 per cent. on the price, and acted as a total prohibition of the import of paper.[2] Thus strongly protected, the American paper industry in the eighteen-fifties met the growing scarcity of rags by turning to the native supplies of soft wood rather than by importing esparto grass from the Mediterranean. Watt and Burgess, after a few tentative experiments with the soda process in England, had emigrated to America about 1854; and the first mill to work under their patents was erected in 1860 by W. W. Harding and Sons at Royer's Ford in Pennsylvania; a larger plant was set up by the same firm five years later at Manayunk near Philadelphia.[3] America developed the soda process earlier, and used—still does use—a much heavier bleach than European papermakers. Esparto was not introduced into their paper-mills until 1907.[4]

These various facts indicate two possible tests; any paper containing esparto must have been made after 1861, and any printing paper containing chemical

[1] L. H. Weeks, *A History of Papermaking in U.S.A.*, 1917, p. 102.

[2] *Ib.*, p. 195.

[3] *Ib.*, pp. 228–30.

[4] *U.S.A. House of Representatives. House Documents. 60th Congress, 2nd Session. Document no.* 1502. *Pulp and Paper Hearings*, Vol. IV. p. 2684; Vol. V. p. 3112. Washington, 1908. Interesting confirmation comes from the *News Bulletin* of the Paper Section of the National Bureau of Standards, U.S.A., for July, 1933. "The dates of the specimens examined, numbering over 200 books and 100 newspapers, cover quite thoroughly the various periods of the transitions in the usage of fibers. . . . Rag fibers were found exclusively until 1867, when the first straw fibers were found, followed by ground wood in 1869 and chemical wood in 1870. . . . The first of the latter type (*i.e.* composed exclusively of chemical wood fiber) was found in a book published in 1889."

wood after 1874. But neither test is quite simple in its application. The microscopic differentiation between esparto and straw is a matter of some complexity, as their fibres are very similar. But esparto has a number of minute hairs growing on the inner side of the leaf, and these appear under the microscope as comma or thorn-shaped cells. "The presence of these hairs," say Messrs. Cross and Bevan in the last edition of their authoritative work on papermaking, "may be taken as conclusive evidence of the presence of esparto."[1] These cells are not found in straw; and we have taken especial care not to characterise any fibre as esparto in which these cells have not been identified. The chemical wood test requires more elaborate qualification, though it holds good for any mixture except one in which esparto is found with minute traces of chemical wood. There are three possible explanations of this combination, and two of them are inconsistent with the 1874 date. If any herbaceous plants had happened to be gathered with the esparto and subjected to the processes of manufacture into paper, their fibres would appear under the microscope as those of chemical wood. It would also have been possible at any time after the installation of esparto cookers for a papermaker deliberately to mix a small proportion of pulverised wood or sawdust with his esparto. It is likely that in the late 'seventies this

[1] It may be of use to quote the whole passage:—"Another characteristic of esparto pulp is the presence of a number of fine hairs which line the inner surface of the leaf (*e*, fig. 10), some of which invariably survive the boiling and washing processes, although the greater portion passes away through the wirecloth of the washing engines. The presence of these hairs may be taken as conclusive evidence of the presence of esparto.

"*Straw.*—Straw pulp resembles esparto pulp in its microscopical features. The hairs above alluded to are, however, absent." C. F. Cross and E. J. Bevan, *A Text-book of Papermaking*, 5th ed., 1920, p. 412.

was actually done with the object of increasing the tensile strength of the paper. But there is no evidence that the practice was introduced before 1870, or that it was ever widespread. By far the most probable explanation, therefore, of the presence of minute traces of chemical wood in an esparto paper is that it was made in a mill which had previously been using wood pulp. In most paper-mills the drainage or backwater from the paper machine is re-used in furnishing the beaters. Under these conditions the next lot of paper made will show traces of the content of the previous lot; so that you would naturally expect to find—and in fact do find—traces of chemical wood in most esparto papers made after the middle 'eighties. But although this is the most likely explanation of such papers, the two other possibilities mentioned above prohibit us from basing any final deduction upon minute traces of chemical wood.

We can now proceed to divide our suspected books into three groups according to the analysis of the fibres which their papers contain. Those containing esparto form the first group; the esparto papers with minute traces of chemical wood form the second; and those with a substantial amount of chemical wood form the third. With two exceptions [1] all of them are printed on cream-wove papers; and it is remarkable that only one [2] of the papers is pure rag, which would have been the only possible content of a printing paper made before 1861.[3] We have, therefore, in the follow-

[1] W. Morris, *Two Sides of the River*, 1876 (cream laid); and D. G. Rossetti, *Verses*, 1881 (Van Gelder handmade).

[2] Wordsworth, *To the Queen*, 1846.

[3] As an additional check we analysed the specimen (no. 168) most closely resembling these papers in Richard Herring's *A Practical Guide to the Varieties and Relative Values of Paper*, 1860. This book gives specimens numbered up to 637 of the main grades in use from tissue-paper to millboard, and was, according to the preface, designed

ing list of the first group drawn a line at the year 1861, because no paper containing esparto could have been made before that date.

Group I: *Pamphlets containing Esparto.*

Lord Tennyson	Morte D'Arthur	1842	Esparto and chemical wood
W. M. Thackeray	An Interesting Event	1849	Esparto
J. Ruskin	The Scythian Guest	1849	Esparto, trace of rag
J. Ruskin	The National Gallery	1852	Esparto and rag
C. Dickens	To be Read at Dusk	1852	Esparto and straw
R. Browning	Cleon	1855	Esparto, trace of chemical wood
R. Browning	The Statue and the Bust	1855	Esparto, trace of chemical wood
J. Ruskin	Catalogue of Turner Sketches in the National Gallery [1]	1857	Esparto, straw and trace of chemical wood
D. G. Rossetti	Sister Helen	1857	Esparto, trace of rag
W. Morris	Sir Galahad [2]	1858	Esparto, trace of rag
1861 - - - - - - - - -	- - - - - - - - -	- - -	1861
J. Ruskin	The Queen's Gardens	1864	Esparto, trace of chemical wood
A. C. Swinburne	Dead Love [3]	1864	Esparto, trace of chemical wood
R. Browning	Gold Hair	1864	Esparto, trace of rag
A. C. Swinburne	Laus Veneris	1866	Esparto
A. C. Swinburne	Cleopatra	1866	Esparto and rag
A. C. Swinburne	Dolores	1867	Esparto, straw and trace of chemical wood
M. Arnold	St. Brandan	1867	Esparto and rag

as the papermaker's equivalent of *The London Catalogue of Books*. This specimen contained nothing but rag; and we found a similar result in Tennyson's *A Welcome*, 1863.

[1] Edition B, see p. 230.

[2] First Issue, see p. 207.

[3] The original edition, see p. 269.

Group I—*continued.*

J. Ruskin	Leoni	1868	Esparto, rag and chemical wood
G. Eliot	Agatha [1]	1869	Esparto, trace of chemical wood
G. Eliot	Brother and Sister	1869	Esparto, small quantity of chemical wood
J. Ruskin	The Future of England	1870	Esparto and chemical wood
J. Ruskin	Samuel Prout	1870	Esparto, trace of rag
J. Ruskin	The Nature and Authority of Miracle	1873	Esparto, trace of chemical wood
R. L. Stevenson	On the Thermal Influence of Forests	1873	Esparto, chemical wood and rag
A. C. Swinburne	The Devil's Due	1875	Esparto, trace of chemical wood
W. Morris	Hapless Love	1876	Esparto
M. Arnold	Geist's Grave	1881	Esparto

The presence of esparto in the papers of pamphlets printed after 1861 is not unnatural; but every one of the ten pamphlets above the line in this list is printed on a paper which *must* have been made from three to nineteen years later than the date of printing given on its title-page; so that there is no doubt whatever that all ten are forgeries.

The case of Tennyson's *Lucretius* must be taken separately, because it purports to have been printed in the United States. Its title-page reads: "Cambridge, Mass. *Printed for Private Circulation*, 1868." But its paper is made of esparto with a trace of chemical wood; and as esparto was not introduced into American papermaking until some forty years later, it is clear that this too is a forgery. Actually its typography [2] shows it to have an English origin, and its paper content puts it into our second group, which consists of those pamphlets with esparto papers which show minute traces of chemical wood.

[1] The second edition, see p. 194. [2] See below, p. 305.

GROUP II: *Esparto Papers with minute Traces of Chemical Wood.*

R. Browning	Cleon	1855	Esparto, trace of chemical wood
R. Browning	The Statue and the Bust	1855	Esparto, trace of chemical wood
J. Ruskin	Catalogue of the Turner Sketches in the National Gallery [1]	1857	Esparto, straw, trace of chemical wood
J. Ruskin	The Queen's Gardens	1864	Esparto, trace of chemical wood
A. C. Swinburne	Dead Love [2]	1864	Esparto, trace of chemical wood
A. C. Swinburne	Dolores	1867	Esparto, straw, trace of chemical wood
Lord Tennyson	Lucretius	1868	Esparto, trace of chemical wood
G. Eliot	Agatha [3]	1869	Esparto, trace of chemical wood
G. Eliot	Brother and Sister	1869	Esparto, small quantity of chemical wood
J. Ruskin	The Nature and Authority of Miracle	1873	Esparto, trace of chemical wood
A. C. Swinburne	The Devil's Due	1875	Esparto, trace of chemical wood

Now the first three pamphlets in this group have already been shown to be forgeries by the esparto test applied in Group I. The last pamphlet, *The Devil's Due*, is probably too late in date for the test to have any validity; there is some independent evidence in its favour and no very serious suspicion against it.[4] But of the remaining seven pamphlets in this group, there is independent and conclusive evidence against five, and very grave doubt about the two others. Nevertheless this test of the traces of chemical wood cannot be considered decisive; although the most likely

[1] Edition B, see p. 230. [2] The original edition, see p. 269.
[3] The second edition, see p. 194. [4] See below, p. 291.

explanation of its presence in members of this group is that their paper was made later than 1883.

Our third group consists of those pamphlets in which we found an unmistakably significant proportion of chemical wood:—

GROUP III: *Chemical Wood Papers.*

Lord Tennyson	Morte D'Arthur	1842	Chemical wood and esparto
Mrs. Browning	Sonnets, Reading	1847	Chemical wood, trace of rag
Mrs. Browning	The Runaway Slave	1849	Chemical wood, trace of rag
E. Yates	Mr. Thackeray, Mr. Yates and the Garrick Club [issue X] [1]	1859	Chemical wood and rag
E. Yates	Mr. Thackeray, Mr. Yates and the Garrick Club [issue Y]	1859	Chemical and mechanical wood
Lord Tennyson	The Sailor Boy	1861	Chemical wood and rag
W. M. Thackeray	A Leaf out of a Sketch Book	1861	Chemical wood and rag
Lord Tennyson	Ode on the Opening of the International Exhibition	1862	Chemical wood and rag
J. Ruskin	Leoni	1868	Chemical wood, esparto and rag
J. Ruskin	The Future of England	1870	Chemical wood and esparto
Lord Tennyson	The Lover's Tale [2]	1870	Chemical wood
Lord Tennyson	The Last Tournament	1871	Chemical wood and rag
R. L. Stevenson	On the Thermal Influence of Forests [3]	1873	Chemical wood, esparto and rag

Four of these pamphlets have chemical wood mixed with esparto, but in each case there is a sufficient quantity of wood to exclude the alternative explanations considered in connection with Group II. The earliest chemical wood pulp available for papermaking

[1] See p. 359.
[2] R. H. Shepherd's first edition according to Wise. See p. 307.
[3] The first edition according to Prideaux. See p. 247.

in England was imported from Bergvik; and that importation did not start until 1874 (even then the first year's supply was less than 500 tons); so that the paper of all the pamphlets in this group must have been made in 1874 or later. The dates at which they purport to have been printed range from 1842 to 1873, which are all impossible; the application of this test proves that all thirteen pamphlets in this group are forgeries.

The results obtained from the application of the esparto test to our first group and of the chemical wood test to our third group are entirely decisive. Such evidence admits neither doubt nor ambiguity; no fresh discovery of author's proof sheets or autographed copies could shake it, for there can be no stronger proof than these paper tests have supplied. If future research should discover any mention of these pamphlets in contemporary correspondence or their original entries in the publishers' ledgers, it would not alter the fact that they are forgeries: it could only show that they were facsimiles or reconstructions of similar pamphlets which were not forgeries. Three of them are of this type [1] and a fourth may be; [2] but of the twenty-two cases proved by these tests, none have contemporary authentication. Nor has the extensive bibliographical research which has been devoted to most of the authors revealed any more than the four facsimiles that we have mentioned. The analysis of the paper has turned our vague suspicion into proved fact, and settled our doubts, not only of the Reading *Sonnets* and the three Ruskins, but of eighteen additional first editions hitherto unchallenged.

[1] Ruskin's *Catalogue of the Turner Sketches in the National Gallery*, 1857; *Mr. Thackeray, Mr. Yates and the Garrick Club*, 1859; and Stevenson's *On the Thermal Influence of Forests*, 1873.

[2] William Morris's *Sir Galahad*, 1858.

CHAPTER V

THE TYPOGRAPHICAL ANALYSIS

ROBERT PROCTOR demonstrated thirty years ago that differences in type design were sufficient to assign books without imprint to their real printers; but his work dealt almost exclusively with the fifteenth century, when printers were their own typefounders.[1] Similar differences distinguish all printing types, but when the trades of printer and typefounder have become separated, the design can only be traced to the founder; and no distinction can be drawn between the different printers to whom a typefounder has supplied identical founts of the same design. Nevertheless, the changing fashions in type design can be precisely traced and dated from the specimen books issued by the typefounders themselves. So that, although in the nineteenth century it is only by an extraordinary chance that a printer can be identified from his type, a typefounder often can be. Even after the application of electrolysis had made it possible to copy an existing type design exactly, the date of original introduction can still be ascertained.

The labour of tracing any design to its source is considerably lightened by the fact that typefounding in England has always been confined to a few firms. The complaint that a ring of founders had the trade to themselves is voiced both before and after the period from 1845 to 1895 with which we have to deal.

[1] Nevertheless, his letter which we reprint in full on p. 208, shows that he was well aware of such possibilities in the nineteenth century.

L. J. Pouchée in 1819[1] set out to break the prices of this ring; and W. Haddon did the same in 1903–4.[2] Actually typefounding was in the hands of eight large firms; so much is clear from the fact that of the 173 specimens which we have been able to trace in this period, 152 come from these eight firms, while the remaining nine firms of which we find record produced only twenty-one specimens between them. It is tolerably certain, then, that the effective introduction of any new design will proceed from one of these eight larger foundries, and, if the design has any success, that it will be rapidly copied by other firms.

The only large-scale innovation in type design that took place in the nineteenth century was the resurrection of "old style." As early as 1840 the Chiswick Press had secured from the Caslon Foundry a fount of the roman of Aldine inspiration which William Caslon had cut some hundred years before. This was used for William Pickering[3] in his edition of Fuller's *Holy War* and two other books, all published in 1840. The use of this "old face" for the next twenty years was almost entirely confined to the Chiswick Press and to the antiquarian reprints which they printed for Pickering. The "old face" is not shown in the Caslon Specimen of 1848, although it is mentioned a little half-heartedly in the preface. It was not until 1852,[4] when A. C. Phemister cut a broader and modernised version of the design for Miller and Richard of Edinburgh, that "old style" came into more general use as a book face. Phemister subse-

[1] See the prefaces to his Specimens of 1819 and 1827 reprinted by W. Turner Berry and A. F. Johnson, *Catalogue of Specimens of Printing Types*, Oxford, 1934, pp. 80–81.

[2] *The Caxton Type Foundry versus the Ring*, 1903.

[3] Geoffrey Keynes, *William Pickering*, pp. 25–6.

[4] Theodore De Vinne, *Plain Printing Types*, New York, 1925, p. 193: the 1900 edition merely says "about 1860." Also S. Morison, p. xli of his introduction to Turner Berry and Johnson, *op. cit.*

quently emigrated to Boston, where he cut similar faces for Phelps, Dalton & Co. and other foundries; and some of these designs were later reintroduced into England.[1] While it is possible to distinguish the original Caslon "old face" from the later recuttings by Phemister and others, it is practically impossible to tell these from one another. This is amusingly demonstrated by Legros and Grant, who print a poem, the verses of which are set in differently mixed founts of "old style"; and they defy any expert to disentangle them.[2] It cannot be done; and as all the pamphlets among those under examination which are printed in "old style" are dated after 1852,[3] it follows that it is not possible to impugn their authenticity on this particular ground.

Most of the pamphlets, however, are set in a "modern style," and an innovation introduced into the designs of these types provided the material for a more fruitful test. The majority of "modern face" romans have only two kerned letters in the lower case, f and j. A "kerned" letter is one in which a portion of the face of the letter extends beyond its body (Figs. *a*, *c*, *d* and *f*). The kerned portion has to be fitted over the shoulder of the adjoining letter, and, if the kern impinges on the face of this letter, a ligature has to be substituted for the two sorts. It is obvious from figure *a* that the thin projection of the kern is both exposed and fragile; and its chief disadvantage to the printer was the frequent necessity of renewing the sorts for f and j as the old ones got broken. This created a natural demand for a kernless type.

[1] De Vinne, *op. cit.*, pp. 193–97.

[2] *Typographical Printing Surfaces*, 1916, pp. 117–18.

[3] With the exceptions of Thackeray's *An Interesting Event*, 1849, and Ruskin's *The National Gallery*, 1852, see below, pp. 347, 348 and pp. 227–229. Both are also condemned by the analysis of their paper.

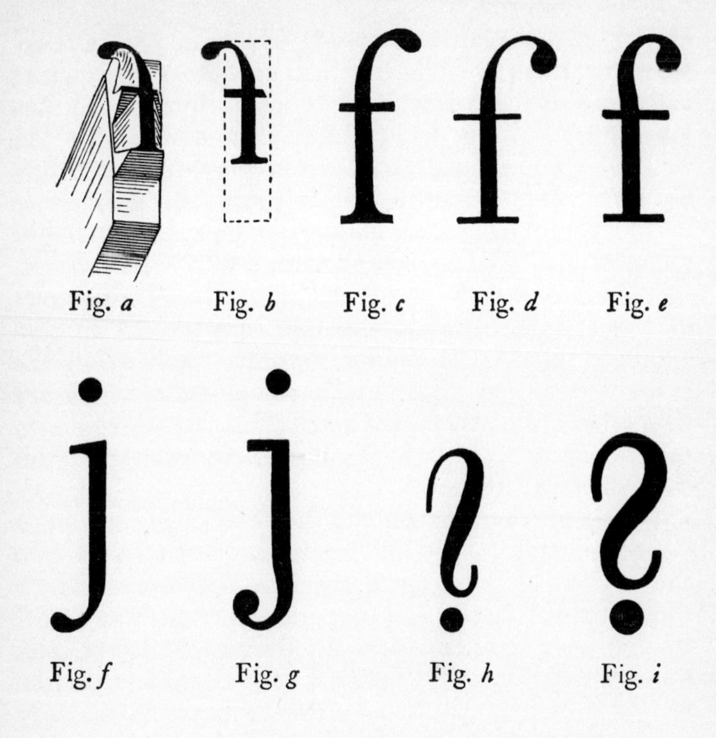

Plate I.—TYPOGRAPHICAL ILLUSTRATIONS

(All figures except *a* and *b* are enlarged approximately eleven diameters.)

a. A kerned letter drawn in perspective. The rectangle from which the printing surface rises is the body of the type: the overhanging portion at the top is the kern.

b. The printing surface of a kerned letter viewed from above. The dotted line shows the dimensions of the body; the portion outside the dotted line is the kern.

c. An 'Old Style' kerned f (Miller and Richard's Long Primer: our fount C).

d. A 'Modern Style' kerned f (Caslon's Long Primer No. 19). This shows the general design in use before the introduction of kernless founts.

e. The 'broken-backed' f of Clay's Long Primer No. 3. It has no kern.

f. An 'Old Style' kerned j (Miller and Richard's Long Primer: our fount C).

g. The 'button hook' j of Clay's Long Primer No. 3. It has no kern.

h. The 'tilting' question mark of Clay's Long Primer No. 3. Note its narrowness, and that its full-point is too far to the left. Its smaller size shows that it is really a bourgeois (9-point) face cast on a Long Primer (10-point) body.

i. The proper question mark for Shanks's Long Primer No. 20.

The idea first occurred to Richard Clay of the firm of R. Clay and Taylor (now R. Clay and Sons): he tried to manufacture such a design by bisecting a double 'ff' ligature and making an electrotype from the first 'f.' The attempt was not satisfactory because the printing surface was too far forward on the body, that is to say, too near the letter in front and too far from the one behind. He then approached the firm of P. M. Shanks & Co., typefounders, of Red Lion Square, who cut for him some time after 1880[1] the first design for a lower-case 'f' without a kern.[2] It is unlikely that Clay would have gone to this trouble if there had been any kernless design on the market at the time. We know that his idea had not been put into execution before 1880, but that it certainly had been by October, 1883.[3] Hence we may be sure that this particular design was conceived and manufactured between these two dates.

The kernless design was made by bending back the main stem of the 'f' and the 'j,' so that the centre of their terminal curves came into the same perpendicular line as the main stem itself. This involved a sharp backward bend in the stem, which makes the letters look as if their backs were broken; and the whole design resembles a button-hook in each case (Figs. *e* and *g*). Its object was to bring the terminal nearer to the centre of the body, and thus

[1] Messrs. P. M. Shanks & Co.'s specimens were hardly ever dated, but by the courtesy of the firm we were shown their file copy for the year 1880, so dated in MS.; and neither the Long Primer No. 20 nor any other type in the specimen shows a kernless design.

[2] This information is derived from two letters dated 19 and 20 Sept., 1933, from Mr. E. H. Jolin, the present typefounder in the employ of Messrs. R. Clay and Sons, to Mr. Cecil Clay, the present head of the firm, to whose courtesy we are indebted for these facts.

[3] The first number of *The English Illustrated Magazine*, printed by R. Clay and Taylor, contains the kernless design in almost mint state.

avoid the necessity of the kern. The breakages had generally occurred in the sizes between eight and twelve point, and the kernless design is mostly confined to these sizes. Although the difference between the two designs does not amount to more than a millimetre or so, it is not difficult, after a little practice, to distinguish between them.

The date of the introduction of this design can be checked by the examination of a comprehensive series of typefounders' specimens. The value of such a check will depend upon the completeness of the series examined and the accuracy with which they are dated. We have examined 152 specimens from the eight larger foundries, and 21, none of which contained this design, from nine smaller firms. These specimens are mostly in the St. Bride Foundation Library, which is particularly devoted to the history of printing, and, on the average over this period, provides a specimen for every two or three years of a foundry's existence. Type specimens are seldom dated; but those from any one foundry can usually be arranged in chronological sequence by their contents, because a specimen showing, for instance, bourgeois founts Nos. 1–17 must normally follow one showing only bourgeois Nos. 1–16. The dated price lists, which are sometimes bound up with the specimens, have enabled us to be still more precise; though we have in some cases been able to correct the conjectural dates given in the printed Catalogue of the St. Bride Library.

Three facts emerged from this examination: first, that no kernless design was shown in any specimen which we examined dated before 1883; secondly, that no less than eight different founts of this design appeared during 1883; and thirdly, that this number was increased nearly fourfold in the next dozen years.[1]

[1] We append a list of kernless founts with the dates of their first appearance in the specimen books of their respective founders :—

The rapidity of this increase gives an overwhelming authority to the observed negative for the years before 1880. One anomalous fact must be mentioned; V. and J. Figgins produced five kernless designs in 1883 and six more by the middle of 1887, whereas P. M. Shanks & Co. had no more than three by 1895. This is not so strange as it seems, because Figgins specialised in display founts and Shanks in type for newspapers, and it does not follow that, because Figgins cut more designs, he sold more type than Shanks. As a matter of fact the two firms were connected by marriage, and have recently (1933) amalgamated; it is at least possible, perhaps even likely, that Figgins cut the punch for Clay's kernless 'f' to Shanks's order. But however this may be, the total result of our examination was to confirm the date for

---

1883. V. & J. Figgins. Long Primer Nos. 11, 13 and 16 (Bible). Small Pica No. 17, Pica No. 12.
P. M. Shanks & Co. Long Primer Nos. 13 and 20.
Miller & Richard offered no kernless fount on January 1, 1883, but drew attention to its appearance in their autumn specimen. Brevier No. 30.

1884. Miller & Richard. Bourgeois No. 30.
The Austin Foundry. Bourgeois No. 3.

1887. P. M. Shanks & Co. Bourgeois No. 21.
Miller & Richard. Long Primer No. 30.
V. & J. Figgins (July 1st). Bourgeois Nos. 11, 12, 14 and 16, Long Primer No. 15, English No. 15.

1889. The Fann Street Foundry. Long Primer No. 6 (recut).
The Austin Foundry. Long Primer No. 1, Small Pica No. 6.

1890. Miller & Richard. Small Pica No. 34.
H. W. Caslon & Co. Long Primer No. 16.

1893. H. W. Caslon & Co. Long Primer No. 21.

1895. V. & J. Figgins. Brevier No. 15.
The Fann Street Foundry. Long Primer No. 10 (recut).
H. W. Caslon & Co. Small Pica No. 23, 12-pt. Pica No. 23.

Stephenson, Blake & Co. of Sheffield (11 specimens), and the Marr Typefounding Co. of Edinburgh (8 specimens) showed no kernless founts before 1895.

the origin of this design which we have given above; and we may, therefore, be doubly sure that no such design was on the market before 1880.

Applying this test to the various pamphlets under suspicion, we found that these sixteen were printed in a kernless fount.

Lord Tennyson	Morte d'Arthur	1842
W. Wordsworth	To the Queen, Kendal	1846
Mrs. Browning	Sonnets, Reading	1847
R. Browning	Cleon	1855
R. Browning	The Statue and the Bust	1855
E. Yates	Mr. Thackeray, Mr. Yates and the Garrick Club (issue B)	1859
Lord Tennyson	Ode on the Opening of the International Exhibition	1862
J. Ruskin	The Queen's Gardens, Manchester	1864
A. C. Swinburne	Dolores	1867
A. C. Swinburne	Siena (2nd ed.)	1868
Lord Tennyson	Lucretius, Cambridge, Mass. (Prefatory Note only)	1868
G. Eliot	Brother and Sister	1869
J. Ruskin	The Future of England, Woolwich	1870
Lord Tennyson	The Lover's Tale (Shepherd's 1st ed.)	1870
Lord Tennyson	The Last Tournament	1871
R. L. Stevenson	On the Thermal Influence of Forests, Edinburgh (1st ed.)	1873

All these sixteen pamphlets are printed in one particular fount, which shows a kernless design with a button-hook 'f.' This in itself is conclusive proof that they were printed from seven to thirty-eight years later than the dates given on their various title-pages. Once the date is shown to be false, the whole purpose of their production becomes suspect; and, particularly in the case of such privately printed opuscula, it is difficult to conceive any other explanation for their existence but that of deliberate forgery.

Besides the button-hook 'f' there was another typographical feature of the Reading *Sonnets* to which

Mr. Morison directed our attention. The question mark (Fig. *h*) is of a most peculiar form; the curve of its upper arm is strikingly narrow, and the whole design appears to tilt forward, somewhat as if it were an italic cast on a roman body. This is not, of course, its real explanation, for the illusion is probably increased by the faulty set of the type which is noticeable in the Reading *Sonnets*. Nevertheless, the lower-case 'f' and 'j' together with the question mark serve to identify a particular fount in which the sixteen pamphlets listed above are printed. The use of this fount would appear to have had a most remarkable range both in time and space. It is in use as early as 1842 and as late as 1893,[1] and at such widely divergent places as London, Manchester, Kendal, possibly Reading, Edinburgh, Woolwich, and Cambridge, Massachusetts. The identification of this fount among typefounders' specimens entirely eluded us, because of the twenty-seven designs of kernless type which we could trace as being on the market before 1895, not one contained this question mark. The obvious explanation of this was that it was a mixed fount, with some sorts from one foundry and some from another. Such a hybrid fount would necessarily be peculiar to one printer and one alone, because the chances are incalculable against these two special founts becoming mixed in this particular way in more than one printing office. This hybrid fount, then, would be a direct clue to the printer of these sixteen forgeries, if it could be found in any book with an authentic imprint. Any comprehensive search of this kind was an obvious impossibility, and the ultimate solution was due to a lucky accident.

In examining "Alaric at Rome. A Prize Poem, by Matthew Arnold. A Type-Facsimile Reprint of the Original Edition, Published at Rugby in

[1] See below, p. 64.

1840. Edited by Thomas J. Wise. London: Printed for Private Circulation Only. 1893," we suddenly recognised the particular hybrid fount used in the Reading *Sonnets*. The broken-backed 'f,' the buttonhook 'j,' the tilting question mark, they were all there; and more meticulous examination entirely confirmed our original impression that both books were printed in exactly the same fount. To enable the reader to test this for himself we show on Plate II opposite a collotype facsimile of a page of the Reading *Sonnets* side by side with the same matter set up in the fount used for this edition of *Alaric at Rome*. The imprint at the end of that book was "London: Printed by Richard Clay and Sons, Limited, Bread Street Hill, and Bungay, Suffolk, 1893." We noticed later that the text of the type facsimile of *Alastor*, 1887, and the notes to the type facsimile of *Hellas*, 1886, both produced for the Shelley Society by the same firm, were also set in this fount.

We thereupon inquired of this famous printing house what the origin of this fount was, and over what period they had used it. On April 28, 1933, they wrote in reply: "The type of *Alaric at Rome* was cast by us in 1876 [1] from matrices supplied by Messrs. P. M. Shanks & Sons, Ltd., 31 Red Lion Square, W.C.1, and designated by us No. 3 Long Primer. We used this type from 1876 to 1893, after which it was replaced by what is now known as Miller & Richard's 17 Long Primer." The type proved to be identical with Shanks' Long Primer No. 20 in every particular but one. The question mark is entirely different. Messrs. Shanks state that their question

[1] This statement was qualified by subsequent inquiry; the fount originally had kerned 'f' and 'j', but the kernless designs were substituted between 1880 and 1883 (see above, p. 59). The first use of the fount in its present form that we have been able to discover is in No. 1 of *The English Illustrated Magazine*, October, 1883.

III.

Unlike are we, unlike, O princely Heart!
Unlike our uses, and our destinies.
Our ministering two angels look surprise
On one another, as they strike athwart
Their wings in passing. Thou, bethink thee, art
A guest for queens to social pageantries,
With gages from a hundred brighter eyes
Than tears, even, can make mine, to ply thy part
Of chief musician. What hast *thou* to do
With looking from the lattice-lights at me,
A poor, tired, wandering singer? . . singing through
The dark, and leaning up a cypress tree?
The chrism is on thine head,—on mine, the dew,—
And death must dig the level where these agree.

PLATE II.

Collotype Facsimile of a page from Mrs. Browning's Sonnets, *Reading, 1847.*

III.

Unlike are we, unlike, O princely Heart!
Unlike our uses, and our destinies.
Our ministering two angels look surprise
On one another, as they strike athwart
Their wings in passing. Thou, bethink thee, art
A guest for queens to social pageantries,
With gages from a hundred brighter eyes
Than tears, even, can make mine, to ply thy part
Of chief musician. What hast *thou* to do
With looking from the lattice-lights at me,
A poor, tired, wandering singer? . . singing through
The dark, and leaning up a cypress tree?
The chrism is on thine head,—on mine, the dew,—
And death must dig the level where these agree.

PLATE III.

The same matter as Plate II printed in Long Primer No. 3 by R. Clay and Sons in May, 1934. No attempt has been made to copy worn or broken letters.

mark (Fig. *i*) is the same as that which has always been sold with the fount; and it therefore follows that the odd question mark of Clay's Long Primer No. 3 is a sport from the matrices of some other foundry. Furthermore, the sixteen pamphlets specified above cannot have been printed by any other firm than Clay's, because they all [1] contain the Clay question mark (Fig. *h*), and not that which properly belongs to the fount as cast by Messrs. P. M. Shanks & Sons, Ltd. (Fig. *i*).[2]

When we laid these facts before Messrs. Clay, they admitted readily enough that the facts which we have just set out proved that they had printed the pamphlets. But they were unable to give us any conclusive clue to the identity of their client, because they had preserved no ledgers earlier than 1911. Nor is there any real reason to suppose that anyone in their employ was privy to the fraud. The facsimiles which they printed for the Browning Society, the Shelley Society [3] and for private circulation by Mr. Wise were all printed on separate sheets from the prefatory matter or notes. There is nothing on the actual leaves of these facsimiles to show that they are reprints; and from their having

[1] Except *Lucretius*, 1868: only the Prefatory Note is set in this fount, and it contains no question mark; but there can be no doubt that it is the same fount.

[2] Examination of their matrices of this design showed that, while those for 'f' and 'j' had been renewed, the question mark was the original strike.

[3] Mr. Wise supervised the production of the facsimiles for both these societies: see *Letters of Robert Browning collected by T. J. Wise*, ed. T. L. Hood, 1933, p. 373. *The First Annual Report of the Shelley Society* says (end of par. 10, p. 15), "To Mr. Thomas J. Wise the Committee also feel greatly indebted. He has had the control of all the Society's printing work. . . ." The inside back wrapper of Part II of the same Society's *Papers* states "An estimate of the cost of producing any of the original editions of Shelley's different works may be had upon application to the Honorary Secretary" [Mr. T. J. Wise].

already done work of this sort, it follows that Messrs. Clay would not have regarded the request for the name of another firm and a false date in the imprint as necessarily involving any malpractice on the part of their now unidentifiable client.

So far we have examined these pamphlets with the single object of determining whether their typography was consistent with the dates on their title-pages. The conclusions that we have reached are definite and final, but they only affect sixteen pamphlets out of some fifty suspects; and we must now turn to a quantitative examination of the founts used for the entire series.

Supposing that they are all the work of one man, it follows that he is unlikely to have had access to more than one, or at most two, large printing houses. Even the largest printers do not have at one time an extensive variety of text types of the same size, so that, if these pamphlets show a wide diversity of text types, the hypothesis of a common origin must be dismissed. Conversely, if, with their widely differing dates and places and printers, they exhibit less than, say, half a dozen different text types between them, the probability, not only that they are forgeries, but that they were forged by one man, is enormously strengthened.

Actually no less than thirty-seven out of fifty-one [1] are printed in one or other of only three text types.

The remainder form one group of four, two groups of three each, one of two, and two singletons in a type larger than any used elsewhere in the series. Within each of these groups the identity of text types is quite unmistakable.

[1] The omission is *Thomas Stevenson*, details of which are given on p. 379.

They may be classified simply: the two most usual sizes for such booklets are Small Pica (about 11 point) and Long Primer (about 10 point); and in each of these an "old style" and a "modern style" may be readily distinguished. The "modern style" Long Primer, which we will call A, has already been identified with Clay's Long Primer No. 3, and a list of the sixteen pamphlets printed in it has been given above on p. 62. The Small Pica "modern style," which we will call B, occurs in eleven pamphlets:—

Mrs. Browning	The Runaway Slave	1849
R. Browning	Gold Hair	1864
C. Dickens	To Be Read at Dusk	1852
G. Eliot	Agatha [2nd ed.]	1869
W. Morris	Sir Galahad	1858
J. Ruskin	The Scythian Guest	1849
J. Ruskin	Samuel Prout	1870
R. L. Stevenson	The Story of a Lie	1882
A. C. Swinburne	Laus Veneris	1866
Lord Tennyson	Lucretius, Cambridge, Mass. (the text only)	1868
W. M. Thackeray	A Leaf out of a Sketch Book	1861

The Long Primer old style (C), which appears to be that cast by Miller and Richard of Edinburgh, is used for the text of ten pamphlets:—

M. Arnold	St. Brandan	1867
W. Morris	The Two Sides of the River	1876
J. Ruskin	Leoni	1868
A. C. Swinburne	Cleopatra	1866
A. C. Swinburne	An Appeal to England	1866
Lord Tennyson	A Welcome to Alexandrovna	1874
Lord Tennyson	The Falcon	1879
Lord Tennyson	The Cup	1881
Lord Tennyson	The Promise of May	1882
W. M. Thackeray	An Interesting Event	1849

The four minor groups comprise:—a Small Pica old style (D), again cast by Miller and Richard, used in four pamphlets,

J. Ruskin	The National Gallery	1852
J. Ruskin	The Nature and Authority of Miracle	1873
A. C. Swinburne	Dead Love	1864
Lord Tennyson	On the Death of the Duke of Clarence and Avondale	1892

Another Small Pica modern style (E) used in

M. Arnold	Geist's Grave	1881
D. G. Rossetti	Sister Helen	1857

Another Small Pica old style (F) used in

R. Kipling	White Horses	1897
R. Kipling	The White Man's Burden	1899
D. G. Rossetti	Verses	1881

and a Pica old style (G) used in

R. L. Stevenson	Some College Memories	1887
Lord Tennyson	The Sailor Boy	1861
Lord Tennyson	Ode on the Opening of the Colonial and Indian Exhibition	1886

Of all the pamphlets included in the series, only two are printed in types which are both peculiar to themselves and of unusually large size. Tennyson's *Carmen Sæculare*, 1887, printed in an old style English (about 14 point), has the same border that is used for *A Sailor Boy* and *A Leaf out of a Sketch Book;* and, actually, looks more recent than any of the others. The attempted facsimile of Ruskin's *Catalogue of the Turner Sketches in the National Gallery*, 1857, is printed in a modern style Pica, and none of the other pamphlets show a modern style fount as large as this; but in any case the piece is proved a forgery on two separate grounds.[1]

This absence of diversity in their text types does not, perhaps, demonstrate more than the possibility that these booklets are all the work of one printer;

[1] See below, p. 230.

but it appears, from the typography of books already proved to be forgeries by their paper, that this printer probably had at least three of these different text types. For the copied vignette common to *A Sailor Boy* and *A Leaf out of a Sketch Book*[1] must have been peculiar to one printer, and he used both fount B (*A Leaf*, etc.) and fount G (*The Sailor Boy*); furthermore, the Prefatory Note to *Lucretius* is set in fount A although without a question mark, while the text is in fount B. It is more than likely, therefore, that founts A, B and G were all in the possession of this one printer.

The display types emphasise the same point. Although they are much more numerous, they are more easily recognisable, and their occurrence links up the various text types. Thus the title of *The Scythian Guest* (B) is set in the same 30-point condensed modern capitals that are used for the title of *Geist's Grave* (E); the type of the fourth line of the title-page of *The Scythian Guest* (B) corresponds to that of the first line of the title-page of *Mr. Thackeray, Mr. Yates and the Garrick Club* (A); the first line of the title-page of *To Be Read at Dusk* (B) with the first line of *Dead Love* (D); the second line of *The Last Tournament* (A) with the first of *An Appeal to England* (C); the first line of *Dolores* (A) with the fifth line of *The Nature and Authority of Miracle* (D); the first line of the cancelled title-page of *Cleopatra* (C) in the Wrenn Library proofs[2] with the heading on p. 11 of Rossetti's *Verses* (F); and so on: examples could be multiplied almost indefinitely. With the exception of fount A it is improbable that any of these types are peculiar to one printer; but, that one printer used them all, is surely demonstrated by the facts set out above. With every fresh link it becomes more and more improbable that more than one printer should

[1] See below, p. 75. [2] See below, pp. 280–284.

have had this particular assortment of text and display types.

We have already shown that fount A is peculiar to R. Clay and Sons, and it was neither difficult nor surprising to ascertain that they also possessed the others. Fount B was used as the text type of the Shelley Society's facsimile of *Rosalind and Helen* (1888). Fount C [1] was used on the front inner wrapper of the Shelley Society's *Papers*, Part I (1888), and fount D as the text type for the same publication. The display type used for the title of *Dolores* is the same as that used for the first line of the title-page of the Shelley Society's *Rosalind and Helen*. Here again it is unnecessary to prolong the catalogue. There was one printer who had all these types, and that was the Shelley Society's printer—R. Clay and Sons.

Our typographical analysis has shown that sixteen of these pamphlets dated from 1842 to 1873 must have been printed after 1880; and that these same sixteen were all printed by R. Clay and Sons. We have further shown that it is extremely probable, though not absolutely proved, that all fifty-one pamphlets were the work of one printer; and that this printer must again have been R. Clay and Sons. We are therefore justified henceforward in regarding every member of the whole series with suspicion. The type test has provided corroboration for the paper test in eleven cases, and has by itself conclusively proved five separate pamphlets to be forgeries.

[1] Tennyson's *The Antechamber*, printed for private circulation in 1906, bears no imprint, but it was printed in this type for Mr. Wise by R. Clay and Sons.

CHAPTER VI

FURTHER TESTS

A NUMBER of further tests remain to be outlined, but none of them are so extensive in their application as those that we have described in the two previous chapters. The only one that is positive and proof in itself is the test of the collation of the text. If an alleged first edition can be shown to include textual alterations made by the author at a later date, it is clear that it must have been produced after those alterations had been incorporated into the text. The pitfall is obvious; and we have only been able to apply this test with any definite results to the work of two authors, Tennyson and Ruskin.

Ruskin wrote two letters to *The Times* in 1847 and 1852, about the National Gallery. They were reprinted as a pamphlet called *The National Gallery* and dated 1852; but this was not known to Mr. Alexander Wedderburn when in 1880 he edited a collection of Ruskin's letters to the newspapers under the title of *Arrows of the Chace*. He took his text direct from *The Times*, and twice felt obliged to emend the version there printed. In arranging the work he placed Ruskin's two footnotes, which had appeared originally in *The Times*, at the foot of the page without distinguishing them from those which he had himself added. Ruskin's own footnotes do not appear in the "1852" pamphlet, and Mr. Wedderburn's emendations do! The conclusion is obvious; the pamphlet was set up from *Arrows of the Chace*, and so cannot have been printed until after 1880.[1]

When Mr. Wise announced his discovery of Ruskin's *The Queen's Gardens*, 1864, in *The Bookman* for February, 1893, he wrote: "The most cursory glance suffices to discover revisions upon every page,[2] but only by a close comparison of texts can it be ascertained how systematic and minute these revisions are—every change a certain improvement, and calculated to enhance the force, the vigour and the beauty of the prose." When that close comparison is made, its results are startling, but hardly in the direction indicated by Mr. Wise. The essay *Of Queen's Gardens* forms the second part of *Sesame and Lilies*; and the texts of the first four editions (1865, 1865, 1866, 1867) of this book are identical: but Ruskin made a number of alterations when it was included in the first volume of his *Collected Works* in 1871. These alterations are mainly directed to clarifying his meaning rather than improving his prose. For example, in 1865 he had written that books for young girls to read should be selected "not for what is out of them, but what is in them": in 1871 he changed this to "not for their freedom from evil, but for their possession of good." There are a number of such changes some of which we have listed on p. 243. Now each change serves to make Ruskin's meaning clearer; and it is inconceivable that he should have reverted to the more obscure expression, if these passages had been originally composed in their clearer form. But in every one of these alterations the 1864 pamphlet agrees with the 1871 text as against the first four editions. The only inference that it is possible to draw is that the 1871 text was the source of the "1864" pamphlet.

[1] *The Works of Ruskin*, ed. E. T. Cook and A. Wedderburn. Vol. XII. p. 396. See also below, pp. 227, 228.

[2] These in fact consist only of omissions from the (1871) text.

Tennyson's *Ode on the Opening of the International Exhibition* is supposed to have been issued as a separate pamphlet in 1862. It was printed seven more times before 1890; but the only version out of these seven which agrees with the separate pamphlet is that in *The Collected Works* of 1889. The differences [1] are not just a matter of commas and capitals, but the alteration of several words and a whole line: the poem shows a continuous evolution that leaves no possible doubt that the "1862" pamphlet derives from the 1889 text.

The case of *The Last Tournament*, 1871, is more complicated: it was first published in *The Contemporary Review* in December, 1871, and later formed the second part of *Gareth and Lynette*, 1872. The separate pamphlet of 1871 corresponds with *The Contemporary Review* in six major variants,[2] and with *Gareth and Lynette* in the minor ones. Mr. Wise has reproduced in another context what can be shown to be the original proof-sheet of the last page of *Gareth and Lynette*; [3] and on this proof the minor variants are inserted in Tennyson's autograph. Thus we know that they were made for the 1872 volume, and any text that contains them must be after that date. So that the "1871" pamphlet, notwithstanding its six *Contemporary Review* readings, must be falsely dated by at least a year.

The editions "printed for the Author" of *The Falcon*, 1879,[4] *The Cup*, 1881,[5] and *The Promise of May*, 1882,[6] may be taken together. In each case the text mainly corresponds to that of the first pub-

[1] See below, pp. 228, 229.

[2] Those given by Mr. Wise, *Bibliography of Tennyson*, Vol. I. pp. 195–6.

[3] *Ib.*, facing p. 193. See below, pp. 316, 317.

[4] See below, pp. 323–326.

[5] See below, pp. 327–331.

[6] See below, pp. 332–335.

lished edition; and in each case proof-sheets, or, as Mr. Wise prefers to call them, "trial-books," have been found bearing a later date, but showing a more primitive text. It is remarkable that Mr. Wise has not recognised the implications of these facts in his study and collation of these "trial-books," which are all in his own library. Indeed he seems to show a perverse ingenuity in explaining away those points he has noticed, while leaving the others obscure. Our knowledge of their text is entirely derived from what Mr. Wise says, and from the single facsimile he gives, which is of a page from the "trial-book" of *The Cup*, 1882.[1] This facsimile shows Tennyson inserting a passage of a line and a half, and then again altering the additional half line. The last version, still further expanded, appears in the 1884 and subsequent editions; but it also appears in the edition "printed for the Author, 1881." Tennyson could not have made the alteration before the "trial-book" was printed in 1882, therefore the "1881" edition must be of later date. It is at least possible that examination of the other "trial-books" might yield an equally serious result.

We have now applied the test of the collation of the text to three Tennysons and two Ruskins; and they are all shown to be falsely dated. But the *raison d'être* of each pamphlet depends upon its date: there can be no reason for an author to reprint privately works that have already been published and are still in print. The only explanation of these falsely dated pamphlets is that they were deliberately manufactured for the rare book market.

We must now turn from these certainties to consider the negative evidence. Although it will not conform to the Euclidean pattern, the quantity of this

[1] *Bibliography of Tennyson*, Vol. I. facing p. 258.

evidence makes an innocent explanation very unlikely. The first negative test concerns illustrations and vignettes. Any printer, preparing an offprint from a volume which contains illustrations from wood or metal blocks, will naturally make use of the same blocks for the offprint that he used for the original volume. If such blocks can be shown to be copies, it must direct very serious suspicion against those offprints in which they occur. The test is not positive, because it is conceivable that the original block might have been mislaid; but this is a contingency so remote that it need not be seriously considered. There are only three pamphlets in our whole series which contain any vignettes or illustrations; they are Tennyson's *A Sailor Boy*,[1] 1861, Thackeray's *A Leaf out of a Sketch-Book*,[2] 1861, and R. L. Stevenson's *Some College Memories*,[3] 1886. The first two are supposed to be offprints from *The Victoria Regia*,[4] 1861. This was an anthology edited by Miss Adelaide Anne Procter, to which the authors contributed their work gratis, as the profits were to be devoted to charity. The volume was printed by Miss Emily Faithfull at the Victoria Press, and both offprints bear her shield-shaped printer's mark on wrapper and title-page. This vignette is the same in both offprints, but it is not the vignette on the title-page of *The Victoria Regia*.[5] We have examined a number of books printed at the Victoria Press, which bear this vignette; but in every case it corresponded to that on *The Victoria Regia*, and differed from the version used

[1] See below, pp. 298, 299. [2] See below, pp. 350–352.

[3] See below, pp. 254–264.

[4] Mr. Wise states that there was also an offprint of Coventry Patmore's contribution to this volume (*Bibliography of Tennyson*, Vol. I. pp. 165–6), but we have been unable to find any other record of its existence.

[5] These differences are described in detail on p. 299, and see Plate IVb.

on the two alleged offprints. Besides the vignette the Thackeray pamphlet contains two full-page woodcuts by the author. The differences between these woodcuts as they appear in *The Victoria Regia* and in the offprint are not so easy to discern, but there is a noticeable breakage of lines in the more heavily shaded portions of the design, particularly on the faces of the nigger boys and the shadows behind them. The simplest, and indeed the only satisfactory, explanation of this difference is that the blocks used in the offprint were photo-engraved reproductions of the original illustrations in *The Victoria Regia*. The same explanation applies to the portrait of Professor Kelland, which appeared as a plate in *The New Amphion*, 1886, from which Stevenson's *Some College Memories* professes to be an offprint. In this case the loss of tone between the original block and its reproduction on the wrapper and title-page of the offprint is even more noticeable: the original is an etching printed from an intaglio surface, whereas the copy is a line block printed from a surface in relief. The printers of *The New Amphion* stated in 1898 [1] that the original etched plate would have been available either to Stevenson himself or the editors of the volume, which makes the use of a reproduction even more curious. These copied vignettes are admittedly only circumstantial evidence of forgery; but the single innocent explanation is very unconvincing for three separate cases.

The argument against the four facsimile editions in our list is an analogous one. Mr. Wise, in referring to the later facsimile of *Dead Love*, used the words "a deceptive reprint, the reproduction of which can hardly have been other than fraudulent." The same remark might be applied to all these facsimile reprints,

[1] *The Athenæum*, Jan. 22, 1898. See below, pp. 255–264.

PLATE IV*a*.—THACKERAY'S NIGGER BOY

The first head is from p. 125 of *The Victoria Regia*; the second from the same sketch as it appears on p. 20 of *A Leaf out of a Sketch Book*. Both are reproduced in collotype, twice their original size. Note particularly in the second head the broken lines on the cheek and above the left eyebrow.

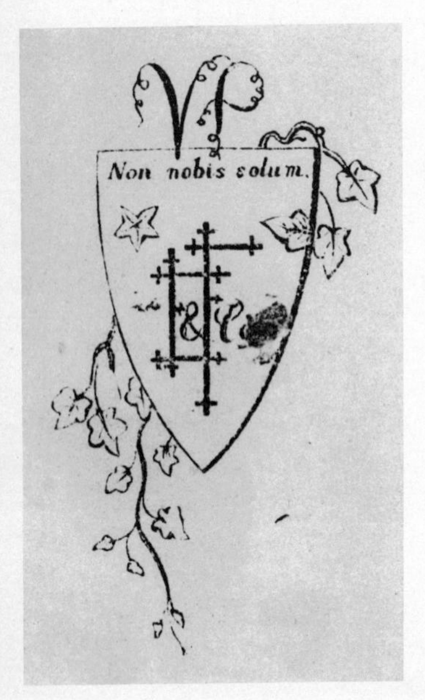

PLATE IV*b*.—THE COPIED VIGNETTE

The first vignette is from the title page of *The Victoria Regia*; the second from that of *A Sailor Boy*. Both are in collotype, twice their original size; their differences are detailed on p. 299. The smudges on each side of the monogram in the first vignette are due to modern ink stains on the British Museum copy.

which, although they will not survive detailed comparison with the original editions, cannot be distinguished from them in ordinary bibliographical description. They are Ruskin's *Catalogue of the Turner Sketches in the National Gallery*,[1] 1857; Edmund Yates's *Mr. Thackeray, Mr. Yates, and the Garrick Club*,[2] 1859; Swinburne's *Siena*[3] (2nd edition), 1868; and George Eliot's *Agatha*[4] (2nd edition), 1869. Their very nature draws suspicion to them. The original edition would presumably have satisfied the private purpose which called it into being; and if a reprint had been needed, it is extremely unlikely that such pains would have been taken to make it indistinguishable from the first edition. Nevertheless, Mr. Wise has come to the rescue of the only two that have so far been challenged. His account of why Buxton Forman printed the second edition of *Agatha* is explicit: we cannot contradict it; but we have set out in detail on p. 195 our four reasons for finding it difficult to believe. Mr. Wise took exactly the same course when Slater challenged the authenticity of the *Siena* facsimile in 1894. He admitted that it was not the genuine copyright edition, but asserted that it was a contemporary piracy by John Camden Hotten, who "it is known . . . sold the booklets readily at five or ten shillings apiece."[5] Actually the type shows that the booklet could not have been produced until at least seven years after Hotten was dead. So that Mr. Wise's attempt to rehabilitate these books has done nothing to lessen the suspicion implicit in their very nature.

Our next negative test was the evidence of the authors themselves, and at first sight this would

[1] See below, pp. 230, 231.
[2] See below, pp. 359, 360.
[3] See below, pp. 287–289.
[4] See below, pp. 194–197.
[5] *Swinburne Bibliography*, I. 178.

appear to be sufficiently conclusive, for there could be no better witness. But an old man cannot always remember accurately the details of his early publications, and the value of his evidence must largely depend upon its explicitness. Furthermore, the author's evidence does not exclude the possibility of contemporary piracy, which is the obvious explanation of the two Kipling pamphlets; for there can be no possible reason to doubt the categorical statement of Mr. Kipling's literary agents.[1]

Swinburne's disclaimer of *Cleopatra* was clear and emphatic: "I am quite positive," he wrote to Mr. Wise in 1888,[2] "quite certain that I never set eyes on the booklet before, nor heard of its existence." But in spite of this Mr. Wise has the hardihood to refer to a cancelled proof of this very book as "evidently rejected by the author."[3] This, of course, may have been a slip on Mr. Wise's part, but it cannot have been on Swinburne's. Even if Swinburne's statement were not supported by other evidence, we should still consider that it made this pamphlet an object of considerable suspicion.[4]

There are three statements by Browning which have a bearing on the authenticity of some of these pamphlets. We have already quoted, at the end of Chapter II,[5] his own account of the circumstances in which he first saw the *Sonnets from the Portuguese*, and there is no need to repeat it here. When Mr. Wise asked him about *The Runaway Slave* in 1888, he wrote: "I never heard of a separate publication,

[1] See below, pp. 204, 205.

[2] *Letters of A. C. Swinburne*, edd. Gosse and Wise, II. p. 189.

[3] *Catalogue of the Wrenn Library*, Austin, Texas, IV. p. 248.

[4] See below, pp. 278–284. Swinburne also denied any knowledge of *Dolores*, 1867, which has been shown to be a forgery; see pp. 285, 286.

[5] See above, p. 35.

and am pretty certain such a circumstance never happened. I fear that this must be a fabricated affair." And when Mr. Wise produced the pamphlet, he fell back on conjecture. "I daresay the fact has been . . ." [1] Our paper test shows that Browning's first thoughts were best, for the pamphlet really is a fabricated affair. In 1874 he wrote to Locker-Lampson: "The business relation between me and Moxon was what you shall hear. He printed, on nine occasions, nine poems of mine, wholly at my expense: that is, he printed them and subtracting the very moderate returns, sent me in, duly, the bill for the remainder of the expense. When I married, I proposed that he should publish a new edition at his own risk, which he declined; whereupon I made the same proposal to Chapman and Hall; or Forster did it for me,—and they accepted. Moxon was kind and civil, made no profit by me, I am sure, and never tried to help me to any, he would have assured you." [2] The nine publications to which Browning refers, are accounted for by *Sordello* (1840) and the eight parts of *Bells and Pomegranates* (1841–46). All Browning's later publications from 1849 to 1868 came from Chapman and Hall, with the exceptions of *Cleon*, 1855, and *The Statue and the Bust*, 1855, which both bear Moxon's imprint. Browning's statement would have aroused suspicion about these two pamphlets in any case, but it could hardly have amounted to more than suspicion without supporting evidence, which, as a matter of fact, is supplied by both paper and type. In a similar way the absence of Ruskin's *The Scythian Guest*, 1849, from the detailed records of that eminent sherry merchant John Ruskin senior, was sufficient for Cook and Wedderburn to denounce it as a forgery; but here again their suspicion, for they

[1] See below, pp. 130, 131.

[2] *The Rowfant Library Catalogue*, Appendix, p. 170.

had no real proof,[1] is confirmed by the analysis of the paper.

Passing now from the negative evidence of authors to that of printers, it is clear that it will be still less conclusive. An author may perhaps be expected to remember what he has published, but a printer could not remember all that he had printed. Even if his ledgers have been preserved intact, it is difficult to be certain that every job done was entered in them. Actually this type of test applies only to two pamphlets.[2] The successors of Messrs. Strangeways and Walden, whose imprint is on Ruskin's *Leoni*, 1868, informed Cook and Wedderburn in 1903 that their ledgers were detailed and intact from 1845 onwards; while they recorded the private edition of Ruskin's *Notes on the Employment of the Destitute and Criminal Classes*, which is also dated 1868, there was no mention of *Leoni*.[3] This evidence, striking though it is, would hardly have been sufficient to condemn the pamphlet without the final proof supplied yet once again by the paper.

While it is difficult to prove from surviving ledgers that an existing firm did not print a particular book, more satisfactory evidence can sometimes be derived from the particular form of imprint which the suspected pamphlet bears. The provision of a suitable printer's and publisher's imprint for each of his creations must have been a delicate task for the forger; and it would have been more than surprising if he had never made a mistake. The case of Swinburne's *Dead Love*, 1864, is a startling example. This pamphlet bears the publisher's imprint of "John W. Parker and Son, West Strand, 1864"; now this

[1] *The Works of Ruskin*, Vol. II. pp. 101–2 footnote, 1903.
[2] Of which one is *Sir Galahad*; see below, pp. 207–210.
[3] *The Works of Ruskin*, Vol. I. p. 288, 1903. See below, pp. 236, 237.

firm changed its style to "Parker, Son and Bourn" on January 1, 1861, and was entirely closed down in October, 1863.[1] It is true that this evidence is still circumstantial, but it could hardly be more damning; and it is the one single instance in which we have accepted such evidence as final. The case of Swinburne's *Laus Veneris*, 1866, is similar, though not conclusive. This pamphlet was supposed to have been printed in January, 1866, but it bears the imprint of "Bradbury, Evans and Co.," a style which that firm did not assume until May 7, 1866. If the pamphlet was produced after that date, its whole *raison d'être*, as explained by Sir Edmund Gosse in his *Life of Swinburne* and Mr. Wise in his *Bibliography*, thereupon falls to the ground; and other considerations seem to indicate that it is a reprint of a much later date from *Poems and Ballads*.[2]

The possibility of making mistakes like these must always have been a source of apprehension to the forger; and it is surprising that he did not more often have recourse to the expedient of inventing a publisher or printer. The publisher's name on Matthew Arnold's *St. Brandan*, 1867, is "E. W. & A. Skipworth." Now a universal negative is notoriously hard to prove, and although we can find no trace of this firm, and no book published by them appears in *The English Catalogue* from 1865 to 1871, it is nevertheless difficult to say outright that such a firm did not exist in London in the year 1867.[3] The evidence is a little stronger against the corporeal existence of Messrs. Hayley and Jackson, whose imprint is found on the title-page of Stevenson's *The Story of a Lie*, 1882.[4] Not only can we trace no other record of their publishing activities, but they do not appear among the

[1] See below, pp. 269–271.

[2] See below, pp. 272–277.

[3] See below, pp. 161, 162. The printers of this pamphlet are equally elusive.

[4] See below, pp. 251–253.

inhabitants of Little Queen Street as recorded in *Kelly's Post Office Directory* for the years 1881 to 1883 inclusive. None the less, it is not entirely impossible for a genuine pamphlet to bear the imprint of a fictitious publisher. A fictitious printer is a more serious matter. Every printer, however small, must have some machinery, and consequently premises of a certain size and length of tenancy; so that, even in the City of London, his name is very unlikely to have been overlooked in a reference book compiled with the elaboration of *Kelly's Post Office Directory*. This appears annually and gives three alphabetical arrangements; one general, one under trades and one under addresses; this last is given in such detail that even unoccupied premises are specified. Neither "J. Andrews, Clements Lane, E.C." nor "R. Charleston and Sons, Ardwick Green (Manchester)," whose imprints appear on *Cleopatra* and *The Queen's Gardens* [1] respectively, are to be found in the Directories; and this may be regarded as tolerably safe evidence that they had no printing establishments at those addresses on the relevant dates.[2] Quite a large proportion of the suspects on our list have no printer's imprints at all; but although this was, and is, illegal, there are a sufficient number of perfectly well authenticated books of this period which also have no printer's imprint, to make it quite unsafe to draw any deductions from its convenient absence in these cases.

There remains one further negative test—that of the auction record. It is not in any sense conclusive, and its pragmatic value only emerges in its cumulative results; but it proved in practice to be the easiest way of deciding whether there was a case to investigate

[1] See below, pp. 278–284, and pp. 232–235.

[2] Nor have we been able to trace the printers who are supposed to have printed *St. Brandan* and *The Story of a Lie*.

against any particular book. The records of books sold at auction have been printed annually in Great Britain since 1887, and in America since 1895. The object of printing them is to inform collectors and dealers of the value of books; so that, although books sold in bundles or for trifling sums are not recorded, and the descriptions of condition leave much to be desired, any inscribed copies or proof-sheets receive special attention because they realise high prices. Thus it is comparatively simple to discover if there are any copies of a particular book authenticated by the author's contemporary autograph. It is not until this test has been put to constant use that one can realise how effective it is, and that the overwhelming majority of collected nineteenth-century books are authenticated in this way. Such a test is particularly applicable to our suspects because, with four possible exceptions,[1] they are all supposed to have been privately printed, that is, printed at the expense of the author to present to his friends.

In general the auction record of a genuine privately printed pamphlet by a collected nineteenth-century author may be expected to show three characteristics:— (*a*) A number of *presentation copies* from the author; (*b*) Evidence of *contemporary binding*; some copies will be found in contemporary calf or half calf or bound up in a volume with other pamphlets. It is, to say the least, unlikely that every copy of such a book will have been preserved by its original recipient with a prophetic tenderness for the pristine state beloved by modern collectors. (*c*) *Scarcity*; an author could hardly have required more than fifty copies for private circulation, and, as pamphlets are not easily

[1] Ruskin's *The Queen's Gardens*; Tennyson's *Ode on the Opening of the International Exhibition*, 1862, *A Welcome to Alexandrovna*, 1874, and *Ode on the Opening of the Colonial and Indian Exhibition*, 1886.

kept if they are not bound, a substantial proportion of these will probably have disappeared. In actual fact the more notable authentic, privately printed pamphlets are real rarities, and often less than half a dozen copies can now be located. A few examples will show how a genuine pamphlet reacts to this test of the auction record. Of Mrs. Browning's early work, *The Battle of Marathon*, 1820, the existence of which Browning himself doubted, about a dozen copies can now be traced; of these, five are presentation copies, and five were in contemporary bindings, old half calf, old russia and so forth. Of Tennyson's *The Window, or The Loves of the Wrens*, printed at Sir Ivor Guest's private press at Canford Manor in 1867, about half a dozen copies are now extant, but these include two presentation copies from the author and a set of the corrected proofs. George Cruikshank's pamphlet, *The Artist and the Author*, 1872, was not privately printed and it is not at all uncommon to-day, but checking the auction record from 1923 to 1930 shows nine separate sales of which no less than five were of presentation copies, and two of these were in contemporary bindings. Many further examples might be cited, but these are sufficient to indicate the type of evidence which consistently supports a genuine pamphlet.

Not a single one of our suspects has an auction record with any of the three points set out above. Not one of them [1] has an author's presentation inscription, or even a contemporary date of acquisition. All of them occur for sale in folded sheets or mint state or expensive modern bindings. Some of them might

[1] With the exception of *Sir Galahad*, of which there was a presentation copy in the Buxton Forman sale, but the inscription was dated 32 years after the alleged date of publication. Mr. Wise also has a presentation copy of this book, but it is undated. The paper test entirely condemns the book.

be called rare, but nearly all are known by more than ten copies; some have been auctioned more than thirty times, and a few were bought by Mr. Gorfin[1] to a total of forty or fifty. This is only a pragmatic test, but it gains in significance when no trace of any of them can be found before 1888. None of the bibliographies before that date, not even those submitted by their compilers for correction to Ruskin and Browning, contain any mention of them: none of the British Museum copies were acquired before then, and no copies can be found with inscriptions of an earlier date. When contrasted with their comparative abundance by the close of the century, this unaccountable lack of pedigree does more than impugn their authenticity. It definitely suggests that they may have been forged in the late 'eighties and early 'nineties.

With the exception of the collation of the text, all the tests outlined in this chapter are negative. They have been applied in detail in the dossiers at the end of the books. Each one of them singly has yielded enough to arouse definite suspicion; but if any contemporary evidence had been found to set against them—if the pamphlet impugned had been given away by the author, mentioned in correspondence, or received at the British Museum, all within a year or two of its putative date—then this negative evidence would have been overborne, and the pamphlet could have been no longer suspect. But in the continuous absence of such evidence (and in spite of extensive research we have found no trace of any), the suspicion aroused by the application of these tests deepens into certainty.

[1] See below, pp. 150, 151, and Appendix II. pp. 371–378.

CHAPTER VII

SUMMARY OF PROVED CONCLUSIONS

WE have described the genesis of our suspicions of these pamphlets, and the circumstances of their common market appearance and general similarity which suggested the working hypothesis that they formed a definite group, probably with a common origin. We have given a detailed account of the various negative tests as applied to the Reading *Sonnets*, supplemented by a discussion of further tests used for other books. We have expounded our researches into the history of paper manufacture and the development of type design during our period, from which we derived the control dates by which these books must be judged. The machinery of detection, in short, has been laid before the reader in full.

In the course of this exposition a number of books have been mentioned as failing to pass one or other of these tests of authenticity, and the general outline of the group will by now be tolerably clear: but the time has come to sum up the total results in such a way that the range of the group and the relative results given by the various tests can be apprehended at a glance.

One of the most remarkable features of the total result is the way in which the different tests corroborate each other. A number of books depend for their ultimate and conclusive proof on one only of the three positive tests, and this is sufficient condemnation. But the larger number are actually convicted on two or more counts; and although these double proofs are unnecessary, their frequency is extremely satisfactory, for the corroboration of, for instance, the type test by the paper test not only fills in the evidence against one particular book, but adds each time another buttress to the solid reliability of the tests themselves. To take only one example: we had been convinced by the preliminary part of the collation test [1] that Tennyson's *Ode for the Opening of the Great Exhibition*, 1862, must be a forgery, before we had even seen a copy—much in the style of Auguste Dupin reconstructing the Murders in the Rue Morgue from newspaper reports. Our first inspection of the book itself provided corroboration of this, in the prompt recognition of the type as Clay's Long Primer No. 3 —the forger's favourite fount. And in due course came the analyst's report of the paper, which contains a considerable proportion of chemical wood.

If we had been able to reverse the order of these three tests, the elaborate business of collating eight different versions of the poem might not have been undertaken; but as it turned out, the expenditure of time was amply justified by the provision of a perfect case of cumulative corroboration.

That we have taken a conservative line in distinguishing between "proved" and "highly suspicious" may be readily perceived by comparing our verdicts with the treatment of four of the Ruskin pamphlets by Messrs. Cook and Wedderburn, the meticulous editors of the standard edition of Ruskin's works. They denounced *The Queen's Gardens* and *The National Gallery* as forgeries, on their collation alone, without any hesitation: we have been able to add proof by type in the former case, and proof by type and paper in the latter. They were almost equally emphatic

[1] Given in full on p. 303.

in their denunciation of *The Scythian Guest* and *Leoni*, on negative evidence only; much more emphatic than we have permitted ourselves to be in many even stronger negative cases. We have been able to confirm their suspicions by the paper test for both books. Indeed, it is remarkable how often, in the course of our investigation, suspicion based on negative evidence, similar to that available to Cook and Wedderburn, has afterwards been turned into proof by the application of one or other of the positive tests. For example, we had felt uneasy about *Cleon* and *The Statue and the Bust* by Robert Browning, both dated 1855. Apart from their presence in the cache, which was, of course, possibly explicable by the story of their occurrence in one of the Moxon sales of 1873 and 1888, they seemed out of keeping with Browning's publishing habits: they bore the imprint of Moxon, whom Browning had left for Chapman and Hall in 1849: they were not accounted for in the number of his works published by Moxon as given by Browning to Locker-Lampson in 1874:[1] they were unknown to Furnivall in 1882, when he was compiling that exhaustive bibliography to whose completeness Browning himself testified:[2] when they were mentioned with other pamphlets by William Sharp in 1890, Furnivall, in his *Corrections*[3] to Sharp's book, asked, "Are not some of these creations of fancy?": no copy of either appeared in the auction room until 1903, and the first reference to their existence seems to be that in Mr. Wise's review of Slater's *Early Editions* in 1894: no cut copies or copies in old binding, or copies with early inscriptions are recorded: no copies are in the British Museum: no copies figured in the Browning sale in 1913. There was, in fact, a body of negative evidence against both

[1] Quoted on p. 79. [2] See below, p. 173.
[3] See above, p. 33, footnote.

these pamphlets sufficient to rouse profound suspicion of their authenticity. This suspicion was deep enough to be thoroughly disquieting, yet not conclusive enough to justify a verdict of forgery; and in such cases the result of the positive tests introduces a most welcome element of certainty. Our tentative verdict was corroborated with overwhelming force by the double evidence of the paper and the type, which condemns both pamphlets beyond appeal.

These two cases are typical of many others; and we submit that if Cook and Wedderburn, with much more cursory tests and none of our knowledge of the existence of this group of forgeries, felt justified in making the statements they did on such data as they had; then the claims of proof in the present work are advanced with adequate caution, and suspicions expressed, in inconclusive cases, with circumspect moderation.

The following lists show the cases fully proved by each of the positive tests, and the asterisks indicate the degree of corroboration by some other positive test or tests. Every book has, of course, been subjected to the more numerous negative tests, and where these have discovered such strongly marked features as inconsistent imprint, a copied vignette, or the expressed ignorance of the author, this higher degree of negative evidence is signalised by an obelus.

Books condemned by their paper.

E. B. Browning.	†*Sonnets, 1847.
	† The Runaway Slave, 1849.
Robert Browning.	†*Cleon, 1855.
	†*The Statue and the Bust, 1855
Charles Dickens.	To be Read at Dusk, 1852.
William Morris.	Sir Galahad, 1858.

* Condemned by two tests.

D. G. Rossetti.	Sister Helen, 1857.
John Ruskin.	†The Scythian Guest, 1849.
	**The National Gallery, 1852.
	Catalogue of the Turner Sketches in the National Gallery, 1857.
	†Leoni, 1868.
	*The Future of England, 1869.
R. L. Stevenson.	*The Thermal Influence of Forests, 1873.
Lord Tennyson.	*Morte d'Arthur, 1842.
	†The Sailor Boy, 1861.
	**Ode for the Opening of the Great Exhibition, 1862.
	*Lucretius, 1868.
	*The Lover's Tale, 1870.
	**The Last Tournament, 1871.
W. M. Thackeray.	*An Interesting Event, 1849.
	†A Leaf out of a Sketch Book, 1861.
Edmund Yates.	Mr. Thackeray, Mr. Yates and the Garrick Club, 1852.

Books condemned by their type.

E. B. Browning.	†*Sonnets, 1847.
R. Browning.	†*Cleon, 1855.
	†*The Statue and the Bust, 1855.
George Eliot.	Brother and Sister, 1869.
John Ruskin.	**The National Gallery, 1852.
	*The Queen's Gardens, 1864.
	*The Future of England, 1869.
R L. Stevenson.	*The Thermal Influence of Forests, 1873.
A. C. Swinburne.	†Dolores, 1867.
	†Siena, 2nd Edition, 1868.

* Condemned by two tests. ** Condemned by three tests.

Lord Tennyson. *Morte d'Arthur, 1842.
**Ode for the Opening of the Great Exhibition, 1862.
*Lucretius, 1868.
**The Last Tournament, 1871.

W. M. Thackeray. *An Interesting Event, 1849.

W. Wordsworth. To the Queen, 1846.

Books condemned by their text.

John Ruskin. **The National Gallery, 1852.
*The Queen's Gardens, 1864.

Lord Tennyson. **Ode for the Opening of the Great Exhibition, 1862.
**The Last Tournament, 1871.
The Cup, 1881.

In only one case, namely Swinburne's *Dead Love*, 1864, do we consider the negative evidence so strong as to be conclusive: here, in addition to all the usual features, we have a publisher's imprint demonstrably out-of-date, and this betrays circumstances of printing which cannot be other than fraudulent.

The following books cannot be proved to be falsely dated; but if not forgeries in the fullest sense of the word, they are established as fraudulent and unauthorised productions designed for the rare book market.

Rudyard Kipling. White Horses, 1897.
The White Man's Burden, 1899.

D. G. Rossetti. Verses, 1881.

R. L. Stevenson. Some College Memories, 1886.

Besides these conclusively proved cases, there are a number of books which we regard as highly suspicious. These escape condemnation outright in-

* Condemned by two tests. ** Condemned by three tests.

asmuch as their type and paper exhibit no inconsistency with the dates on their title-pages, while their collation accords with the expected text. They are found, however, in quantity, in company with the proved forgeries: they exhibit all the characteristics of the proved forgeries in bibliographical status and auction record: each is similar in format to *at least* one [1] of the proved forgeries: many are aspersed by negative evidence of their authors or by the absence of their printers from the directories. On the other hand, not one of them is supported by any particle of authenticating evidence whatsoever, and not one has a pedigree going further back than 1890.

Practically every one of these could have been pushed into the "proved" class by a little special pleading. Nevertheless, we have been content to label them only as profoundly suspicious. They are dealt with at full length in Part III. This list runs as follows:—

Matthew Arnold.	Saint Brandan, 1867.
	Geist's Grave, 1881.
Robert Browning.	Gold Hair, 1864.
George Eliot.	Agatha, 2nd Edition, 1869.
John Ruskin.	Samuel Prout, 1870.
	The Nature and Authority of Miracle, 1873.
R. L. Stevenson.	The Story of a Lie, 1882.
A. C. Swinburne.	Laus Veneris, 1866.
	Cleopatra, 1866.
Lord Tennyson.	A Welome to Alexandrovna, 1874.
	The Falcon, 1879.
	The Promise of May, 1882.
	Carmen Sæculare, 1887.

[1] E.g. *The Nature and Authority of Miracle* has the same, rather unusual, display type on its title-page as *The National Gallery*.

Beyond this class again comes a larger number of books which resemble the forgeries in one way or another and were preserved in quantity in the same hands as the forgeries at an early date; whose general record is unconvincing; which are not supported by any authenticating features: but against which there seems an insufficient weight of incisive evidence to justify treating them at length. The outer edges of the group are of necessity somewhat blurred; and in spite of our efforts to establish its extent and composition as certainly as possible, there remains this unauthenticated residue. We cannot find anything definite against these books: but we cannot find anything in their favour. It is quite possible that further research may disclose evidence which will put them beyond suspicion, but until that evidence is produced their genuineness must remain in doubt. These cases, remanded for further investigation, are discussed in collective postscripts attached to their several authors in Part III, and there is no need to tabulate them here.

This brief survey of the results of a long and many-sided investigation reveals a state of affairs which may well shock the most cynical commentator on the pitfalls of book-collecting; and we ourselves, who should be inured to it after many months of delving amongst forgeries and suspected forgeries, retain the capacity if not for surprise, at least for dismay.

With all its drudgery, detective work has a great intellectual fascination. Weeks might be spent in conscientiously wading through published correspondence or auction records, in search of a reference or a presentation copy, with the moral certainty that no such thing existed; but there have been redeeming moments of excitement, such as the identification of the forger's favourite type with Clay's Long Primer

No. 3, or the arrival of the analyst's report on the paper of the Reading *Sonnets.*

But the satisfaction of every piece of work completed brought with it regrets. If a book is a forgery, the sooner it is exposed the better: yet one cannot but sympathise with the many collectors who have treasured copies of it. In the earlier stages of the Reading *Sonnets* investigation, when it was suspect, but not proved, it was clearly necessary to compile as complete a census as possible of surviving copies, and an appeal to owners for details of condition, provenance, etc., brought a number of courteous and informative replies. It is an unhappy duty to requite this courtesy with proof that the book is a forgery: but nevertheless it is a duty, if not to the present owners, at least to all potential purchasers—not to mention the general public, which has for nearly forty years been deceived by a totally fictitious account of the origin of this famous book.

If we ourselves are beyond being surprised at the results of our investigation, we are fully alive to the fact that their unexpected nature is likely to induce not merely shock but incredulity in the minds of some of our readers. A man who has always accepted a certain book is nevertheless prepared (even against his inclination, if he owns a copy) to believe it spurious, provided that the proof seems to him satisfactory. But if it is not a question of a single book, but thirty or forty, what then? We are perfectly confident that in every case where proof is claimed, that proof *is* satisfactory: but the very magnitude of the numbers involved is bound to provoke some scepticism in anyone unprepared for such a wholesale exposure of clay feet among the accepted idols. The sceptic will then very properly ask: "When was this fraud perpetrated? and by whom? How did these books achieve their position? and why have they remained unchallenged so long?" We have dealt in Part I of this book with the deduction and detective work. We are therefore devoting Part II to the reconstruction of the circumstances in which these forgeries were conceived, the method by which they were executed and the steps which were taken, by the forger and by his unwitting accessories after the fact, to establish them on the road to their past or present eminence. Parts of the reconstruction are of necessity conjectural, for the passage of time has obliterated several interesting details; but we are able to answer three of the four questions posed above, and the main outline is reasonably clear.

PART II
RECONSTRUCTION

CHAPTER VIII

THE MODERN FIRST EDITION MARKET, 1885–1895

WE are all familiar with the type of book-collecting which flourished at the beginning of the nineteenth century and which was chronicled with such agreeable enthusiasm by the Rev. Thomas Frognall Dibdin. Dibdin loved a lord almost as much as he loved an Aldine on blue paper, and his pleasure in any connection between the two is not only inoffensive in its simplicity but is positively communicated to the readers of his comfortable quartos. The first quarter of the century was indeed a heroic period of book collecting, and the figures of the Duke of Roxburghe, Lord Spencer, the Marquess of Blandford, the Duke of Devonshire, Sir Mark Masterman Sykes, Richard Heber, W. H. Miller, Thomas Grenville, Beckford with his eccentric millions, the celebrated Roxburghe Club—all these seem to-day more than life size. It was the Golden Age, infinitely removed from our present collecting preoccupations both in the kind of books which stirred its enthusiasm and in its spacious and aristocratic atmosphere. Shakespeare folios and quartos were, it is true, held in some estimation, but it was the Valdarfer Boccaccio which caused the real sensation at the Roxburghe sale in 1812, making a price record for a single book which stood for seventy-two years. The magnificence of early printing and early illustration, the work of the classic binders, all the physical splendour of books—these were the main objects of their zealous pursuit; and although the earliest specimens of English, French and Italian literature were eagerly sought, an Aldine on vellum or a really tall Elzevir of the "right" date commanded ten times the price of the first edition of *Gray's Elegy*, while the *Essay on Man* could be had for a few shillings.

The existence of this state of affairs is, as we have remarked, perfectly well realised. What is not so generally apprehended is, how slow was the transition to the type of collecting which is characteristic of the last fifty years. It is only necessary to survey the activities of the great men of the middle of the century —Holford, Utterson, Halliwell, Lord Ashburnham, Huth, Tite, Offor, R. S. Turner, Thorold and the rest—to see how little attention was paid to the first editions of any authors later than Milton, and how comparatively little attention was paid to any first editions in English literature as such. Caxtons, yes; and the early editions of the rare early English books. But that special magic which we regard to-day as inseparably connected with the firstness of a first edition had not yet taken hold. The great libraries of Dyce and Forster, now at South Kensington, contain, it is true, a large number of first editions of date later than 1700; among them a sprinkling of the books of their contemporaries; but to read through the catalogues [1] is to feel that they were no first edition collectors in our sense.

The beginnings of the change can be seen fairly clearly, however, in the 'seventies. B. M. Pickering was advertising first editions of the Romantic poets and even Tennyson, as early as 1870, and Blake was beginning to be collected. As the distance in time between collectors and the objects of their enthusiasm

[1] Published in 1875 and 1888 respectively.

lessened, their interest took on a more personal colour, and the sentimental element became gradually stronger. Collectors were interested in the lives and habits of their favourite authors; they paid more attention to minor productions; they visualised the arrival of the first copies on the author's breakfast table—a powerful influence in the creation of a taste for "original condition."

This sentimental approach is seen at its strongest in the rapid strides of Dickens and Thackeray towards collecting eminence, and their popularity is a salient feature of the later 'seventies. Burns, of course, had always enjoyed a peculiar personal as well as literary position in the hearts of his countrymen, and it is not surprising to find that his was the place of honour on the shelves of most of the members of the flourishing Scottish school of collectors which had its centre in Glasgow.

Besides this general movement—in advance of it, in fact, and even more significant of what was to come—at least two great collectors of the modern school were at work—Locker-Lampson and MacGeorge. Of the former Mr. de Ricci has written:[1] "The library formed by the poet Frederick Locker . . . was unique of its kind. The owner's object—and it is indeed strange that nobody should have had the idea before him—was to secure the masterpieces (and the masterpieces only) of English literature, from Chaucer to Swinburne, in the first original edition of each work." That Locker-Lampson as a matter of fact included a large number of books of his chosen authors for their rarity, and historical, rather than purely literary, importance—Crabbe's *Inebriety*, for instance, and *Pauline*—only goes to stamp him more clearly as a pioneer of the modern school of collecting. The MacGeorge library, in common with others in the bibliophile city

[1] S. de Ricci, *English Collectors of Books and MSS.*, 1930, p. 174.

of Glasgow, was described fairly fully in 1885 by Thomas Mason,[1] and after being properly dazzled by its scope and splendour, one is struck by the astonishing judiciousness of its selection as viewed by to-day's standards. It is probable that this is less an indication of MacGeorge's remarkable foresight than of the immense influence over the succeeding generation which was exerted by these pioneers. In the dozen or so other Glasgow libraries described we find an abundance of Dickens, Thackeray, Cruikshank, Bewick, a fairly good showing of the Romantics, several notable collections of Ruskin and Tennyson: and this is a fairer reflection of the taste of the day in moderns.

Another potent factor in the development of book collecting was the foundation of those societies for the study of various authors which were so notable a feature in the literary life of the 'eighties. After the Chaucer, Shakespeare, and Early English Text Societies came the Wordsworth Society (1880), the Browning Society (1881), the Shelley Society (1886) and the numerous Ruskin Societies which, beginning in Manchester in 1879, sprang up all over the country. Their activities not only extended the study of the author's works, but also, in the case of the more recent, of their thought and lives. Prominent in the formation of these societies was F. J. Furnivall: and another branch of his work had an even more direct influence on the course of collecting. He was an ardent promoter of author-bibliographies, a type of publication hardly attempted previously except by Richard Herne Shepherd,[2] and the steadily increasing

[1] *Public and Private Libraries of Glasgow*, 1885.

[2] *E.g.* of Carlyle [1881], Dickens [1880], Ruskin [1879] and [1882], Swinburne [1883], 1884 and 1887, Thackeray [1881]. *Tennysoniana*, 1866, 1879; *Bibliography of Tennyson* (posthumous), 1896. Furnivall's own *Bibliography of Robert Browning* appeared in the Papers of the Browning Society in 1882.

output of these from 1890 onwards, almost all of moderns,[1] was both proof of the new trend and encouragement to its adherents.

The contrast between 1890 and 1860 is vividly exemplified by a comparison of those two standard manuals for collectors—Burton's *The Book Hunter*, 1862, and Slater's *Early Editions*, 1894. It takes no more than a glance to show the reader two different worlds—Burton's ideal the Roxburghe Club, Slater's the Ashley Library: and it is almost incredible that so much can have happened in so short a time. It is hardly too much to describe this change as a revolution, and Slater's book is in effect the revolutionary primer. If Locker-Lampson and MacGeorge were the pioneers, the leading figures of the effective period were Gosse, Prideaux, Thomas J. Wise, Buxton Forman, W. B. Slater, and, across the Atlantic, C. B. Foote, John H. Wrenn and W. H. Arnold. The decade 1880–1890 seems to have been the crucial period, and *Early Editions of Some Popular Modern Authors* was designed to help the scores of lesser collectors who by the early 'nineties were clamouring in the wake of the leaders. Slater had advanced the revolutionary theory as early as 1891,[2] but the later book is a much more detailed affair. He lists works by thirty-two authors; five of whom [3] are mere pegs for collected illustrators. Of the remaining twenty-six, no fewer than thirteen are represented in Part III of the present work.[4] For the rest, Jefferies, Lever

[1] *E.g.* T. B. Smart's Matthew Arnold, 1892; Wise and J. P. Smart's Ruskin, 1889–1893; Wise's Browning, 1896, and Swinburne, 1897; Temple Scott's William Morris, 1897; Buxton Forman's William Morris, 1897; etc., etc.

[2] *Round and About the Bookstalls*, p. 101 and *passim*.

[3] These are A'Becket, Apperley, Combe, Egan and Albert Smith.

[4] The only authors in Part III who are not in Slater are Wordsworth and Kipling.

and Surtees support the novel, though the two last are valued at least as highly for their illustrations as their text: Burns, Byron, Leigh Hunt and Shelley represent the Romantics: and Barham (? plates again), Bridges, Dobson, Gosse, Lang and Locker the lesser moderns. Poetry has a noticeable advantage over prose, if the "plate" books are discounted, but that was a taste in which readers of the time concurred with collectors against the general preference of the present day.

Reactionaries, of course, were not wanting to criticise the new movement, nor was Slater's primer entirely to the liking of the left wing of the movement itself; and the opposite views are clearly exposed by the reactions which the book provoked in the Press. *The Athenæum* during March and April 1894 contained a running controversy in its correspondence columns between Slater and C. E. S. Chambers, with various others intervening. Chambers picked many holes on points of detail, but his chief complaint lay against the selection of authors, which, however natural, was less justifiable in view of Slater's qualifying title. The full-length review of the book which appeared on May 26 describes the authors listed as "fashionable rather than popular," and the reviewer accuses Slater of catering to "the bric-à-brac collector" on the ground that less than half his authors had "produced works which have the least chance of taking a permanent place in literature." The book, he exclaims indignantly, contains "no fewer than ten living authors." And so on. He also convicts him of carelessness and inaccuracy in a number of places.

William Roberts, in *The Fortnightly Review* for March 1894, took an even stronger line, under the heading, "The First Edition Mania," [1] and though

[1] The main body of this (the controversial passages being omitted) was reprinted in his *Rare Books and their Prices*, 1896, pp. 29–50.

he does not actually mention Slater's book anywhere, his article is an attack on everything it stood for.

"The craze for first editions," he wrote, "is not by any means a recent one, although it may be said to have now reached its extremest form of childishness. Time was when the craze existed in a perfectly rational form, and when the first editions in demand were books of importance and books with both histories and reputations, whilst their collectors were scholars and men of judgment. Now, every little volume of drivelling verse becomes an object of more or less hazardous speculation, and the book market itself a stock exchange in miniature." He speaks scornfully of "flatulent little *biblia abiblia*" and "rubbishy tracts by living authors," and refers darkly to operators "working the market." He also has something to say about "too-zealous persons who feed their own vanity by hanging on to the coat-tails of eminent men and claim the title of public benefactors by 'resurrecting' from a well-merited obscurity some worthless tract or obsolete and ephemeral magazine article, and trumpeting it about as a masterpiece."

As an example to illustrate his statement that "the history of book-collecting has never offered such a fruitful source of ridicule as it does at present, because never before has the apotheosis of the infinitely little been so pronounced," he cites Norman Gale. "Mr. Gale's books of rhymes began to appear in 1885, and at the present time a complete set of the first editions of his booklets, about twenty volumes on large and small paper, is catalogued at £100—the published price of many of which did not exceed three shillings and sixpence . . . in fact," he concludes, ". . . the first edition craze generally is nothing more or less than barefaced gambling from beginning to end." The collector of to-day who reads Roberts' article will probably disagree with much of it; but at least he can congratulate himself that he had no opportunity of speculating in Norman Gale, whose first editions have now mostly retreated to their published prices—and no takers.

The spokesman of the modern school was Mr. Wise. In an article in the April 1894 number of *The Bookman* he replied to Roberts' tirade, convicting him of a number of inaccurate statements and adducing the hard facts of prices given under the hammer as evidence for the strength of the demand for modern firsts. He ended with a spirited defence of Ruskin first editions in particular; and the justice of this claim was implicitly admitted by Roberts, who introduced an ungrudgingly warm paragraph on the subject when he reprinted the bulk of his article two years later.

Mr. Wise had broken a lance in defence of Browning in the course of this reply, observing *inter alia* that "*Cleon*,[1] *Gold Hair*[2] and *The Statue and the Bust*[3] are worth ten or twelve guineas *each*"; and in his review of Slater's *Early Editions* in the May number of *The Bookman* he is equally vigorous in the championship of those minor rarities which roused Roberts to such intemperate language. Slater had gone much too far for the conservatives, but in the eyes of the left wing he had not gone far enough. "Compositions," wrote Mr. Wise, "which now find a fitting path to publicity through the medium of the periodical press were formerly printed separately, and circulated in the shape of a tract or pamphlet. A guide to such ephemera would be of the utmost value to dealer and collector alike." In the course of his review he indicates the extent of Slater's shortcomings in this respect by references to Matthew Arnold's

[1] See p. 177. [2] See p. 181.
[3] See p. 179.

Saint Brandan [1] and *Geist's Grave*,[2] Morris' *Sir Galahad* [3] and *Hapless Love* [=*Two Sides of the River*],[4] Ruskin's *The Scythian Guest*,[5] *War*, and *The Queen's Gardens*,[6] Rossetti's *Verses* [7] and *Sister Helen*,[8] and Tennyson's *Lucretius* [9]: none of which Slater had mentioned at all. He also corrects him on the points of Browning's *Gold Hair* [10] and George Eliot's *Agatha*; [11] and of Swinburne's *Siena* [12] he remarks that "the 'masterly pirated reprint' of *Siena* described on p. 294 is a creation of the author's fancy, these 'forged copies' being none other than examples of the first published edition of the pamphlet, Hotten, 1868."

These two views give a sufficiently clear picture of the contemporary trend in book collecting, and the situation in the modern first edition market during the latter half of the nineteen-twenties affords so close a parallel that we can have little difficulty in recapturing something of the atmosphere of the decade 1885–1895. New vistas were opening before the collectors' eyes, each with a glint of Eldorado at the end. Mr. Wise records, in the review quoted above, that in 1892 a washed copy of *The Scythian Guest* [5] was sold for £42, a figure which probably seemed no more ridiculous to the enthusiast then than £210 for *Jocelyn* by John Galsworthy, given under the hammer in 1929, did to some of us. The collecting public was eager, credulous and greedy. It was particularly keen on the obscurer rarities of its favourite authors, and since the obscurer and more trifling they were the greater their *réclame*, it followed that the first few copies of such things which came to light were apt to fetch very large prices indeed. A parallel case occurred in 1931, when the first copy to be sold of Rupert

1 See p. 161.
2 See p. 163.
3 See p. 207.
4 See p. 211.
5 See p. 225.
6 See p. 232.
7 See p. 218.
8 See p. 215.
9 See p. 305.
10 See p. 181.
11 See p. 194.
12 See p 287.

Brooke's schoolboy poem, *The Bastille*, made £70 at Sotheby's.

Those whose business it is to supply such demands naturally ransacked their stock for anything of the kind which they might unearth, and there were eager buyers, both trade and private, for anything offered; without too much regard, perhaps, to its provenance. There were, it is true, a fair number of pamphlet issues in the output of the fashionable authors of the moment: but, as these really were rare, there were not nearly enough. If only some others could be discovered, what pleasure and what profit would be provided for all concerned!

At the time of the Italian Renaissance, when new works and new manuscripts of known works were being unearthed every month, and hailed with joyous enthusiasm by a public newly awakened to the pleasures of humane letters, there lived an ingenious Dominican, Annius by name. He observed that though the supply of these things was fairly abundant, the demand was always in excess of it. So he provided, and then discovered, a number of manuscripts of hitherto unknown works by various attractive authors, including Archilochus, Cato and Fabius Pictor, the lost predecessor of Livy: and the fact that these were rather quickly exposed only proves that his execution was not up to the standard of his conception.

This simple formula could be even further simplified if no original composition were required: and to meet the crying needs of the book collecting renaissance of 1890, all that was necessary was to discover editions, so long as they were first editions. To look back at these feverish and speculative conditions in the book market is to see that it would have been almost surprising if there had *not* been some collateral descendant of Annius to perceive this golden opportunity. There was one such man, who is the hero (or villain) of the present work: there may, of course, have been others. The remarkable thing is, not that the circumstances produced a forger, but that the quality of his work was so extraordinarily high as to deceive not only his contemporaries but a whole generation of bibliographers and collectors. At the time, the thing was, comparatively, easy money: the fish were rising, he found (after a few experiments) the right fly, and they swallowed it with a regularity and unanimity which must have been to him exceedingly satisfactory. But the man was something of an artist. His formula for production was so effective that he was wisely content to eschew any great virtuosity in variation; and the mistakes that he did make were nearly always in the small details of type and paper, which, then as now, were the undisputed province of the technical expert. Yet, considering the scope of his operations, his success has been no greater than his talents deserved.

CHAPTER IX

THE FORGER'S METHOD

IT seems to us clear that the group of forgeries under discussion must almost certainly be the work of one man. It is, of course, impossible to prove this, but there are three arguments which make any other conclusion extremely unlikely. First, the earliest discoverable provenance of them all is the same. This does not postulate any necessarily close connection between the manufacturer and the wholesale distributor, but it does enable us to assign an early date to their common location. Secondly, sixteen out of the thirty fully proved forgeries—over half, in fact—have been shown to be the work of one printing house,[1] while other groups of proved and suspect books are printed in identical founts of type which, though not restricted to that same printing house, were in use there during the period in question.[2] Thirdly, and even more significant, the formula of forgery is unique, and this carries the common quality of the group back through the distributor, through the printer, to the mind which conceived them.

This formula, which is as simple as it is effective, consisted in taking some suitable piece from a published volume, printing it in pamphlet form with an earlier date, and thus *creating* a first edition. There are exceptions to the policy of pre-dating—*Cleon* and *The Statue and the Bust*, for instance, bear the same

[1] See above, p. 62.   [2] See above, pp. 69, 70.

date as *Men and Women* from which they were taken, while *Dolores*, dated 1867 and taken from *Poems and Ballads*, 1866, ranks only as "first separate edition." In many cases,[1] poems were chosen which had originally appeared in collected volumes by different authors, periodicals, or daily papers, and this, with its vague suggestion of protecting copyright, gave an added plausibility to a pamphlet issue for private circulation. With a few minor variations of method, then, this principle was consistently followed by the forger throughout the period during which he was at work, and it had the success that such a brilliant idea deserved. Periodical publication is almost ignored by collectors, so that the pamphlet ranked as a first edition: it preceded the published volume in which its contents (almost always) [2] afterwards appeared: it had the great merit to the collector of being "privately printed," whether explicitly or by implication: above all, it avoided, for the forger, the disadvantage of the fake reprint, in that it had no original to be compared with—it was an independent original itself.

Apart from technical tests this formula, if strictly followed, is practically proof against detection. It is impervious to textual criticism except for two eventualities—the survival of proof sheets of the later volume, which may betray an earlier state of the text; or the emergence, after the creation of the forgery, of a genuine article in the bibliographical place which it had usurped. The forger was unfortunate in that cases of both these eventualities have occurred.[3] He had presumably been unaware of the existence of the Metaphysical Society's pamphlet issue of Ruskin's

[1] *Cleopatra*, *An Interesting Event*, *To be Read at Dusk*, *The Runaway Slave*, *Sister Helen*, *Some College Memories*, *White Horses*, *The White Man's Burden*, *Saint Brandan*, etc.

[2] Swinburne's *Dead Love* and *Cleopatra* were not republished.

[3] For the former see *The Last Tournament* and *The Cup*, below, pp. 315, 327.

The Nature and Authority of Miracle, which indeed only came to the notice of Messrs. Wise and Smart while their Bibliography was in process of publication (1889–1893): as also of Stevenson's genuine offprint, from the Proceedings of the Royal Society of Edinburgh, of his paper *On the Thermal Influence of Forests*. The genuine Macmillan pamphlet issue of Tennyson's *Carmen Sæculare*, 1887, seems to have been obscure until July 18, 1900; and Matthew Arnold's offprint of *Geist's Grave*, from *The Fortnightly Review* of January, 1881, was not known, apparently, until a copy (with a presentation inscription from the author) appeared at Sotheby's on November 10, 1930.[1] Otherwise the only occasions when the test of the collation of the text yielded any significant result were due to the forger's carelessness. For instance, in Tennyson's *Ode for the Opening of the International Exhibition*, 1862, he used the 1889–96 text, which differs in different respects from all the previous versions. In *The Queen's Gardens*, 1864, he adapted the text of 1871, which had been extensively revised by Ruskin *after* the first published version of 1865; and here Mr. Wise unfortunately added to the confusion by stating that this was probably the text of the lecture as delivered by Ruskin.[2] That is exactly what one would have expected anyone of the forger's intelligence to have given us, and it is surprising that he overlooked the report of the lecture in the *Manchester Examiner and Times*, December 16, from which he might have safely reprinted.[3]

Apart from these lapses, the forger used his formula with discretion, and it is indeed a remarkably skilful

[1] See also *The White Man's Burden*, *The Cup*, *The Falcon*, *The Promise of May*, *The Last Tournament*, *A Welcome to Alexandrovna* in Part III.

[2] *The Bookman*, Feb. 1893, p. 145: Bibliography, II, 220: Ashley Catalogue, IV, 182.

[3] See also *The National Gallery*, below, p. 227, for a similar case.

one; simple, and, as the event proved, eminently convincing. The significant thing about it in our present context is that nobody else has ever used it. It is unique, and peculiar to him, and its impress on these pamphlets is the clearest of indications that they are all the product of a single mind.

The formula once evolved, it remained to choose suitable material for its exploitation; and when we come to examine the principles of the forger's selection, we find, as we should expect, that it is a faithful reflection of the collecting taste of the modern school of 1885–95. The literary importance of the pieces chosen was a secondary consideration; indeed prudence probably dictated the avoidance of major works, and the attractive trifle was sure of an even readier welcome from those whom William Roberts called first edition maniacs. There are a number of well-known things in the list: the *Sonnets from the Portuguese*, part of *Sesame and Lilies*, *Dolores*, *The Last Tournament*, and so on. There are the mere trivialities, like the preliminary edition of Ruskin's *Catalogue* and Stevenson's *On the Thermal Influence of Forests*, which yet seemed serious enough in 1890. But the main bulk of the group is made up of pieces which lie between these two extremes; interesting, curious or favourite examples of their authors' work, which were minor perhaps, but not obscure; of some importance, but not too ambitious.

In the selection of authors the forger was faced with a situation of some delicacy. With the market he had in mind, it was no use going outside the list of fashionable "moderns," and although at that date this list consisted of authors who had "arrived" rather than (as to-day) those who were merely "coming" he had to avoid forging books by any author who might notice and expose the fraud. In the majority of cases he exploited the work of authors who were dead. Mrs. Browning, Dickens, George Eliot, D. G. Rossetti and Thackeray, of course, had died well before he began; and there is no evidence known to us that any of the forgeries of Arnold, Robert Browning, or Tennyson were produced before the death of their authors, in 1888, 1889 and 1892 respectively. This leaves Ruskin, Stevenson, Swinburne, William Morris and Mr. Kipling.

Ruskin, however, had his first attack of brain fever in 1878; and although this was of short duration, from 1885 onwards he had only intermittent intervals of lucidity during which he was able to work, and he wrote no more after June 19, 1889. The first part of Wise and Smart's Bibliography appeared in September, 1889, so that although the parts were duly despatched to Brantwood, Ruskin could not have examined them with any critical attention.[1]

Stevenson left England in 1887 for ever, a sick man; and his lack of interest in his own opuscula is shown clearly enough by the fact that although he was in Edinburgh in that year, he paid so little attention to the printing of *Ticonderoga* as to be able to write later that he had never even seen a copy.[2]

Swinburne's health was delicate; and although he lived on for many years, the strictness of his seclusion at "The Pines" and Watts Dunton's complete control of everything he did are too well known to need any stressing here. He was, however, "a bit of a bibliophile" (to use his own words), and there was obviously a possibility that someone might show him any putative example of his early work. This did in fact happen, and his reactions to Mr. Wise's inquiries are considered below.

There remains only William Morris, who lived in

[1] Cf. The *Works* of Ruskin, edited by Cook and Wedderburn, I. 288.

[2] See below, p. 266.

full possession of his health and faculties until 1896. The forger must have summed him up as sufficiently careless of such things as thirty-year-old pamphlets of his own, to justify taking a risk: and in fact we find that Morris was credulous and amiable enough not only not to be surprised at, but actually to inscribe, a copy of *Sir Galahad*, which his friend Harry Buxton Forman showed him in 1890.[1] He also inscribed a copy of Swinburne's *Dead Love* to Westland Marston.

In addition, then, to his intimate knowledge of the taste of the day and the condition of the market, the forger is seen as skilful in his choice of material and circumspect in his choice of authors. He also shows a knowledge of literary history and a degree of bibliographical skill which stamp him as familiar with the relevant specialist publications and in close touch with the most up-to-date information. He knew who was Mrs. Browning's most intimate friend, and where she was living in 1847; he knew something of Swinburne's relations with his publisher, John Camden Hotten; he knew something, though not quite enough, of Tennyson's ceaseless revision of his texts, and his habit of having his poems printed in proof form for his own use in recasting towards their finally published state. But his knowledge was more significantly extensive than this. The numbering of the stanzas, for instance, might so easily, by an oversight, have betrayed the true status of *Gold Hair*:[2] but the change is noted by Furnivall in his *Bibliography* in the privately printed Browning Society papers; so that presumably the forger had access to these. He knew of the textual differences between the versions

[1] The status of two other inscribed copies is not absolutely clear: see below, p. 210.

[2] Three stanzas were inserted in *Gold Hair* in the second and subsequent editions of *Dramatis Personæ*, the volume in which it was first published.

of *The Last Tournament* in *The Contemporary Review* and in *Gareth and Lynette*.[1] He knew the date and place at which Ruskin gave the lectures *Of Queen's Gardens* and *The Future of England*: these, however, were given in a list in *Igdrasil*, the journal of the Ruskin Reading Guild. It seems likely, therefore, that the forger was, if not a member of these societies, at least in touch with their work.

In general, he showed a very high degree of bibliographical expertise and ingenuity. Almost every one of his productions is plausibly set in the list of its author's output, conforms to probability in its place and date, and boasts some kind of *raison d'être*. Considered intrinsically and separately, no one of them strikes a suspicious note, and it is little wonder that the group has remained for so many years secure and unchallenged.

In the matter of the selection of publisher's and printer's imprints for the pamphlets his record is again impressive. That he realised the difficulties is shown by the large number of cases in which there are none; and in the majority of instances where he employed the names of firms which really existed, they are unassailably appropriate. He did, however, make mistakes, and in view of the number of possible pitfalls it would be surprising if he had not. Swinburne's *Dead Love*, as already pointed out, bears the imprint of an extinct publisher.[2] Browning's *Cleon*, 1855, and *The Statue and the Bust*, 1855, both have Moxon's name on the title-page; but Browning had gone over to Chapman and Hall with the *Poems*, 1849, and as they were also the publishers of *Men and Women*, 1855, from which both these poems were taken, it would have been more politic to have attributed the pamphlets to them. And had he known of

[1] See below, p. 317.
[2] See above pp. 80, 81 and compare also *Laus Veneris*, p. 272.

an explicit statement made by Browning in a letter to Frederick Locker [1] in 1874, he would have been even less likely to confuse the logical sequence of imprints. On the other hand, he put Bell and Daldy's name on Morris' *Sir Galahad*, 1858, presumably because they published *The Defence of Guinevere*, its parent volume of the same date. But the printing of the two is very different, and unfortunately the publishers' records give tell-tale negative evidence against the book. He was similarly unfortunate over the absence of *Leoni* from the printers' records.

But if these mistakes are fewer than might be expected, in view of the difficulties involved, the forger was undoubtedly running a serious risk in inventing firms. He provided what seem to be purely fictitious imprints for *Saint Brandan*, *The Queen's Gardens*, *Cleopatra* and *The Story of a Lie*, and in relying on the impossibility of establishing an absolute negative on points of this kind, he neglected the potential importance as evidence of such exhaustive compilations as Kelly's Directories.

There are in this group of forgeries only four [2] fakes in the ordinary sense—that is, facsimiles of genuine books. These are difficult to date for first appearance, since in early references they cannot be distinguished from their originals. But at least two [3] of the four were in circulation before 1893, and one would like to believe that they were of considerably earlier date—prentice efforts, in a medium which is

[1] We have quoted the passage above, on p. 79. It was not published until 1900.

[2] *Agatha* (2nd Edition), 1869, *Siena* (2nd Edition), 1868, Ruskin's *Catalogue of the Turner Sketches*, 1857, and *Mr. Thackeray, Mr. Yates and the Garrick Club.*

[3] *Siena* was presented by Mr. Wise to the British Museum on December 9, 1893; and both this and *Mr. Thackeray, Mr. Yates and the Garrick Club* are printed in Clay's Long Primer No. 3, the use of which was discontinued in that year.

both conventional and dangerous and which he soon deserted in favour of the much better one he had himself invented.

When we come to consider the details of technical production, we are again compelled to pay a tribute to the forger's skill. He did not bargain for the microscopic examination of the paper which has played such havoc with these books, and there was little reason, at the time, to expect it. To a layman, even to a sceptical layman, there is nothing unusual or improbable in the appearance of most of the pamphlets.[1] With the exception of Rossetti's *Verses*, 1881, they are all printed on cream wove papers; and although many of these show a glossy finish characteristic of 1890 rather than 1860, this is a very nebulous ground for suspicion and quite unlikely to attract any attention. As long as he kept away from watermarked paper, the forger was safe as far as the layman was concerned: and with the exception of Rossetti's *Verses*, not a single book in the group has any watermark at all.

Typographically, too, the separate books are plausible enough to the casual eye. The minute details which indicate some datable evolution in type design are only visible to the specialist, and how unremarkable the printing of the group is, is convincingly witnessed by the fact that only once has any of its members attracted attention on this ground, and then from a specialist.[2]

But once the whole series is placed side by side, their typographical similarities become obvious: and we have already [3] explained why it is practically cer-

[1] There are one or two exceptions. Tennyson's *Carmen Sæculare*, for instance, looks more like 1910 than 1887, in paper, type and layout, though its mention by Livingston proves that in fact it must have been in circulation at any rate before 1901.

[2] Morris' *Sir Galahad:* see below, p. 270.

[3] See above, pp. 69, 70.

tain that Messrs. R. Clay and Sons printed them all. The identity of their types was a danger that the forger could hardly have avoided: it was not likely to be noticed, and even if it was, it was no proof of forgery. For, once he had the unsuspected entrée of one large printing house, it would obviously have been running a greater risk to transfer his operations elsewhere. Nevertheless, he showed considerable fertility in his handling of the type available: the pamphlets show much variety in their display, even though the same types are used. Some of the exceptions are clearly intentional: *The Falcon*, 1879, *The Cup*, 1881, and *The Promise of May*, 1883, bear the same imprint and are meant to look like the work of one printer. But the similarity of Ruskin's *The National Gallery*, 1852, to *The Nature and Authority of Miracle*, 1873, was a definite blunder. No one who puts the two side by side can fail to notice their resemblance. The capitals on the title-page, the text type and the general display are all the same. It is impossible to believe that this pair were printed by two different printers twenty years apart. The forger's typographical resource is most clearly shown in copying a genuine pamphlet. *The Runaway Slave*, 1849, imitates *Two Poems*, 1854; the arrangement of the stanzas, the rule surrounding the text pages, and the setting of the title all correspond. Both are set in a Small Pica modern face type; but these types are not the same. Such close resemblance without identity is in itself suspicious; but it is none the less an impressive demonstration of typographical mimicry.

We come now to the problem of the identity of the forger. The first candidate whose claims must be examined is John Camden Hotten, to whose unauthorised activity *Siena*,[1] *Dolores* and *Cleopatra* have

[1] *Literary Anecdotes*, II. 322.

long been attributed on the strength of their imprints. He was also believed [1] to have been responsible for the piratical issue (1862) of Tennyson's *Poems MDCCCXXX. MDCXXXIII*, on the ground that he was convicted of marketing it. Swinburne himself said of him: "The moral character of the worthy Mr. Hotten was—I was about, very inaccurately, to say—ambiguous. He was a serviceable sort of fellow in his way, but decidedly what Dr. Johnson would have called 'a shady lot,' etc.": [2] and his reputation generally was not a good one. By swindling Swinburne out of royalties, as he is supposed to have done over *Notes on Poems and Reviews*, second edition, 1866,[3] he qualified as a pirate, but that is not the same thing as a forger; and as he is not likely to have been concerned with spurious issues of any other author on our list, it will suffice to see whether he could have perpetrated those of which he is already accused. And since it has already been established that *Siena* and *Dolores* were not printed until after 1880, it is clear that Hotten was innocent of these two at any rate, for he died in 1873; and in this case there seems very little ground for connecting him with *Cleopatra*.[4]

Another possibility is Richard Herne Shepherd, a character very well known in the book trade in the 'seventies and 'eighties. A heavy drinker, who lived for many years at the Bald-Faced Stag, in the Finchley Road, Shepherd was a publisher's hack, working chiefly for the firm of Hotten; a bookseller's "run-

[1] *E.g.* there is a MS. note by Locker-Lampson in the Rowfant-Kern copy of the book which reads: "I hope I do not do Mr. Hotten the bookseller injustice, but I am told he was the pirate of this volume." The piracy has also been attributed to John Dykes Campbell, and Mr. Wise (*Bibliography of Tennyson*, II. 8) supports this with circumstantial detail on the authority of Campbell himself.

[2] Quoted in *Literary Anecdotes*, II. 314.

[3] *Ibidem.*

[4] See below, p. 278.

ner," to the trade in general and B. M. Pickering in particular; and a "literary chiffonier" on his own account. It is true that he printed and marketed these "ragpickings" without any regard for the rights of their authors, so that Tennyson had to prosecute him for pirating *The Lover's Tale* in 1875;[1] but he seems to have been inspired by a perfectly genuine idea of the importance of unreprinted pieces by such authors as Thackeray, Mrs. Browning and Longfellow. He was, in fact, something of a scholar, and his editions of Elizabethan dramatists earned him the approval of Swinburne, which took the practical form of allowing him to print and publish such pieces as *The Jubilee*, *A Word for the Navy*, etc. He was also the author of numerous bibliographies,[2] and Mr. Wise, to whom we owe practically all the unfavourable details about his character and operations, shows some lack of generosity in his attitude towards these pioneer ventures.

The points against Shepherd are:—

(i) He is known to have published piracies of Tennyson and other authors.

(ii) He is stated by Mr. Wise[3] to have been responsible for the circulation of *Dolorida*, a leaflet containing a poem possibly by Swinburne.[4]

(iii) The format of Rossetti's *Verses*, 1881[5]—a pamphlet certainly unauthorised and probably falsely dated—is somewhat like that of the Swinburne pamphlets issued by Shepherd and Rignall under the style of Ottley, Landon & Co. in the late 'eighties. *Verses* stands apart from the physical tendencies of the group as a whole, with its Van Gelder paper and three copies on vellum. But its similarity to the Shepherd publications is no more marked than its similarity to (for

[1] See below, p. 309.
[2] See above, p. 102.
[3] *Literary Anecdotes*, II. 374.
[4] See below, p. 282.
[5] See below, p. 218.

instance) the Ashley Library privately printed pamphlets, which have the above-mentioned characteristics; and it could form at best a very slender thread to connect Shepherd with the group as a whole.

The points in favour of Shepherd are:—

(i) He included none of these forgeries in his bibliographies; whereas he did include both his piracies of *The Lover's Tale* (giving quite frankly the details of its suppression) and *Dolorida*. This is such an obvious method of establishing a forgery that it is hardly conceivable that he should have neglected it.

(ii) One of his admitted piracies was copied by the forger. The 1870 edition of *The Lover's Tale*,[1] which Mr. Wise calls Shepherd's first edition, is, in fact, printed in Clay's Long Primer No. 3, and is a supplanter manufactured to oust the genuine Shepherd piracy of 1870 from its position as the first published edition.

(iii) There is no evidence that he ever had any connection with R. Clay and Sons; and the enjoyment of a regular and established custom there is an essential attribute of the forger.

(iv) He could not have been responsible for the two Kiplings, since he died in 1895, and it is almost impossible that he should have been responsible for *The Falcon* and *The Cup*, of which even Mr. Wise had never heard in 1896.[2]

(v) There is no evidence that, with all his piracy of *texts*, he ever falsely *dated* a book.[3]

The weight of evidence is overwhelmingly against the possibility of Shepherd having forged these books: and having disposed of these two possibilities, it remains to admit the disappointing fact that we have no

[1] See below, p. 307.

[2] *Literary Anecdotes*, II. 266.

[3] See below, p. 313.

conclusive evidence of the forger's identity. A number of his characteristics emerge from a study of his work, and to those enumerated earlier in this chapter must be added another, and a rather peculiar one: a rigorously firm belief in the principle of small profits and quick returns.

He knew well enough that the creation of a plausible first edition was only half the battle—the remaining half was to get it established. He had laid all the clues ready to be picked up, he had provided all the necessary internal confirmation for the so likely circumstances in which these pamphlets purported to have been printed; and he could be reasonably sure that the desirability of his creations would speedily be emphasized by high prices in the auction rooms and in the trade. But the things needed an influential sponsor: they needed bibliographical canonisation: they needed a position of eminence so secure that there would be no chance of anyone asking possibly awkward questions.

This was a delicate moment in the course of the forger's plans, and his surmounting of it was masterly. It was clearly imperative to introduce the pamphlets into the hierarchy of the modern movement: once on the shelves of such collectors as Gosse, Wise, Slater and Buxton Forman, the rest would be plain sailing.

Whether it was some prescient instinct of his future eminence as a collector and bibliographer, or merely a happy accident, which resulted in the forger's connection with Mr. Wise at this point, we shall never know. But it seems quite certain that he was successful in planting the forgeries on Mr. Wise, in bulk, over a period of at least fourteen years. As events proved, he could have chosen no more influential person for his purpose—the bibliographical and commercial promotion of the forgeries; and he was certainly alive to the vital importance to his scheme of some such unwitting "accessory after the fact." Nevertheless, even a very modest estimate of the financial returns due to the creative artist, even a fervent desire to turn over his productions quickly and cheap, hardly explain his prices as far as they can be inferred. What he received for how many copies we cannot say: but unless Mr. Wise was content to lose heavily on the resale of a large quantity of them in 1910–12 [1] (and there was no reason, in the state of the market, why he should have been), the forger's original prices must have been very moderate indeed. This is extraordinary, in view of the high degree of skill, care and risk involved in their manufacture; it is almost incredible, when we consider the auction record of some of the pamphlets even before the series was complete.

Mr. Wise's gullibility may seem extraordinary today, but it must be remembered that neither the general efficiency of bibliographical scrutiny nor his own experience as a collector were so great forty years ago. We cannot give any details of the methods used to foist the forgeries on to Mr. Wise, and in only one case has he given a full account of his discovery of a cache of any of them. The pedigree of the Reading *Sonnets*, as given by Dr. Bennett, is complete, and the whole story as related by Mr. Wise perfectly detailed and circumstantial. But the book is a forgery.

It is perhaps odd that Mr. Wise did not detect the nature of the "old and broken half calf," which covered "Miss Mitford's own copy," and which was subsequently replaced by new morocco; but such apparently impeccable provenance must have disarmed suspicion. The facts force us to question either Dr. Bennett's story or Mr. Wise's; and although Bennett seems to have been a blameless character,

[1] See Appendix II.

and he could not possibly have been responsible for many of the other forgeries (since he died in 1893), the possibility must be faced that he was a deliberate accomplice of the forger's in planting the book on Mr. Wise.

As for the rest, the story of "remainders" doubtless did a good share of the work. This was plausible enough, for there have been such remainders of perfectly genuine books: *e.g.* Shelley's *We Pity the Plumage*, 1843, Tennyson's *A Welcome*, 1863,[1] the Brownings' *Two Poems*, 1857, and Stevenson's *The Pentland Rising*, 1866.[2] The only appearances of such remainders to which Mr. Wise actually refers are attributed to the two sales of Moxon & Co.'s stock. The first of these took place in 1873, soon after Ward, Lock took over the business; the second in 1888, which was apparently a final clearing out. But these sales could only be made to account for the Moxon books in the cache, namely, *Cleon*, *The Statue and the Bust*, *The Runaway Slave*, *Laus Veneris*, besides the genuine Tennyson's *A Welcome*, 1863; and it ought not to have escaped Mr. Wise's observation that the first two of these were printed in identically the same fount of type, not only as the Reading *Sonnets*, but also the Shelley Society's *Alastor*, 1887, and the notes to the same Society's *Hellas*, 1886, of which Mr. Wise himself had superintended the printing by Clay.

Apart from this, the Moxon sale story was probably not much easier to verify then than it is to-day. We have been unable to trace the catalogue of the 1873 sale at all: and that of the 1888 sale, which took place at Hodgson's, contains at the end a number of miscellaneous lots which might have contained anything. But it does not appear from Mr. Wise's

[1] See W. H. Arnold, *Ventures in Book Collecting*, pp. 20, 21.
[2] See *Book Prices Current*, 1899, p. 529.

statements [1] about these sales that he took any pains to verify the story: at any rate the information he supplies is vague in the extreme.

But, be that as it may, this story only pretends to account for four books: and forty odd titles are left without any explanation at all. Plausibility alone is hardly enough to establish such a large and varied list of books appearing in considerable numbers, with apparently no provenance whatever. Yet Mr. Wise seems to have accepted without suspicion what must have been a steady stream of three or four "remainders" a year for fourteen years; and we have no evidence that he carried out any such inquiry into their origins as common sense, let alone bibliographical duty, plainly demanded. How disastrous this initial negligence has been is now overwhelmingly clear.

[1] *Bibliography of Swinburne*, I. 103; *Ashley Catalogue*, I. 118; etc.

CHAPTER X

ESTABLISHING THE PEDIGREES

THE actual dates between which the forger was engaged in production cannot, of course, be precisely determined. Kipling's *The White Man's Burden* shows that he was at work as late as 1899, and the evidence of paper and typography affords a conclusive earliest date possible for others; while some sort of *terminus ad quem* can be deduced from the first appearance, in the auction records and books of reference, of the various titles in our list.

The Reading *Sonnets* claims priority here, for Mr. Wise has dated the dispersal of Dr. Bennett's cache in 1886;[1] and it must have been shortly followed by *The Runaway Slave*,[2] shown to Browning in 1888. Then the Moxon sale, which Mr. Wise so readily believed to have been the source of some dozen of the forgeries, took place in 1888; and the same year gives us the earliest first-hand evidence apart from Mr. Wise's own accounts, in the shape of two British Museum reception dates—*The Runaway Slave*, purchased in August, and *Brother and Sister* in October—and the letters from Swinburne to Mr. Wise respecting *Cleopatra*. The next year brought to light copies of *Siena* and *Agatha*, both in a miscellaneous sale at Sotheby's in December; and in August, 1890, a copy of *Saint Brandan* was purchased by the British Museum.

[1] This date was not, however, divulged until 1918.

[2] See below, p. 169.

In 1892 the two Matthew Arnold pamphlets found a place in T. B. Smart's Bibliography. Slater's *Early Editions* (1894), although it dealt with all our authors except two, mentioned comparatively few of the forgeries; but the three Robert Brownings, the Reading *Sonnets*, *The Runaway Slave*, Thackeray's *An Interesting Event* are all included; not in the main lists, but in small type notes at the end of their respective sections. Several of the Swinburnes are accorded the more prominent position, as is *Brother and Sister*, with a significant note.[1] From 1895 onwards we find three or four additional titles in every year's auction records, though no copy of the Reading *Sonnets* seems to have come under the hammer until 1901.

It is apparent, then, that by the turn of the century most of the members of the group had achieved a respectable, some a sensational, standing in the auction market,[2] and such evidence as is available confirms similar conditions in private trading. For instance, a copy of *The Scythian Guest*, together with a vellum copy of one of Mr. Wise's privately printed volumes of Ruskin's letters, now in the John Rylands Library, Manchester, was purchased in 1893 for no less a sum than £63.[3] But except for the brief comments of " rare " or " very rare " in catalogues, we have little but bare figures (however significant) as indications of the ranking of these books; and for

[1] See p. 192.

[2] *E.g.* Browning, *Gold Hair* £9, 1899; Dickens, *To Be Read at Dusk* £8 15*s*., 1893; Ruskin, *Leoni* £6 15*s*., 1897; Stevenson, *Thermal Influence* £14, 1897; *Some College Memories* £12, 1897; Swinburne, *Cleopatra* £9, 1891; Tennyson, *Lucretius* £12, 1896; *The Last Tournament* £31 10*s*., 1900; *The Falcon* £52, 1899; *The Cup* £46, 1899; *Carmen Sæculare* £31, 1899; Thackeray, *An Interesting Event* £7 10*s*., 1899.

[3] Tregaskis were asking 25 guineas for a copy of Dickens *To Be Read at Dusk* in 1891, and Robson £30 for *Laus Veneris* before 1896 (*Literary Anecdotes*, II. 305).

their bibliographical and general status we have to fall back on Mr. Wise.[1]

Mr. Wise was in possession of what must have been a considerable stock of the books in the group, and just as the excitement of acquisition had lulled his suspicions of their origin, so now the pride of possession prompted him to do his best for such interesting finds. He was in a position to contribute information, as authoritative as it would be welcome, to the compilers of bibliographies of many of the authors concerned. T. B. Smart, for instance, was a friend, as well as brother to J. P. Smart, Mr. Wise's collaborator in the Ruskin Bibliography; he mentions Mr. Wise's copy of *Alaric at Rome* and his plans for the facsimile edition in his Bibliography of Matthew Arnold (1892, p. [77]), and the Ashley Library copy of the book bears a presentation inscription. It is therefore not surprising to find the two Arnold pamphlets duly described.[2]

Then in 1898 we find Mr. Wise describing himself as "the bibliographer of Stevenson," [3] and although he never produced such a bibliography, Prideaux in 1903 acknowledges his obligation "to Mr. Thomas J. Wise, whose materials for a Bibliography of Stevenson were generously placed at my disposal." [4] All the forged or suspect Stevenson pamphlets in our list figure in Prideaux.

Livingston, too, in 1901, writes in the Introduction to his list of Tennysons: "We have been favoured and much aided in preparing the description of this

[1] E.g. *Bibliography of Ruskin*, 1889–93; *Bibliography of R. Browning*, 1897; *Bibliography of Tennyson*, 1908; *Bibliography of E. B. Browning*, 1918; *Bibliography of Swinburne*, 1919; *The Ashley Catalogue*, 2 vols., 1905–08; the same, 10 vols., 1922–30; *A Browning Library*, 1929; *A Swinburne Library*, 1925; *Literary Anecdotes of the Nineteenth Century*, 1895–6; articles and reviews in *The Bookman*, 1893–4.

[2] They were dropped, however, from his second edition (1904). See below, pp. 161, 163.

[3] See below, p. 260. [4] Preface to his *Bibliography*, p. xiii.

set by having the privilege of consulting the proof sheets of a part of Mr. Wise's Bibliography," which he describes as about to appear "in one of the forthcoming volumes of *Literary Anecdotes*." All but one [1] of the forged or suspect Tennyson pamphlets on our list figure in Livingston.

As to D. G. Rossetti's *Verses*, 1881, Prideaux' *Additions* [2] to W. M. Rossetti's Bibliography expressly quote Mr. Wise as authority for this supplementary item.

Beyond these, and aside, of course, from Gosse's fictitious second-hand story about the Reading *Sonnets*, Mr. Wise's own works are the standard authorities for almost all the books with which we are dealing,[3] and we may therefore proceed with confidence to an inspection of his statements about their origins, their bibliographical status and the external evidence for their authenticity—the first item of which, naturally, will be that of such of their authors as were available for inquiry.

On August 1, 1888, Robert Browning wrote to Mr. Wise,[4] in respect of *The Runaway Slave*: "I never heard of a separate publication, and am pretty certain such a circumstance never happened. I fear that this must be a fabricated affair," etc. Two days later, after inspecting Mr. Wise's copy, he wrote: "I daresay the fact has been that, on the publication of the Poem in America, the American friends (in London) who had been instrumental in obtaining it, wrote to the Authoress (in Florence) for leave to reprint it in England, and that she of course gave her consent—probably wrote the little advertisement.

[1] *On the death of the Duke of Clarence* [1892]. [2] See below, p. 218.

[3] George Eliot is hardly an exception, since the first, and until recently standard, bibliography acknowledges the Ashley Catalogue as its source for details of *Brother and Sister* and *Agatha*. See below, pp. 191, 193.

[4] *Ashley Catalogue*, I. 100.

The respectability of the Publisher and Printer is a guarantee that nothing surreptitious has been done." Browning shows a touching, though quite natural, innocence of what our forger was capable of in the way of false imprints, but it may be observed that he does not offer any confirmation of the book whatever. Since Mr. Wise inquired of Browning about this book and *The Battle of Marathon* in 1888, it is curious that he did not at the same time make similar inquiries about the Reading *Sonnets*, in which Browning would obviously have been far more interested. As for the three pamphlets of Browning's own poems, which were supposed to have come from the Moxon sale in 1888, we can only assume that they did not come into Mr. Wise's possession until too late for inquiry of their author, who died at Venice on December 16, 1889.

Swinburne, however, lived on long after the discovery of the various forgeries of his work: and the forger was either very bold or uncannily conversant with the circumstances when he undertook them. Mr. Wise asked him about *Cleopatra*, in 1888, and the net result of his two letters in answer [1] was the words: "I am quite certain, quite positive, that I never set eyes on the booklet before, nor heard of its existence." What could be plainer than that?

Mr. Wise, however, on the strength of two variations in the text between the pamphlet and the version printed in the *Cornhill*, sets aside Swinburne's statement and declares that the author must have corrected the proofs of the pamphlet—how else account for two "superior" readings? He also refers to a set of proofs found afterwards at "The Pines," but he gives no specific account of these nor does he record that the corrections in question appeared in them.[2]

[1] See below, p. 279.

[2] The Wrenn proofs of this (see below, p. 281), show the *Cornhill* reading in the first case, the pamphlet's final reading in the second; and these at any rate were not corrected by the author.

Swinburne was equally ignorant of the existence of the second edition of *Siena*. His information about the original privately printed edition was precise enough, but as for the other, he could again only "suggest"[1] that Hotten was responsible for the roguery. We know his opinion of Hotten,[2] and when he was faced with the thing for the first time this must have seemed to be the only explanation. But when Mr. Wise adds: "It is known that he [Hotten] sold the booklets readily at five or ten shillings apiece," he must be relying on some even less satisfactory evidence, for, as we have seen,[3] Hotten was dead before it was even printed.

Dolores is in similar case. "Why it should have been reprinted separately," wrote Mr. Wise in 1896,[4] "can only be conjectured. Mr. Swinburne himself has no recollection of the circumstances under which it was produced."

Swinburne, in short, was unable to throw any light whatever on these books. This is natural enough, of course, in view of what we now know about them; but ought it not to have seemed just a little odd to Mr. Wise? Swinburne knew all about the original *Siena*; and *Under the Microscope*, 1872, a genuine pamphlet of very similar format and status, is several times mentioned in his correspondence.[5] He might reasonably have forgotten the existence of one pamphlet —but three? Mr. Wise must have been very sure of them to have remained undisturbed by such extensive ignorance.

Finally, we come to Ruskin, who is heavily represented on the list and who lived on to 1900. It is

[1] *Literary Anecdotes*, II. 321; *Bibliography*, I. 178; *Ashley Catalogue*, VI. 75.

[2] See p. 120. [3] See p. 120.

[4] *Literary Anecdotes*, II. 316.

[5] *Ashley* VI. 99 *et seq.*; *Letters*, edd. Hake and Rickett (1918), p. 88.

not recorded that copies of the forgeries of his work were shown to him, by Mr. Wise at any rate, but the Bibliography of his Works, by Messrs. Wise and Smart, was published during the years 1889 to 1893. Cook and Wedderburn,[1] however, state that whereas R. H. Shepherd's Bibliography (two editions, [1878] and [1881]), which did not include any of the forgeries, was examined with care by Ruskin, when the later one "was also sent to Brantwood . . . it does not appear that Ruskin was at that time able to give it his personal attention." The reason for this has been referred to above, and if Ruskin's health did not permit him to read it himself, it is not surprising that no one else at Brantwood detected the cuckoo's eggs which were now established in that well-filled nest.

He was even less likely to have seen an article in *The Bookman* for February, 1893, in which Mr. Wise [2] announced at some length the discovery of *The Queen's Gardens.* Its rarity and desirability were perhaps legitimate objects for emphasis, but he was less happy in the importance he claimed for it on textual grounds, as Cook and Wedderburn pointed out ten years later with such scathing emphasis.[3] This article, however, enables us to date the appearance of the pamphlet with some degree of accuracy; and the fact that *The Scythian Guest* and *The Queen's Gardens* were included only in the addenda seems to show that they both emerged between 1889 and 1893.

Apart from the personal inquiry of their authors; blankly unconfirmatory in the case of Swinburne, partial and unconfirmatory in the case of Browning, and merely implied, in the offering of the Bibliography,

[1] Vol. I. p. 288.

[2] This article is signed "W," but any doubt of its authorship is removed by the reference to "the editor of the new Ruskin Bibliography" in an unmistakably personal context; and it is, in fact, acknowledged in the *Bibliography*, Vol. II. p. 203.

[3] See p. 234.

in the case of Ruskin; Mr. Wise engaged his full powers as bibliographer and authoritative collector in the establishing of his finds. If his behaviour in face of Swinburne's reactions savoured of Nelson with the telescope to his blind eye, he had no commanding officer to consider in the case of other authors. He was in a position to lay down the law, and he did so with an assurance which in the circumstances was even less justifiable in its direction than in its force. In reviewing Slater's *Early Editions* in 1894 he picked out for special mention, as having been omitted or misdescribed by Slater, no less than twelve of these books:[1] and he was not content merely to note their existence. He emphasised (*a*) their rarity and (*b*) their price, quoting figures in most cases. "*Gold Hair*," he wrote, "is a privately printed pamphlet of the greatest rarity, and the sale of no copy has ever been recorded by Browning specialists. There would be no difficulty in finding buyers for half a dozen copies at *twice* the £5 at which it is here reported to be selling." And of *Sister Helen*: "This latter is one of the rarest items in modern poetical literature, and a clean copy would be worth at least £15 of anybody's money." And again: "*The Queen's Gardens*, 1864, only some two, or perhaps three, examples are known; a good copy ought certainly to be valued at ten or a dozen guineas." Now apart from any question of the bibliographical status of these pamphlets, if he had by then acquired his stock of them, this was tantamount to an advertisement of it; and whether the prices he quoted were fair estimates or not, he knew very well that many of these books were not by any means as rare as he made out. How many of each he had at this time we have no means of knowing; but we do know that even fifteen years later his stock of *The Queen's Gardens* amounted to at least seven copies, and

[1] See above, p. 107.

of *Gold Hair* to at least nineteen; while of *Geist's Grave*, which he described in the same article as a "rarity," he was still in a position in 1910 to sell as many as forty-three to Mr. Gorfin. It is impossible to escape the conclusion that Mr. Wise's zeal for the bibliographical establishing of these books, both in this review and elsewhere during the following years, had a partly commercial motive; and even if this went side by side with the pride of the discoverer, the fact that the establishing was done mainly under his own name, while his marketing of the books was carried on largely through agents, gives the whole affair a rather unhappy colour.

In 1895–6 there appeared the two volumes of *Literary Anecdotes of the Nineteenth Century*, edited by W. Robertson Nicoll and Thomas J. Wise. This collection contains, besides much other interesting and valuable matter, several sections which are relevant to the present inquiry; namely, *Materials for a Bibliography of the Writings in Prose and Verse of Robert Browning; Elizabeth Barrett Browning and her Scarcer Books; The Building of the Idylls, a Study in Tennyson; A Bibliographical List of the Scarcer Works and Uncollected Writings of Algernon Charles Swinburne*. Of these contributions, none of which are signed, the second is by Harry Buxton Forman; the last was acknowledged by Mr. Wise in the preface to his *Bibliography of Swinburne* in 1919; the first appeared separately in the same year, in parts, with his name on the title-page; and the third is attached to his name by Livingston in 1901 as if his authorship was common knowledge. Now books with which we are dealing figure fairly prominently in every one of these bibliographical studies, as may be seen by the frequent references throughout the present work, and the authoritative acceptance and description of them in a publication of this kind undoubtedly played a large part in establishing them in the eyes of the literary and collecting world.

In 1896, too, Gosse's *Critical Kit-Kats* carried his story of the origin of the Reading *Sonnets* to a wider public than it had apparently reached on its first appearance two years before. This was examined at length in Chapter II, and there is no need to do more here than fit it into its chronological place in the establishing movement. In view, however, of what we now know of Mr. Wise's position in regard to these books, it is obvious that he must have known who Gosse's anonymous and inventive informant was. Now that we know his story to have been fictitious, the revelation of his identity, so long and inexplicably concealed, has become a matter of public interest.

By 1898 it is probably true to say that the main body of the group were fairly well established, bibliographically as well as commercially. And in that year their sponsor was called upon to deal with two public attacks.

The *Athenæum* during January and February contained a correspondence on the question of the authenticity of *Some College Memories*. This was impugned by Messrs. Constable of Edinburgh; defended by the editorial comment, quoting " a bibliographer of note "; attacked by Constable in greater detail; defended with a fine dogmatism by Mr. Wise; and finally aspersed in a sarcastic letter from Frank T. Sabin, one of the most notable booksellers of his day. There was no reply to Sabin's letter: indeed, to anyone who reads the correspondence [1] it must seem obvious that there could be no reply. Mr. Wise had done his best, but the brief was too poor for anything except bluffing.

On January 22 of the same year, there appeared a

[1] Reprinted in full below, pp. 255–262.

short note[1] by Robert Proctor, the greatest typographical scholar of his age and a friend of William Morris, giving his reasons for believing Morris's *Sir Galahad* to be a fake. These, though perhaps less numerous than the arguments against *Some College Memories*, were cogent enough in all conscience and came with all the weight of a great authority. It was perhaps the most peaceful course to leave this note unanswered; for indeed, as we shall point out later, these casual denunciations do disappear, leaving almost no trace behind in the consciousness even of those interested in such things. Yet it is strange that Mr. Wise, so vigorous in defence of *Some College Memories* in the same columns, did not reply to Proctor. He had referred to it in his review of Slater, in 1894, as one of "the two most difficult of Mr. Morris's books to procure"; he described it without misgivings in his catalogue in 1905[2] and he had a stock of at least seventeen copies in 1910. All these facts testify to his belief in its genuineness, and in view of his decisive attitude in similar cases his silence over *Sir Galahad* is strange. It is all the stranger inasmuch as he had ready to his hand an argument to back up his own statement, in the shape of two copies of the book containing inscriptions in the author's hand. One of these belonged to Buxton Forman,[3] and this inscription was dated 1890: the other was in Mr. Wise's own collection. The inscription in this copy—*Ford Madox Brown from his friend William Morris*—is not dated at all, and as it appears from the description[4] to be possibly not on an integral leaf of the book itself, it may be that it could not be conclusively proved to belong to *Sir Galahad* at all.

But whatever was the reason which prevented

[1] Reprinted below, p. 208. [2] I. 115.
[3] Sold April 1920 at the Anderson Galleries in New York.
[4] *Ashley Catalogue*, III. 161.

Mr. Wise from putting Proctor right on this point, the occurrence of these inscriptions does definitely concern us. Where Proctor suspected, we know that *Sir Galahad* is a forgery, and the proof has been duly propounded in Chapter IV. Consequently there must be some explanation of these inscriptions. There is, and it is a tolerably simple one. We have stressed above the conclusive evidence for authenticity provided by a copy of a book presented by the author (or indeed by anyone else) at or near the date of issue; but just as the prudent collector discriminates between a copy "presented" and one merely "inscribed," so, and even more rigorously, must the sifter of evidence distinguish between these valid inscriptions of contemporary date and others which are dated years later or have no date at all. Authors often are, or were, before autograph hunters became so numerous, accommodating people: very few would at that date have refused to put their name in a book for a friend, and the mild vanity in being collected, when collecting moderns was still an unfamiliar pursuit, would have made such a thing even easier. Many of us remember Clement Shorter's collection of Hardy's first editions: almost all had inscriptions from the author, but they were mostly dated years, decades later than the books themselves. They had been inscribed on request.

Similarly, no doubt Buxton Forman in 1890, much pleased with his recently acquired *Sir Galahad*, begs an inscription from the author. Morris, with his head full of future Kelmscotts and neither remembering nor probably much interested in a pamphlet thirty years old, is only too glad to oblige a friend. More, he signed copies of *The Two Sides of the River*, one for Forman and another which is now in the Ashley Library; neither of them dated. And in the same way, Swinburne, who paid no more attention to the pamphlets shown to him than to say he knew nothing about them, and to exclaim at the fantastic prices they fetched, naturally had no objection to putting his signature on Mr. Wise's copy of *An Appeal to England*, or writing a little note in *Cleopatra* giving his inaccurate recollection of the picture which had originally inspired the poem.

But if such signatures as these have little bearing, beyond the most superficial appearance of hall-marks, on the authenticity of the books in which they are written, what are we to conclude from a specific signed statement like that provided by Alexander Strahan for Mr. Wise's two copies[1] of *The Last Tournament*? That this book is a forgery we know;[2] and yet Strahan, whose imprint is on the title-page, writes on the half-title, "Of this private edition of The Last Tournament not more than 20 copies were printed." There are only two explanations of this. Either Strahan confused this, in after years, with the so-called "trial-book" of [? 1868], which he would have known about and of whose printing number he could truthfully make such a statement: or he knew what the book was, and used the word "private" with a meaning the ordinary reader could not be expected to understand; and this suggestion is both less pleasant and less likely. Yet Strahan wrote a presentation inscription (also undated) in Mr. Wise's copy of Tennyson's *Ode for the International Exhibition*, 1862, a book with which he was in no way connected and one which is proved a forgery on several counts.[3] It looks, in fact, as if Strahan must have been either privy to the nature of these two books, or else unusually, almost improbably, careless and obliging.

But whether supported by inscriptions such as

[1] Reproduced in facsimile in *Bibliography of Tennyson*, I. 194 and *Ashley Catalogue*, VII. 129.

[2] See below, pp. 315–319. [3] See pp. 301–304.

these, or faced by the blank ignorance of Browning and Swinburne, or attacked in print by Proctor, Constable and Sabin, Mr. Wise pursued a course of unswerving dogmatism. He was in a position to interpret Swinburne's reactions in as little unfavourable a light as possible, and he did so: nor can it pass unnoticed that there is a marked increase of assurance in the descriptions of the pamphlets on our list in the *Bibliography* (1919), *The Ashley Catalogue* (Vol. VI. 1925) and *A Swinburne Library* (1925), when compared with *A Bibliography of the Scarcer Works* (1897). Similar instances of increasingly positive confidence, of amplified detail in pedigrees, are numerous, and may be observed in many entries in Part III. The Reading *Sonnets* is perhaps the outstanding case, as will be remembered from Chapter II, and *Cleopatra* [1] and *Some College Memories* are also among the more remarkable witnesses to Mr. Wise's capacity for overcoming any doubts he may—or at least ought to—have had. *Some College Memories*, for instance, was shown quite clearly to be spurious in the *Athenæum* correspondence of 1898,[2] and Mr. Wise, who unconvincingly defended it, made no reply to the final letter of aspersion: yet in *The Ashley Catalogue* he states, without reference or qualification, that it was printed "with the Author's consent and approval."

The stately sequence of now standard bibliographies carried everything before them—Tennyson (1908), Mrs. Browning (1918), Swinburne (1919); and the ten volumes of *The Ashley Catalogue*, together with those amplified sections of it published under separate titles like *A Browning Library*, have enjoyed in the collecting world an equal bibliographical prestige with the bibliographies proper. The two categories are, indeed, more closely akin than is entirely satisfactory for either. For on the one hand we find in the

[1] See pp. 278–284. [2] Reprinted in full below, pp. 255–262.

catalogue of one man's collection (superb though it be) frequent instances of bibliographical dogmatism which do not properly belong there; while on the other hand the bibliographies are far more intimately connected with, far more exclusively based upon, that single collection than is appropriate to their wider scope and more authoritative status.

It is owing to the latter circumstance as much as the former that Mr. Wise's acceptance and sponsoring of these forgeries has done such incalculable harm to the bibliography of the authors represented in the present book. His original negligence in authenticating his finds: his purchase of them in bulk and subsequent gradual dispersal of them through commercial channels: his disingenuousness in emphasising the rarity of books which he knew well were not rare in the strict sense at all—all these things have inflicted damage in plenty on innumerable collectors all over the world, who have for years paid good money—and in some cases a good deal of it—for books which are, in fact, worthless except as curiosities. But far more serious in its import and far-reaching in its extent is the damage done to the integrity of bibliography as a whole. Mr. Wise, by his credulity, by his vanity in his own possessions, by his dogmatism, by abuse of his eminence in the bibliographical world, has dealt a blow to the prestige of an honourable science, the repercussions of which will be long and widely felt.

He was deceived where he ought not to have been deceived; and if thirty or so spurious books have been established as genuine by the influence of his authority, how can the credit, not only of his own great mass of bibliographical work, but of much else as well, fail to be seriously shaken?

Like the thirteenth stroke of a faulty clock, which discredits the accuracy of the hours which have gone before, the spuriousness of these books must inevitably cast aspersions on many similar books which are, in fact, genuine. If these, so plausible, so well-established, are forgeries, what can we trust? If Mr. Wise, one of the most eminent bibliographers of our time, can be so extensively wrong, who can we be sure is right?

In the whole history of book collecting there has been no such wholesale and successful perpetration of fraud as that which we owe to this anonymous forger. It has been converted into an equally unparalleled blow to the bibliography and literary criticism of the Victorian period by the shocking negligence of Mr. Wise.

CHAPTER XI

MARKETING THE FORGERIES

WE have already pointed out that the earliest reference that we have found to any of these pamphlets is Mr. Wise's discovery of the Bennett cache of the Reading *Sonnets* in 1886. Two further forgeries are mentioned in Mr. Wise's correspondence with Browning and Swinburne in 1888; and in the same year some of them were bought by the British Museum. As it will be convenient to consider all the British Museum acquisitions together, we give here a complete list:

16 Aug. 1888. Mrs. Browning, The Runaway Slave, bought from E. Schlengemann for £5 5*s*.
23 Oct. 1888. George Eliot, Brother and Sister, bought from E. Schlengemann for £3 3*s*.
12 Apl. 1890. Swinburne, Dead Love, presented by Mr. Wise.
12 Apl. 1890. Swinburne, Laus Veneris, presented by Mr. Wise.
12 Apl. 1890. Swinburne, An Appeal to England, presented by Mr. Wise.
13 May 1890. Swinburne, Cleopatra, bought from Otto P. Rubeck for £5 5*s*.
16 June 1890. Ruskin, The National Gallery, bought from Otto P. Rubeck for £2 2*s*.
16 June 1890. Ruskin, The Nature and Authority of Miracle, bought from Otto P. Rubeck for £2 2*s*.

20 Aug. 1890. Arnold, St. Brandan, bought from Otto P. Rubeck for £2 2*s*.

13 Sept. 1892. Tennyson, Lucretius, bought from F. G. Aylward of Hereford.

9 Dec. 1893. Swinburne, Siena [2nd ed.], presented by Mr. Wise.

12 Nov. 1894. Morris, Two Sides of the River, bought from J. E. Cornish of Manchester, with other books, for £3 3*s*.

12 Nov. 1894. Rossetti, Verses, bought from J. E. Cornish of Manchester, with other books, for £3 3*s*.

8 Jan. 1898. Kipling, White Horses, presented anonymously.

11 March 1899. Tennyson, The Cup, presented by Mr. Wise.

11 March 1899. Kipling, The White Man's Burden, presented anonymously.

11 March 1899. Tennyson, The Promise of May, presented by Mr. Wise.

8 July 1899. Tennyson, The Sailor Boy, presented by Mr. Wise.

8 July 1899. Thackeray, A Leaf out of a Sketch Book, presented by Mr. Wise.

10 Oct. 1903. Tennyson, Ode on the Colonial and Indian Exhibition, presented by Mr. Wise.

10 Oct. 1903. Tennyson, Carmen Sæculare, presented by Mr. Wise.

9 Jan. 1904. Tennyson, A Welcome, 1874, presented by Mr. Wise.

11 May 1907. Tennyson, The Falcon, presented by Mr. Wise.

9 Feb. 1908. Tennyson, On the Death of the Duke of Clarence and Avondale, 1892, presented by Mr. Wise.

19 Apl. 1919. Swinburne, The Devil's Due, presented by Mr. Wise.

14 June 1919. Swinburne, Dolores, presented by Mr. Wise.
14 Oct. 1924. Arnold, Geist's Grave, bought from Bernard Quaritch, Ltd., with other books, for £2 5s.
Jan. 1926. George Eliot, Agatha [2nd ed.], presented by Mr. Wise.

The generosity of Mr. Wise is outstanding;[1] but our inquiry must be directed towards some independent source of supply, which may indicate the real origin of the forgeries. The copy of *Geist's Grave* bought from Messrs. Quaritch was one of the forty-three copies acquired by Mr. Gorfin under circumstances which are discussed later. The firm of J. E. Cornish are well-known booksellers; their two pamphlets were bought by the Museum together with several other books, and there is no reason to suppose that the seller did not acquire them in the ordinary course of trade. We have been able to ascertain no facts about F. G. Aylward of Hereford who sold the copy of *Lucretius*. E. Schlengemann, from whom the Museum bought their first examples of the forgeries in 1888, was, we are informed, at that date an employee of Herman Rubeck, an essential oil merchant, of 59 Mark Lane, London, E.C., and the Otto P. Rubeck, who sold four more of the forgeries to the Museum in 1890, was the son of the same gentleman. This same Otto P. Rubeck also sold the copy of Thackeray's *An Interesting Event*, which is now in Viscount Esher's library, to Messrs. B. F. Stevens and Brown on Dec. 8, 1892. On inquiring of this firm, we were

[1] This is still further emphasised by the fact that all fifteen of these pamphlets in the Cambridge University Library were presented by Mr. Wise in August and September, 1916; and of the four in the Bodleian Library, one (see p. 203) was an anonymous gift, one (see p. 240) was bought from Mr. Gorfin, and the other two were presented by Mr. Wise in February, 1917.

told that, although their records of that date were no longer preserved, they remembered having purchased from the same source a number of the Tennysons and Swinburnes on our list. But all this only takes us round in a circle, because from the mid-eighties until after the War, the cashier, manager and later part proprietor of the Rubeck firm was Mr. Thomas J. Wise.

Faced with this dead end, we again examined the auction record of the whole group; and we were impressed by two features. First, that a curiously large proportion of the sales in which they occurred were of anonymous properties; thus, of the thirty-one records of *Laus Veneris*, twenty-two were in anonymous sales; eighteen out of twenty-seven records of *Cleopatra* were anonymous property, and so on. Secondly, that nearly all the sales, whether anonymous or not, seemed to show a substantial number of the forgeries; they occur in groups which cannot be accounted for by an interest in any one author. Thus at Sotheby's on May 12, 1897, seven were included in the "Other Properties" offered with the library of Sir Cecil Domville, Bart.; at Puttick and Simpson's on June 14, 1897, "The Property of a Collector" contained fourteen; and "The Valuable Library of a Gentleman living in Yorkshire," sold at Sotheby's on June 10, 1903, contained no less than twenty-three, besides some duplicates and nearly a dozen of the special issues on vellum of Mr. Wise's private pamphlets. Turning to the sales which were not anonymous, we find the greatest number of forgeries occurring in the libraries of Sir Edmund Gosse (20; Sotheby's, Dec. 1928–May 1929, to which must be added the copy of the Reading *Sonnets*, which Mr. Wise says that Gosse had earlier sold for £50); John Morgan of Aberdeen (24; Bangs & Co., New York, April 1,

1902 and Sotheby's, March 25, 1908); Rev. Stopford Brooke (8; Sotheby's, July 18, 1910, and this does not include his copy of the Reading *Sonnets*, which Mr. Wise says that he sold separately for £40); P. M. Pittar (12; Sotheby's Nov. 4, 1918); and Harry Buxton Forman (30; Anderson Galleries, New York, March 15, 1920; another forgery and ten duplicates were in the second part of the library sold by the same firm in the following month).

The provenance of the copies in the anonymous sales, which must represent about two-thirds of the total, is now impossible to discover, as none of the auctioneers seem to have preserved their ledgers. Nor does the acknowledged ownership of copies in England help to indicate any possible alternative source of supply. Mr. Wise wrote, referring to his discovery of a bundle of the Reading *Sonnets*, "They were bought by Harry Buxton Forman, Robert Alfred Potts, Sir Edmund Gosse, the Rev. Stopford A. Brooke, John Morgan of Aberdeen, Mr. Walter Brindley Slater, and other friends to whom I hurried the good news."[1] The auction record would seem to suggest that the good news of other finds may have been treated in the same way.[2]

The American collections in which the forgeries were most strongly represented before the War appear to have been those of W. H. Arnold (8; and the three Tennysons were apparently duplicates;[3] Bangs & Co., New York, 1901); Edwin N. Lapham (22; sold for $1766.50; Anderson Galleries, New York, Dec. 1–3, 1908);[4] Henry W. Poor (15; in five sales at the Anderson Galleries, Nov. 1908–April 1909); and to

[1] *A Browning Library*, 1929, Preface. See above, p. 17.

[2] The libraries of R. A. Potts and W. B. Slater do not seem to have been sold under the hammer.

[3] See W. H. Arnold, *Ventures in Book Collecting*, 1923, pp. 22 and 255.

[4] His copy of the Reading *Sonnets* came from Mr. Gorfin.

these must be added the libraries of Harry Elkins Widener (25; mainly from the Lapham and Poor sales) now at Harvard, and of John H. Wrenn, now in the library of the University of Texas at Austin. It was in the Arnold sale that copies of the Reading *Sonnets* and Tennyson's *The Falcon* and *The Promise of May* first appeared in the auction room on that side of the Atlantic. The first of these we know to have been secured through Mr. Wise, and perhaps some of the others, because Mr. Arnold writes, "Through the kind offices of my new, but now dear old, friend the distinguished collector and bibliographer, Mr. Thomas J. Wise . . . I obtained one Tennyson rarity after another, most of which were at that time unknown to American collectors."[1] But wherever Mr. Arnold got his copies of the forgeries, they are much less important for our purpose than those in the Wrenn Library. This alone rivals the Ashley Library in containing a complete series of the forgeries; indeed it also contains proof sheets of two, and duplicates of several more. Mr. Wise himself tells how he collaborated with Wrenn for nearly twenty years, and claims that "quite a substantial portion of the books now safely and finally housed at Austin were purchased by me in this country."[2] These facts are a tribute to the wide and powerful influence which Mr. Wise has for so many years exercised on the book collecting world; but they do not indicate any alternative provenance for the forgeries.

There is one further angle from which the question of provenance may be considered. In the case of such a rare and highly priced book as the Reading *Sonnets*, it is possible to trace the provenance of a large proportion of the extant copies; and we hoped that inves-

[1] Arnold, *op. cit.*, p. 14.
[2] *Catalogue of the Library of J. H. Wrenn*, 1920, Preface.

tigation of this might show some alternative to Dr. Bennett's bundle as the original source of the booklet. Our results have been set out in detail in Appendix I.[1] Of the seventeen copies in the first group, which consists of those the present location of which is known, no less than seven derive from Mr. Wise or the Bennett bundle. Of the nineteen copies in the second group, which we cannot locate, six more come from this same source. This gives a total of thirteen out of thirty-six; but it must be remembered that some of the first group may be duplicated in the second, so while, as far as our researches go, thirty-six is a maximum figure, thirteen is an irreducible minimum. But the odd fact here is not that so many copies derive from the Bennett bundle, but that none of the remaining twenty-three have a pedigree that can be traced further back than 1897, so that all thirty-six copies may have come from that one cache. Actually not one can be shown to have come from any other source; all may have come from there; and more than a third of them certainly did. The significance of this is not that some copies passed through the hands of Mr. Wise, but that we can trace no alternative source for any of the copies of this forgery.

We must now return to an earlier stage of our investigation. We have described in Chapter I how the occurrence of these forgeries together in recent anonymous auction sales first directed our attention to them. When we began to suspect that Mr. Herbert Gorfin was their owner, we naturally imagined it to be possible that he was also their forger. But Mr. Gorfin was born in 1878, so that he was only ten years old when the earliest independent evidence of their existence is found; and we know that all of them had been produced by the time he was twenty-one. A

[1] See below, pp. 363–368.

few minutes' conversation was sufficient to convince us not only that Mr. Gorfin was not the forger, but that he had not the slightest idea that he was selling forgeries. Once he was convinced, he gave us all the information that he could; not only this, he lent us copies of many of the pamphlets that we had not been able to examine before, and this book could not have been as comprehensive without his straightforward co-operation.

Mr. Gorfin joined the firm of H. Rubeck & Co. as office boy in 1892, and with a short interval remained in their employ until in 1912 he set up as an antiquarian bookseller in Charing Cross Road, later moving to Lewisham. From 1898 until the War he acted as Mr. Wise's agent on commission in selling copies of nearly all these pamphlets, as well as autograph manuscripts of the Brontës, George Borrow and Swinburne. When he decided to set up as a bookseller, he purchased from Mr. Wise all that he understood to be left of the various "remainders" of these forgeries. In this way between November 23, 1909 and May 10, 1912 he invested nearly £400 of his savings, and he has shown us documentary evidence of some of these transactions. A full list which he has supplied will be found in Appendix II.[1] Not unnaturally he regarded this purchase as an investment for his old age; and his moderation, his discretion in putting them on the market, was successful in maintaining their reputation for rarity and price until the last two or three years.

The quantities that he purchased from Mr. Wise are astounding: 57 copies of *White Horses*;[2] 50 copies of *To be Read at Dusk*;[3] 43 copies of *Geist's Grave*;[4] 41 copies of *The National Gallery*;[5] 36 copies

[1] See below, pp. 371–373.
[2] See below, p. 201.
[3] See below, p. 185.
[4] See below, p. 163.
[5] See below, p. 227.

of *The Nature and Authority of Miracle*;[1] 30 copies of *The White Man's Burden*;[2] 27 copies of *On the Thermal Influence of Forests*;[3] and so on: we have printed the list in full at the end of the book.[4] But it must not be supposed that all the remainders which Mr. Gorfin bought on these occasions were forgeries. We discuss below in a note to Appendix II how far the fact that Mr. Gorfin bought a quantity of any pamphlet from Mr. Wise renders that pamphlet *ipso facto* an object of suspicion. But some of them are undoubtedly genuine. They may be divided into four categories: first, those that are genuine; secondly Mr. Wise's publications, etc.; thirdly, those that are highly suspicious; and fourthly, those that are proved forgeries. In the first category there are 89 copies of seven different works; in the second, 52 copies and two bundles of nine booklets edited by Mr. Wise; in the third, 214 copies of ten highly suspicious pamphlets; and in the fourth, 344 copies and one bundle of nineteen proved forgeries. So that it is not a question of two or three forgeries in quantity being sold with a number of other remainders, but, of the total sold to Mr. Gorfin by Mr. Wise, four-fifths are open to the gravest suspicion, and practically half are proved forgeries.

At this point we felt that it was imperative that we should inquire of Mr. Wise the source or sources from which he had acquired these "remainders."

Accordingly we informed him fully of the course and methods of our investigation and at his request supplied him with a list of the pamphlets concerned. We find it difficult to believe that Mr. Wise cannot now guess the identity of the forger; but, as long as it remains a guess, he has followed a very proper course

[1] See below, p. 242.
[2] See below, p. 203.
[3] See below, p. 247.
[4] See below, pp. 371–373.

in making no suggestion; and unfortunately the state of his health has prevented him from giving us the information, which he was good enough to promise, about the source of the "remainders."

This part of our investigation has led to no conclusive result, but it forms an integral part of a revelation too serious to suppress. Literary students are at work on the study of these authors; book collectors are buying these books; and the sooner the extent of this fraud is marked out and assessed, the sooner will the damage to bibliography be made good. By withholding our discoveries even for a year or two, we feel that we should be assuming a responsibility far greater than any that we shall incur by their publication.

PART III

DOSSIERS

PRELIMINARY NOTE

IT must be remembered that the conspectus of the auction records attached to each book is based on *Book Prices Current*, *Book Auction Records* and *American Book Prices Current*, supplemented in some cases by reference to sale catalogues and by personal knowledge. These records are not exhaustive, and omissions were no doubt more frequent during the earlier years of their existence. The *number* of copies noted as sold by auction represents, therefore, a conservative estimate, but in view of the much higher prices fetched by presentation or inscribed copies of any first edition, it is highly unlikely that any such, had they appeared, would have escaped inclusion. We are confident, therefore, that if our totals err on the side of moderation, our notes of the absence of inscribed copies are reliable.

ABBREVIATIONS

THE abbreviations for the bibliographies of each particular author are given in the introductory notes. The only general abbreviations are:—

Slater. J. H. Slater, Early Editions of Some Popular Modern Authors (1894).

Ashley. The Ashley Library Catalogue, by Thomas J. Wise (1922–1930).

Wrenn. Catalogue of the John H. Wrenn Library at Austin, Texas, edited by Thomas J. Wise (1920).

Matthew Arnold

THE only authoritative bibliography of Matthew Arnold is Smart's, of which there are two editions, (i) *The Bibliography of Matthew Arnold* . . . by Thomas Burnett Smart, London, J. Davy & Sons, 1892 [Smart A]. (ii) The revised edition of the same in vol. 15 of the De Luxe Edition of Arnold's *Works*, Macmillan, 1904, pp. 341–400 [Smart B].

SAINT BRANDAN

Saint Brandan. / By / Matthew Arnold. / London : / E. W. & A. Skipworth. / 1867.

8vo, brown wrappers, printed in black, uncut.

Imprint on p. 11—"London: Printed by J. S. Seaton and Co., 1867." Printed on cream wove paper in a Long Primer old style type.

First published in *Fraser's Magazine*, July, 1860 (Vol. LXII, pp. 133–4): afterwards in the 1867 edition of *New Poems.*

Smart A (1892), p. 14: not mentioned by Slater (1894): mentioned by Mr. Wise in *The Bookman* (1894) as "a rarity": omitted from Smart B (1904).

The British Museum copy (11647.ee.26) was purchased on August 20, 1890, from Otto P. Rubeck, for two guineas. The copy in the Cambridge University Library (Syn. 6. 91. 20) was presented by Mr. Wise in 1916: there is no copy in the Bodleian. Ashley I. 11 (wrappers, uncut). Wrenn I. 41 (two copies).

The first copy to appear at auction fetched three guineas in 1896 (June 18, Sotheby, Miscellaneous sale). The highest price was £6 10*s.* in 1929 (June 20, Hodgson, Miscellaneous, lot 380), and the lowest was 5*s.* in 1919 (February 17, Sotheby, Miscellaneous, lot 358). Normal prices in England have ranged from 30*s.* to £4, and the only four copies recorded in America ranged from $9 to $7 in 1897 and 1915 respectively. Of the total of twenty-five sold, eighteen were in original wrappers, two rebound, uncut, with the wrappers bound in, and in five cases the condition is not stated. No inscriptions of any kind are recorded.

Mr. Gorfin purchased sixteen copies from Mr. Wise at 3*s.* each on April 12, 1910.

The paper on which this pamphlet is printed is made of esparto and rag, a perfectly normal content for 1867.

The text type is that listed as B in our schedule.[1] It is identical with that of six proved forgeries and four other suspects in the group.

The omission of this book from Slater is not perhaps very disturbing, but the fact that Smart, having included it in 1892, dropped it altogether from his 1904 edition, implies some sort of undeclared suspicion of its authenticity.

The imprint of *E. W. and A. Skipworth* struck us as unfamiliar, and we found on investigation that no such firm is recorded in *Kelly's Directory* for 1866, 1867 or 1868, nor do any books with this imprint figure in the English Catalogue during those years. The name of *J. S. Seaton and Co.* is also unmentioned by Kelly. Both publisher and printer claim London for their location, and, though not conclusive, this double absence from Kelly is peculiar.

Conclusion.—The pamphlet has a uniformly bad auction record; its type is by no means reassuring; it is similar in bibliographical status and in the earliest discoverable provenance of copies in quantity, to the numerous proved forgeries in the group. Since it has no single piece of authenticating evidence to set against this accumulation of sinister features, it must be pronounced highly suspicious.

[1] See above, p. 67.

GEIST'S GRAVE

Geist's Grave / By / Matthew Arnold / London / Printed only for a few Friends / 1881

8vo, lavender-grey printed wrappers, uncut.

No imprint. Printed on cream wove paper, in a Small Pica modern style type.

First published in *The Fortnightly Review*, January, 1881: some offprints of this (2 leaves only, pp. 1–3 text, p. 4 blank) were done for the author's use: afterwards in the 1881 edition of the *Poems*.

Smart A (1892), p. 14: omitted by Slater (1894): mentioned by Mr. Wise in *The Bookman* (1894) as "a rarity": omitted from Smart B (1904).

The British Museum copy (11632.aa.68) was purchased for £2 5*s*. on October 14, 1924, from Messrs. Quaritch, who had bought it from Mr. Gorfin: the copy in the Cambridge University Library (Syn. 6.91.20[2]) was presented by Mr. Wise in 1916: no copy in the Bodleian: Ashley I. 11 (wrappers, uncut)—a note is added, "the majority of copies are found with the edges trimmed."[1] Wrenn I. 41.

The first copy recorded in the sale room fetched £2 4*s*. in 1897 (June 14, Puttick's, A Collector, lot 14). The highest price was $45 in the R. B. Adam sale in 1926 (February 15, Anderson Galleries, lot 16), and the lowest five shillings in 1919 (February 17, Sotheby, Miscellaneous, lot 357). Copies made £3 12*s*. and £5 10*s*. in 1902 and 1903, but the price in 1905 dropped to £1 15*s*. and remained about this level in England until 1928, when it began to rise sharply. The few American records are higher, never falling below the 1927 level of $15. Of the twenty-one copies recorded, seventeen were in original wrappers and in four cases the condition is not given. No inscriptions of any kind are recorded.

---

[1] We have been unable to find any copy in original state with trimmed edges. Mr. Wise's own, and those purchased from him by Mr. Gorfin, are uncut.

Mr. Gorfin purchased 29 copies from Mr. Wise at 5*s.* on April 15, 1910, and 14 more at the same price on April 18, 1910.

The text type is identical with that of *Sister Helen*, being the one described under E in our schedule. An identical display type, also, is used on the title-pages of this book and *The Scythian Guest*.[1]

Conclusion.—The late putative date of this pamphlet precludes any considerable chance of useful evidence from the paper: and in fact it proves not to be remarkable, the content being pure esparto. The book's record, however, is full of ominous features. To begin with, its whole *raison d'être* is removed by the existence of the offprint from *The Fortnightly*, though it should be noted that the first recorded copy of this did not turn up until 1930 (November 10, Sotheby, Miscellaneous, lot 285, with an autograph inscription " with kind regards, M.A." £16 10*s.*), and it seems to have been previously entirely unknown.[2] It was silently dropped by Smart from the second edition of his Bibliography. Its auction record is highly unconvincing. It conforms to our forger's formula in every respect of format and bibliographical status, and its typographical affinities rivet this similarity even more firmly. It is found in very bad company, both in the sale room and in Mr. Wise's stock, and a phenomenal number of copies were transferred to Mr. Gorfin in 1910.

No single piece of evidence of authenticity can be discovered to offset this accumulation of negative evidence against it: and though not a proved forgery, it must be declared highly suspicious.

[1] See above, p. 69.

[2] We can trace only two other copies as having appeared since, both similarly inscribed. One was in Catalogue 323 of B. H. Blackwell, No. 231; the other is in the library of Mr. Michael Holland.

Elizabeth Barrett Browning

THE bibliographical authorities for the two books by Mrs. Browning discussed here are as follows. (i) Edmund Gosse, *Critical Kit-Kats*, 1896 [Gosse]. (ii) H. Buxton Forman, *Elizabeth Barrett Browning and her scarcer books*, 1896 [Forman]. (iii) Thomas J. Wise, *Bibliography*, 1918 [Wise].

The Reading *Sonnets* has been fully dealt with in Chapter II, so that only a skeleton outline of the mass of negative evidence is called for here.

SONNETS FROM THE PORTUGUESE

Sonnets. / By / E. B. B. / Reading: / [Not for publication] / 1847.

Small 8vo, uncut: perhaps pinkish wrappers, traces of which survive on the spines of some copies.

No imprint. Printed in Clay's Long Primer No. 3, on a cream wove paper.

Published in *Poems*, 1850 (2 vols., Chapman & Hall).

Gosse (1896), pp. 1–3: Forman (1896), *passim*: Wise (1918), pp. 72–75.

No copies in the British Museum, Bodleian or Cambridge University Library, nor, so far as we can discover, anywhere else in England except the two in the Ashley Library (I. 97–99). A census of traceable copies will be found in Appendix I.

The first copy to appear at auction fetched $440 in the W. H. Arnold sale (May 7, 1901, Bangs & Co., lot 29). Nineteen sales are recorded, some copies, however, having appeared more than once. The highest price was $1250 (February 19, 1930, American Arts, Miscellaneous, lot 20); the lowest £33 in 1906 (March 21, Sotheby, Miscellaneous, lot 353). The average price works out at just over £98 per copy.

This was one of the books sold by Mr. Gorfin on commission for Mr. Wise.

The paper is composed of chemical wood, with a trace of rag, which cannot have been manufactured before 1874, and is very unlikely before 1883.

Certain letters of the type in which the book is printed were not cut for Clay until after 1880.

Conclusion.—It is eminently satisfactory that the large body of negative evidence against this book, detailed in Chapter II, should be so conclusively clinched by the available positive evidence. It is condemned, both by its type and its paper, as having been produced more than thirty years later than the date on its title-page.

THE RUNAWAY SLAVE

The / Runaway Slave / at Pilgrim's Point. / By Elizabeth Barrett Browning. / [*ornament*] / London: / Edward Moxon, Dover Street. / 1849.

8vo, pale buff printed wrappers; uncut in all copies seen by us; "more usually trimmed," according to Mr. Wise.

Contents—*Advertisement* (Prefatory Note) following title; and text of the poem.

Imprint on p. [27]—"London: / Bradbury and Evans, Printers, Whitefriars." Printed on a smooth deep cream wove paper; in a Small Pica modern style type.

First printed in *The Liberty Bell*, Boston, 1848; subsequently in the *Poems* of 1850.

Slater (1894), p. 43, "the pamphlet is very rare": Forman (1896), pp. 20–22: Wise (1918), pp. 84–94.

The British Museum Copy (C.39.g.30) was purchased on August 16, 1888, from E. Schlengemann (see above, p. 145): no copy in the Cambridge University Library, or in the Bodleian: no copy in the Browning sale, 1913: Ashley I. 99 (wrappers, uncut): Wrenn I. 125, three copies and a set of proof sheets (see below).

The first copy appeared at auction in 1889 and fetched £3 in original wrappers (June 12, Sotheby, J. S. Streatfield sale). Twenty-eight copies in all are recorded; the highest price being $115 in 1920 (April 26, Anderson Galleries, Buxton Forman sale, lot 86), the lowest 28*s*. for one of the three copies which came up together in a Miscellaneous sale at Sotheby's, February 17, 1919. The average price 1890–1915 was £3–£4, more recent prices usually ranging between £5 and £7. Of these copies twenty-one were in original wrappers; six were bound, uncut (with wrappers in five cases); of one the condition is not stated. No inscriptions of any kind are recorded.

This was one of the books in Mr. Wise's stock, as handled on commission by Mr. Gorfin, who finally purchased "about ten copies" in 1910.

Robert Browning's letter (1888), stating that he had never heard of this separate publication, was pretty certain such a circumstance never happened, and feared that it must be a fabricated affair, is quoted above, p. 130.

The paper on which this book is printed is composed of chemical wood fibre, with a trace of rag: this cannot have been manufactured before 1874, and is much more likely to have been made after 1883.

The type (B in our schedule) is the same as that used for five other proved forgeries and five of the suspects in the group.

Conclusion.—Forman (*loc. cit.*) suggests that it was from this piece that Mrs. Browning's sister Arabel got the idea for *Two Poems* (Chapman & Hall, 1854), the pamphlet printed for sale at her charity bazaar: for *The Liberty Bell* had been sold under similar circumstances, and the format of *The Runaway Slave* and *Two Poems* is noticeably similar. In fact the inspiration, if any, was in the opposite direction: *The Runaway Slave*, which is conclusively proved a forgery by its paper, was very likely suggested to the forger's mind by the genuine piece.

The Runaway Slave and Swinburne's *Cleopatra* seem to be the only cases amongst the books we are discussing in which proof sheets survive; both in the Wrenn Library. The note in the catalogue[1] under the present entry reads as follows: "The pages throughout are freely corrected and many differences in the text may be observed between this and the

[1] This, the Librarian states, was written by the editor, Mr. Wise.

regular published copy." The Wrenn Librarian, however, informs us that beyond a number of "marks indicating typographical changes," the only textual alteration is the correction of *mangos* (stanza XXX, line 5) to *mangoes*; the latter being written in the margin, in a hand which we have been unable to identify from a photostat.

The provenance of these proofs is given in a pencil note in Mr. Wrenn's hand as "Underwood, 10/4/1908,"[1] but the Librarian writes further, "I have traced the sale through Mr. Wise." Mr. Wise's reference to the "remainder" of copies of *The Runaway Slave* is given above (p. 125); but who Underwood was, and how he came to have the proofs of this forgery, and what account he gave Mr. Wise of their further provenance, has not been explained. The possession of proof sheets of a fraudulently printed book is a far more serious matter than a mere dozen or so copies of it, and Mr. Wise's position as the earliest discoverable handler of them will remain an embarrassing one until he chooses to provide further details about their previous history.

[1] See also this gentleman's place in the provenance of the *Cleopatra* proofs, discussed on pp. 280–284, below.

Robert Browning

THE important Bibliographies of Browning are three. (i) *A Bibliography of Robert Browning, 1833–1881*, by F. J. Furnivall, in *The Browning Society's Papers*, 1881–4, pp. 21–116 [Furnivall]. Browning himself corrected the proofs of this; and with considerable care, as may be seen in the series of letters from him to Furnivall printed in *Letters of Robert Browning collected by Thomas J. Wise*, 1933, pp. 194–208. (ii) A bibliography by John P. Anderson, at the end of William Sharp's *Life of Browning*, 1890 [Anderson]. (iii) *A Complete Bibliography . . . of Robert Browning*, by Thomas J. Wise. Issued in 8 parts, 1896–7, this is an uncommon book; but as it is included (under the title *Materials for a Bibliography*, etc., and with no indication of authorship) in the first volume of *Literary Anecdotes of the Nineteenth Century*, the page references to that more accessible work are given below [Wise].

A note which refers to the three books discussed here must be quoted from Mr. Wise (*op. cit.*, I. 378). "As a matter of minor bibliographical detail it may be mentioned that copies of the separate print of *Gold Hair*—as also of the separate issues of *Cleon* and *The Statue and the Bust*—occasionally occur bound up at the end of cloth copies of the first collected edition of *Christmas Eve and Easter Day*; they may, however, have been so inserted in such copies only of the books as were given away as presents by their author."

No examples of such insertion are recorded, nor does Mr. Wise himself apparently possess them. If they exist at all, the insertion must be due, in two of the three cases at any rate, to a hand very different from the author's.

An earlier reference must also be mentioned. William Sharp, in his rather rhapsodical and inaccurate *Life of Browning*, 1890, mentions (p. 173) five pamphlet issues of Browning's poems. *Two Poems*, 1854 (by R. B. and E. B. B.), as having been printed for sale in a charitable cause;[1] *Prospice*, of the separate issue of which there is no other record, nor are copies known to exist; and the three pamphlets discussed here. These, he says, were printed "either for transatlantic copyright or when the verses were not likely to be included in any volume for a prolonged period. These leaflets or half-sheetlets . . . are among the rarest 'finds' for the collector, and are literally worth a good deal more than their weight in gold." These remarks sound very much like the inaccurate suppositions of a biographer tacked on to information supplied from some other source; as in fact they are. Furnivall refers to this passage in his *Corrections*[2] to the book, p. 3, with these words: "Are not some of these creations of fancy? See Mr. Anderson's *Bibliography*, p. ii, col. 2" [where it is noted that *Gold Hair*, *Prospice* and *Under the Cliff* were all in fact piratically printed in *The Atlantic Monthly* from advance sheets of *Dramatis Personæ*].

[1] The authenticity of *Two Poems* is attested by copies with contemporary presentation inscriptions: cf. also Browning's letter to Furnivall about it, February 17, 1882 (*Letters of Robert Browning* (1933), p. 209).

[2] See above, p. 33, footnote.

As for Sharp's other suggested reason for the pamphlets, it needed no Furnivall to point out that all three of the pieces with which we are concerned were included in volumes in the very same year in each case.

CLEON

Cleon / By / Robert Browning. / London: / Edward Moxon, Dover Street. / 1855.

Small 8vo, uncut. Perhaps coloured paper wrappers: the large majority of copies are merely folded, without wrappers.

Imprint—" London: Bradbury and Evans, Printers, Whitefriars " on verso of title. Printed in Clay's Long Primer No. 3 on cream wove paper.

Published in *Men and Women* (2 vols., Chapman & Hall, 1855).

Unknown to Furnivall (1882): Anderson, p. ii: mentioned in a note by Slater (1894), p. 55: Wise (1896), I. 373.

No copy in the British Museum, the Bodleian, or the Cambridge University Library: no copy in the Browning sale, 1913: Ashley I. 118 (morocco, uncut. " The original plain coloured paper wrappers are preserved "): Wrenn I. 130 (two copies).

The first appearance at auction was on June 10, 1903 (Sotheby's, lot 34), when a copy in calf, uncut, fetched £7. Between then and the end of 1932, fifteen copies have been sold in the rooms, the highest price being $50 (April 23, 1919, Brooks, lot 208, and April 26, 1930, Holden, lot 118; both at the Anderson Galleries), the lowest 18*s*. (February 17, 1919, a Miscellaneous sale at Sotheby's, lot 365). Prices have usually been between £4 and £8. Nine copies in sheets, folded, uncut; one copy, condition not stated. None of these copies had wrappers, and those preserved with Mr. Wise's are apparently the only ones recorded. None had inscriptions of any kind.

Mr. Gorfin purchased two copies from Mr. Wise at £1 on April 20, 1910, and twelve more copies at the same price two days later.

Browning's letter to Locker, quoted on p. 79, is strong presumptive evidence against the genuineness of the Moxon imprint: but as Mr. Wise believed (*Bibliography of Swinburne*, I. 103) that the "remainder" of the book only came to light in the Moxon sale of 1888, it seems unlikely that copies were in circulation in time for the author to be shown them, for authentication or the reverse.

The paper is composed of esparto with a trace of chemical wood, and therefore could not have been manufactured until after 1861 at the very earliest.

Certain letters of this type were not cut for Clay until after 1880: it is the same as that of the Reading *Sonnets* and fourteen of the other forgeries (A in our schedule).

Conclusion.—This book is condemned both by its paper and its type as a forgery.

THE STATUE AND THE BUST

The / Statue and the Bust. / By / Robert Browning. / London: / Edward Moxon, Dover Street. / 1855.

Small 8vo, uncut. Occasionally in plain coloured wrappers: the large majority of copies are merely folded, without wrappers.

Imprint—" London: / Bradbury and Evans, Printers, Whitefriars" —on verso of title. Printed in Clay's Long Primer No. 3, on cream wove paper.

Published in *Men and Women* (2 vols., Chapman & Hall, 1855).

Unknown to Furnivall (1882): Anderson (1890), p. iii: mentioned in a note by Slater (1894), p. 55: Wise (1896), I. 373.

No copy in the British Museum. The copy in the Cambridge University Library (Syn. 4.91.55[1]) was presented by Mr. Wise in 1916. No copy in the Bodleian: no copy in the Browning sale: Ashley I. 118 (morocco, uncut, wrappers preserved): Wrenn I. 130.

The first copy to appear in the auction room (1903) was the succeeding lot to the first copy of *Cleon* (see p. 177); it was in the same condition, and was bought by the same purchaser for £6 5*s*. Thirteen copies altogether are recorded. The highest price (by far), $200, was brought in the Kern Sale (January 7, 1929, Anderson Galleries, lot 108, with a two-page A.L.S. laid in; folded, uncut): the Holden copy (April 28, 1920, American Arts, lot 299) made $111, brown morocco uncut, an autograph laid in. The lowest price was £2 in 1922 (Sotheby, February 21, Miscellaneous, lot 554) for a folded copy. The usual price has been between £4 and £8. Of these copies one was in wrappers; nine folded, uncut; three in modern bindings, uncut. No inscriptions of any kind are recorded.

Mr. Gorfin purchased eighteen copies from Mr. Wise on April 18 and 22, 1910, at £1 each.

The evidence of Browning's letter to Locker applies as strongly here as against *Cleon* (*q.v.*).

The paper is composed of esparto with a trace of chemical wood, and therefore could not have been manufactured until after 1861 at the very earliest.

Certain letters in this type were not cut for Clay until after 1880: it is the same as that used for the Reading *Sonnets*, *Cleon* and thirteen of the other forgeries.

Conclusion.—The book is condemned both by its paper and its type as a forgery.

GOLD HAIR

Gold Hair: / A Legend of Pornic. / By / Robert Browning. / 1864

8vo, uncut. Occasionally in plain wrappers: the large majority of surviving copies are merely folded, without wrappers.

Imprint on verso of title-page—"London: Printed by W. Clowes and Sons, Stamford Street and Charing Cross." Printed in a Small Pica modern style on a cream wove paper.

First printed in *The Atlantic Monthly*, xiii, pp. 596–599 (1864). Subsequently published in *Dramatis Personæ* (Chapman & Hall, 1864).

Unknown to Furnivall (1882): Anderson (1890), p. ii: mentioned by Slater (1894) in a note: Wise (1896), I. 376–378, "reserved for private circulation only."

No copy in the British Museum: the copy in the Cambridge University Library (Syn. 4.91.55[2]) was presented by Mr. Wise in 1916: no copy in the Bodleian: no copy in the Browning sale: Ashley I. 119 (morocco, uncut, wrappers bound in): Wrenn I. 131 (morocco, uncut).

The first copy to appear at auction was sold on July 3, 1899 (Sotheby, Thorold and others, lot 318, morocco, uncut) for £9. Twenty-two copies in all appear in the records, the highest price being $49 (Holden sale, lot 120, Anderson Galleries, April 26, 1920), the lowest 18*s.* (February 17, 1919, Sotheby, Miscellaneous, lot 367). Normal prices have ranged between £3 and £8. Of these copies twelve were folded, uncut; nine in modern bindings, edges, where mentioned, always uncut; of one the condition is not stated. No inscriptions of any kind are recorded. None of these copies had wrappers, and those preserved with Mr. Wise's copy are apparently unique.

Mr. Gorfin purchased nineteen copies from Mr. Wise on April 18 and 26, 1910, at £1 each.

The paper is composed of esparto, with traces of rag, which is not inconsistent with the date on the title-page.

The text type (B in our schedule) is identical with that used for six proved forgeries and four other suspects in the group.

Conclusion.—No evidence is provided by the collation of the three relevant texts (*The Atlantic Monthly*, the pamphlet and *Dramatis Personæ*), the differences being insignificant.[1] The printers named in the imprint have no detailed records covering the date in question. In the absence, therefore, of any positive evidence, the case must be declared non-proven. The auction record, however, is uniformly bad; the stock remaining in 1909 was large; and the book's earliest discoverable provenance is the same as that of the large number of definitely proved forgeries. It conforms to the forger's formula in all respects, and its type is not in its favour. In these circumstances it cannot but be regarded with considerable suspicion.

[1] In the *second* edition of *Dramatis Personæ* (1864) three extra stanzas were introduced into this poem, taking their places as Nos. 21, 22, 23, and throwing out the numbering of subsequent stanzas.

Charles Dickens

TO BE READ AT DUSK

To be Read / at / Dusk. / By / Charles Dickens. / [*French rule*] / London: / [*rule*] / 1852.

8vo; some copies are said to have wrappers, but all those that we have been able to examine were in folded sheets, unsewn and uncut.

There is no publisher's imprint; the printer's imprint on the reverse of the last leaf is "London: / Printed by G. Barclay, Castle St. Leicester Sq." Set up in a leaded Small Pica modern style. Printed on cream wove paper.

This story was first published in *The Keepsake*, 1852, pp. 117–131. The printer's imprint to that volume is the same as that given above.

Not mentioned by James Cook in *The Bibliography of the Writings of Charles Dickens*, 1879; C. P. Johnson in *Hints to Collectors of . . . Charles Dickens*, 1885; or R. H. Shepherd in *The Bibliography of Dickens* [1886], although he does mention (p. 29) its appearance in *The Keepsake*.

Attention was first drawn to it in a letter from Charles P. Johnson to *The Athenæum*, No. 3316, May 16, 1891. "Every Dickens collector knows that this tale appeared in *The Keepsake* in 1852, under the editorship of Miss Power. I question, however, whether it is known that it was also issued, as was Thackeray's 'An Interesting Event,' in a separate pamphlet. By courtesy of Mr. and Mrs. Tregaskis, the booksellers in Holborn, I am able to describe this pamphlet. . . . I fear that the pamphlet is only interesting to the bibliographer, as the collector can hardly hope to possess a volume so rare as I believe this to be."

F. G. Kitton, *The Minor Writings of Charles Dickens*, 1900, p. 82, " only one copy known " ; J. C. Thomson, *Bibliography of the Writings of Charles Dickens*, Warwick, 1904, p. 79 ; *The Franklin Club Exhibition*, St. Louis, February, 1912, no. 33 (the property of F. W. Lehmann) ; *The Grolier Club Exhibition*, New York, no. 177, pp. 124–5 ; A. S. W. Rosenbach, *A Catalogue of the Writings of Charles Dickens in the Library of Harry Elkins Widener*, Philadelphia, 1918, p. 71 ; J. C. Eckel, *The Bibliography of Dickens*, 1932, pp. 176–7.

No copy in the British Museum, the Bodleian Library, or the Cambridge University Library. Ashley II. 40. Wrenn II. 64.

Messrs. Tregaskis were asking 25 guineas for the copy mentioned in C. P. Johnson's letter to *The Athenæum* in 1891. Two copies appeared at Sotheby's in 1893 (lot 519, 7 June ; lot 548, 12 December) and fetched £8 15*s.* and £5 7*s.* 6*d.* respectively. Another copy fetched £5 at Sotheby's as lot 925 on 18 May, 1903. All these three copies were in modern morocco with uncut edges. A copy fetched $101 in sheets as lot 336 in the Lapham sale in New York in December, 1908 ; and another $115, bound by Zaehnsdorf, in the Whiton sale, also in New York, in February, 1911. No more copies seem to appear until March, 1932, both at Hodgson's. The first on March 2, the condition of which is not described, fetched £11 ; and the second, which was uncut and unopened, £9.

On May 2, 1910, Mr. Gorfin bought two copies from Mr. Wise at 30*s.* each ; on May 14 of the same year fourteen more copies at the same price ; on the 21st of the same month another twelve copies at thirty shillings each. On August 11 the same year twenty-one more copies for £20. He bought a further single copy for thirty shillings on April 30, 1912. This makes a total of fifty copies for £67 10*s.*

The pamphlet is printed in the modern style Small Pica which we have scheduled as B (see p. 67). Five suspects and five other forgeries are printed in this type.

The analysis of the paper showed that it is composed of esparto and straw : as esparto was not introduced into the manufacture of paper until 1861, nine years after the date on which the pamphlet was supposed to be printed, there can be no doubt that it is a forgery.

Conclusion.—The fact that this pamphlet was not discovered until 1891 would have been curious, but the evidence of the paper is entirely decisive.

George Eliot

THE bibliographical authorities for George Eliot are three. (i) The bibliography by John P. Anderson, at the end of Oscar Browning's *Life*, Walter Scott, 1890 [Anderson]. (ii) The bibliography by P. H. Muir, in *Bibliographies of Modern Authors*, Third Series, 1931 (pp. 41–58) [Muir]. (iii) *Victorian Lady Novelists*, by Morris L. Parrish, London, Constable, 1933 [Parrish]. Reference has also been made to the *Life of George Eliot* by her husband, J. W. Cross.

BROTHER AND SISTER

Brother and Sister / Sonnets / By / Marian Lewes / London / For Private Circulation Only / 1869.

8vo, blue printed wrappers, some copies entirely uncut, some trimmed.

There is no imprint. The book is printed on cream wove paper, in Clay's Long Primer No. 3.

Published in *The Legend of Jubal*, 1874.

Not in Anderson (1890): Slater (1894), p. 125 (see below): Muir, 6: Parrish, p. 24.

The British Museum copy (C.40.g.12) was purchased on October 23, 1888, from E. Schlengemann (see p. 145), for 3 guineas: the copy in the Cambridge University Library (Syn. 6.91.20[20]) was presented by Mr. Wise in 1916: the Bodleian copy (280.e.2844) was presented by Mr. Wise on February 15, 1917. Ashley II. 106–7 (morocco, uncut, original wrappers preserved): Wrenn II. 118 (morocco, uncut, wrappers preserved).

The first copy to appear at auction fetched £2 8*s*. in 1897 (June 14, Puttick's, A Collector, lot 125[a]). Thirty copies in all are recorded. The highest price was £9 (May 23, 1928, Hodgson, Miscellaneous, lot 170); the lowest, £2 2*s*. (December 21, 1905, Puttick's, Misc., lot 10). Normal prices range between £3 and £8. Of these copies, two were in morocco, uncut, the wrappers bound in: twenty-six in original wrappers, uncut: of two the condition is not stated. No inscriptions of any kind are recorded.

Mr. Gorfin purchased twenty-three copies from Mr. Wise in 1910, for £20, and one further copy at 18*s*. on April 30, 1912.

Slater (*loc. cit.*) added to his description of the book the following note: "This work is supposed to be a fictitious and antedated edition reprinted from 'The Legend of Jubal and Other Poems,' 1874, in which the Sonnets perhaps really first appeared." In his prefatory note, however, he refers to this hesitating utterance of suspicion as follows: "I am assured on the highest authority that there is no foundation for the assertion, actual proof of the writing and printing of the Sonnets being available." He does not give any details of this actual proof; and he excuses himself for the original statement by saying that "the British Museum Catalogue contains a note to the same effect." This note is not in the present catalogue.

The paper is composed of esparto, with traces of chemical wood; this content, although improbable before 1883, is not impossible.

Certain letters of the type in which this book is printed were not cut for Clay until after 1880.

Conclusion.—Slater had practically copied the note in the old British Museum Catalogue, which, except for beginning "This appears to be a fictitious edition reprinted," etc., has precisely the same wording. The original authority for this note is unfortunately not now discoverable, but it was removed from the catalogue on the ground that Mr. Wise believed it to be quite unfounded. This, together with the mention of Mr. Wise by name in acknowledgment for a precisely similar correction in the previous sentence of Slater's preface, suggests a possible identity for his "highest authority." Since the pamphlet is a forgery, it is not surprising that the "actual proof" of the printing has never been made public.

Note.—There is a facsimile of this forgery, which we have had no opportunity of examining. Mr. William A. Jackson, to whom we are indebted for the knowledge of its existence, informs us that a comparison of the two discloses the following features as characteristic of this facsimile: (i) No rule at the end of the text. (ii) No full-point after III at the head of the third sonnet. (iii) The half-title comes after the title, and was apparently so imposed. (iv) The ornaments at the corners of the frame on the wrapper are fleur de lys instead of interlaced rules. (v) The wrapper itself is of coarser paper and is almost flush with the text page, whereas in the original forgery it is usually about $\frac{3}{8}''$ short at the foot. These distinguishing notes were taken from copies in the library of Mr. Carl H. Pforzheimer.

AGATHA (Second Edition)

Agatha. / By / George Eliot. / London: / Trubner & Co., 60, Paternoster Row. / 1869. / [All Rights reserved.]

8vo, uncut, without wrappers; stitched, according to Wise and Muir; all copies we have examined were unstitched.

Imprint on verso of title—"Taylor and Co., Printers, / Little Queen Street, Lincoln's Inn Fields." Printed on a cream wove paper, in a Small Pica modern style.

First printed in *The Fortnightly Review*, August, 1869; subsequently in *The Legend of Jubal*, Blackwood, 1874.

There are three editions of this which closely resemble each other. The twenty-seven textual differences by which they can be distinguished are given in full by Mr. Parrish (pp. 24, 25), and though he describes them merely as variant copies it is clear that they represent three separate printings. A is the genuine first edition: it is attested by contemporary reception dates in the British Museum and the Bodleian, and copies occur (*e.g.* Mr. Parrish's) in binder's cloth, with cut edges, and in similar condition appropriate to their date and format. B is the present pamphlet. C we have had no opportunity of examining, and its existence was not generally known until the publication of Mr. Parrish's book in 1933. It may be identical with a facsimile whose occurrence has been rumoured in the U.S.A., and if so it may be connected with a similar facsimile of the forged *Brother and Sister* (see p. 192, footnote).

A and B were undifferentiated by Anderson (1890) and Slater (1894), and Mr. Wise's statement in 1922 (Ashley II, 106) gave the first distinction between the two and the accepted account of the circumstances of their printing. This, which was merely quoted by Mr. Muir (No. 9[a]), runs as follows:

"*Agatha* was seen through the press upon behalf of the authoress by Mr. Buxton Forman.[1] Of the first edition twenty copies only were printed. These, however, proved insufficient to meet the demands of friends who clamoured for them, and a second batch of fifty copies were ordered. . . . Mr. Forman claimed that these later copies were a 'second issue of the first edition'; but as the types from which they were printed were reset, they undoubtedly form a *second edition* of the poem."

Mr. Wise's account of the genesis of this "second edition" is explicit, but there are four reasons why we regard it as unconvincing. (i) The paper shows, in its main content of esparto, traces of chemical wood, which, though not impossible in minute quantities, is still highly unlikely at this date. (ii) If the author's friends "clamoured" for copies, it is odd that there should be no mention of it in Cross's exhaustive *Life*. (iii) In spite of the clamouring friends, Mr. Wise (not Forman or George Eliot's heirs) was in possession of twenty-one at least of the fifty printed, as late as 1912. (iv) There were two copies of *Agatha* in the Buxton Forman Sales (March and April, 1920, Anderson Galleries, part 1 lot 267, part 2 lot 316). Both were certainly of the "second" edition, as the descriptions in the catalogue show: both were sold as "the rare first edition." Contrary to what one might expect, there were no bibliographical notes by Forman

[1] Forman had died in 1919.

in either copy, nor is there any mention in the catalogue of the existence of another issue or edition, whether second or not.

The British Museum copy (C.57.d.46) was presented by Mr. Wise in 1926: no copy in the Cambridge University Library or in the Bodleian. Ashley II. 106 (morocco, uncut). Wrenn II. 118 (morocco, uncut). This copy is described in the catalogue, which was edited by Mr. Wise in 1920, as "First edition," but the Librarian confirmed our surmise that it was the second.

The auction record of this book is confused, owing to the fact that all copies, whether of first, second or third edition, seem to have been indiscriminately described as first, even after Mr. Wise's announcement in 1922. But if we rule out all rebound copies as being possibly firsts (and no single copy in boards [1] has ever been sold in the rooms), we find the following to be the record of copies whose stitched or merely folded condition proclaim them as clearly second or third. The first copy was sold in 1899 for £2 6*s.* (March 20, Puttick's, Miscellaneous, lot 233[a]). Seventeen in all are recorded. The highest price was $35, in the Brayton Ives sale (April 7, 1915, American Arts, lot 314): the lowest was the first copy to appear. Normal prices ranged between £3 and £6. Of these copies ten are explicitly described as "unstitched"; the remainder—"unbound, as issued," etc.—may have been stitched. No inscriptions of any kind are recorded.

Mr. Gorfin purchased nineteen copies from Mr. Wise for £15 on March 15, 1912.

The text type is that described under B in our schedule: it is identical with that used for six proved forgeries and four other suspects.

Conclusion.—The grounds for our suspicions of this book have been outlined above, and our inspection of its auction record and early provenance did nothing to allay them. Furthermore, it is printed in the same fount of type as six of the proved forgeries and four

[1] The original binding of the first edition, according to Mr. Wise.

other suspects,[1] which, although not positive evidence, at least proves that its typography is not inconsistent with the hypothesis that it is a member of the group. There is no single authenticating feature to set against this body of negative evidence; and the pamphlet must be set down as highly suspicious.

[1] See p. 67.

Rudyard Kipling

THERE are four important bibliographies of Kipling: (i) The bibliography by John Lane appended to Richard Le Gallienne, *Rudyard Kipling. A Criticism.* London, 1900 [Lane]. (ii) *A Bibliography of the Works of Rudyard Kipling* by E. W. Martindell. This was first issued in 1922. We have cited "A New Edition, much enlarged," London, 1923 [Martindell]. (iii) Mrs. Flora V. Livingston, *Bibliography of the Works of Rudyard Kipling*, New York, 1927. This is the authoritative bibliography [Livingston]. (iv) *Catalogue of the Works of Rudyard Kipling.* Exhibited at the Grolier Club from February 21 to March 30, 1929. New York, 1930 [Grolier Club].

WHITE HORSES

White Horses / By / Rudyard Kipling / London / Printed for Private Circulation / 1897

8vo, printed lilac wrappers, back wrapper blank, edges trimmed.

No publisher or printer mentioned, but copyright notice on the reverse of the title-page. Printed in an old style Small Pica, on a cream wove paper.

This poem first appeared in *Literature*, Oct. 23, 1897: reprinted in *The New York Tribune*, Oct. 31, 1897. It first appeared in book form in *With Number Three*, Santiago de Chile, 1900 (unauthorised). The first authorised appearance in book form was in *The Five Nations*, 1903.

Lane (1900), p. xviii. Martindell (1923), no. 69, p. 55. "The First Edition." Livingston (1927), no. 139, p. 170. "This is not a copyright edition, as has often been stated, but a pirated edition; and judging from the number of copies reported, there must have been many printed. 'The White Man's Burden' was also issued in the same form. Both were printed without the author's permission." Grolier Club (1930), no. 226, p. 68.

The British Museum copy (C.59.b.22) was presented anonymously on 8 Jan. 1898. No copies in the Bodleian Library or the Cambridge University Library. Ashley III. 34. Wrenn III. 43.

This pamphlet first appeared in the auction room on April 4, 1921 (Sotheby, lot 91), when it fetched £15. We have traced twenty-two sales at auction in England and America since 1921; in only ten cases was the condition stated, but all of these were in original wrappers. Its price has varied between £10 and £20, but its high-water mark was in 1928, when it fetched $130 (Anderson Galleries, Jan. 16), £25 (Hodgson's, May 23, lot 167), and £24 (Hodgson's, Dec. 6, lot 96). The lowest price was £5 5*s*. at Hodgson's on June 8, 1932, when it was bought in by Mr. Gorfin, whose anonymous property it was.

Mr. Gorfin bought fifty-seven copies from Mr. Wise on May 10, 1912, for about two shillings each.

In addition to the statement of Mrs. Livingston, we have been categorically assured by Mr. Kipling's literary agents, Messrs. A. P. Watt & Co., that Mr. Kipling never sanctioned this production.

This pamphlet is printed in the type which we have scheduled as F.

Conclusion.—Although this is the first separate edition, undoubtedly executed in 1897, it is nevertheless a piracy specially and successfully designed for the rare book market.

THE WHITE MAN'S BURDEN

The / White Man's / Burden / By / Rudyard Kipling / London / Printed for Private Circulation / 1899

8vo, printed lilac paper wrappers, back wrapper blank, edges trimmed.

No publisher or printer mentioned, but copyright notice on the reverse of the title-page. Printed in an old style Small Pica, on a cream wove paper.

The real copyright edition is *The White Man's Burden A Poem by Rudyard Kipling Copyright MDCCCXCIX by Rudyard Kipling All Rights Reserved The Doubleday and McClure Company MDCCCXCIX*. This was printed in an edition of ten copies by Gilliss Bros. in New York on 28 January, 1899.

The poem was printed in *McClure's Magazine*, February, 1899; *Literature*, February 4, 1899; *The Times*, February 4, 1899; and *The New York Tribune*, February 5, 1899. It first appeared in book form in *With Number Three*, Santiago de Chile, 1900 (unauthorised). The first authorised appearance in book form was in *The Five Nations*, 1903.

Martindell (1923), pp. 61–62. Livingston (1927), no. 196, p. 209. " This is not the copy-righted edition, as has been stated so often, but a pirated edition, and many copies were printed." Grolier Club, (1930), no. 275, p. 79.

The British Museum copy (C.59.g.15) was presented anonymously 11 March, 1899. The Bodleian copy was presented anonymously 13 Feb., 1899. The copy in the Cambridge University Library (Syn. 6.91.20[17]) was presented on 1 Sept., 1916, by Mr. T. J. Wise. It bears a note in his autograph on the wrapper: " printed, I believe, in Chicago . . ." Ashley III. 35. Wrenn III. 43.

This pamphlet first appeared in the auction room on April 4, 1921

(Sotheby's, lot 93, £15). We have been able to trace fifteen sales since 1921: in nine cases the condition is given, and all of these were in original state. Its price has varied between £8 and $120, which was given at the Anderson Galleries on January 16, 1928. Twelve out of the fifteen records are American.

Mr. Gorfin bought thirty copies from Mr. Wise on May 10, 1912, for about two shillings each.

Messrs. A. P. Watt & Co. made the same statement about this pamphlet as about *White Horses*.

The type in which this pamphlet is printed is the one we have scheduled as F.

Conclusion.—Although the number possessed by Mr. Wise in 1910 must lend considerable authority to any statement which he makes about this pamphlet, the date of the reception of the Bodleian copy, no less than its typography, rules out any possibility that it could have been printed in Chicago. It is not the first edition; but the English forger—or pirate—could not have been aware of the New York copyright edition, as it was reprinted in England within nine days of its appearance in *The Times*. Nevertheless, the pamphlet seems to have had a certain success in the rare book market, in spite of the fact that, since 1927, it has been known to be a piracy.

William Morris

THE principal bibliographies of Morris are two. (i) *A Bibliography*, by Temple Scott, London, Bell, 1897: published in March [Scott]. (ii) *The Books of William Morris* described by H. Buxton Forman, C.B., London, Hollings, 1897: published in November [Forman]. Reference is also made to *William Morris: his Art, his Writings and his Public Life* by Aylmer Vallance, London, Bell, 1897: published in October.

SIR GALAHAD

Sir Galahad / A Christmas Mystery. / By / William Morris. / London: / Bell and Daldy, 186, Fleet Street. / 1858.

12mo, uncut. Described by Scott as "sewed": all copies in original state which we have been able to examine are folded, unsewn.

No imprint. Printed on a cream wove paper, in a Small Pica modern style type.

This is the so-called genuine first edition. The existence of "an unauthorised facsimile reprint" was announced, but it was not distinguished, by Scott: Forman describes its paper as "thinner and whiter" and states that there are a number of typographical differences, of which he notes one—*hauberk* at p. 16, l. 3, where the "first edition" was *hauberke*.

Published in *The Defence of Guenevere* (Bell and Daldy, 1858).

Unknown to Slater (1894): mentioned by Mr. Wise in *The Bookman* (1894): Scott, p. 1, "The only copy I have ever seen is that from which the above description and collation were obtained": Forman, p. 33, "It is but a thin little pamphlet, and cannot be traced in the books of Messrs. George Bell & Sons, the imprint of whose predecessors, Messrs. Bell & Daldy, it bears. Neither is it traceable at the Chiswick Press, at which the Oxford and Cambridge Magazine and Morris' first two volumes of poetry were printed. It does not, however, look like Chiswick Press printing, and so small a thing may have been got done elsewhere."

No copy in the British Museum: no copy in the Cambridge University Library: no copy in the Bodleian: Ashley III. 161, a rebound copy with an undated autograph inscription, *Ford Madox Brown from his friend William Morris*, apparently not on a leaf of the book itself: a copy in the Buxton Forman sale (1920) carried an autograph inscription, *H. Buxton Forman from William Morris, Nov. 23 1890*: Wrenn III. 179, two copies in morocco, uncut, one being inscribed on the fly-leaf *D Ward with William Morris kind regards.*

The first copy to appear at auction made £3 12*s.* 6*d.* in 1897 (June 14, Puttick's, A Collector—this sale contained a long run of proved or suspected forgeries). The highest price for an ordinary copy was $65 in the Kern sale (January 21, 1929, Anderson Galleries), the lowest 24*s.* for one of three copies in a miscellaneous sale at Hodgson's on December 11, 1929. Normal prices in England have ranged between 30*s.* and £3 10*s.*, with higher figures for the few sold in America. Of the sixteen copies recorded, six were in modern morocco or calf, uncut, nine folded unstitched, and of one the condition was not stated. The only inscription of any kind was that in the Buxton Forman copy described above. This copy made $110.

Mr. Gorfin purchased sixteen copies from Mr. Wise on April 21, 1910, for £7 10*s.* and one further copy at 10*s.* on April 30, 1912.

Aspersions were cast on the date and authenticity of this pamphlet as early as 1898, when *The Athenæum* of January 22 contained the following letter from Robert Proctor, the typographical expert and an intimate friend of Morris:

British Museum.

" Mr. Temple Scott and Mr. H. Buxton Forman in their bibliographies of William Morris agree in assigning the place of honour among his works to a separate edition of ' Sir Galahad, a Christmas Mystery ' which is assumed to be earlier in date than the ' Guenevere ' volume, in which it is included. Mr. Forman further distinguishes two editions of ' Sir Galahad,' a genuine original, and a later unauthorised reprint. I have recently had the opportunity of examining a copy of the former, which purports to be published in 1858, the year of ' Guenevere,' by Bell and Daldy, the publishers of that volume. All that is known about it seems to point to its being itself an unauthorised and later reprint from the ' Guenevere ' of 1858, the imprint being taken bodily from that work. The types in which it is printed differ wholly from those used by the Chiswick Press for ' Guenevere '; and, after what Mr. Forman has said on p. 33 of his book [see above], it may be considered certain that it was not printed there. But for all Morris's other literary ventures at this period he employed the Chiswick Press; and it is therefore extremely improbable that different printers should have been used by him for two books so intimately connected, and both published, as is alleged, by the same firm in the same year. Moreover (Forman, p. 33), the books of Messrs. Bell do not, any more than those of the Chiswick Press, contain any trace of such an edition having been ever undertaken by them; and, what is even more convincing, neither Mr. Morris's family nor any of his most intimate friends had ever seen or heard of the tract before the publication of Mr. Aylmer Vallance's *Art of William Morris* last spring.

R. PROCTOR."

It is worth noting that Vallance, in the book mentioned in the last sentence, refers to the pamphlet in the briefest terms (p. 26) and that he explicitly based himself on Scott for all his bibliographical details. Now Scott had only seen one single copy (see above); and since in his preface he acknowledges the help of Vallance, F. S. Ellis, Gleeson White, F. H. Evans and Buxton Forman, it follows (*a*) that the single copy must presumably have been Forman's, which Morris had inscribed for him in 1890, and which, since Scott describes the book as "sewn," must have been afterwards bound, (*b*) that none of the others mentioned possessed a single copy between them. This corroborates Proctor's final sentence.

The paper on which this book is printed is composed of esparto with a trace of rag. It therefore cannot have been manufactured until after 1861.

The text type (B in our schedule) is identical with that used for five other proved forgeries and five suspects in the group.

Conclusion.—This pamphlet is conclusively proved a forgery on its paper content, and this is supported by the strong negative evidence summed up by Proctor in 1898. His indictment becomes the more damaging from the fact that no one made any attempt to rebut it. Scott perhaps was hardly in a position to do so, with his negligible knowledge of the book; but if Buxton Forman possessed an inscribed copy it is in the highest degree curious that he did not produce it as evidence of authenticity—so curious, in fact, that one wonders whether perhaps it could not stand examination. The inscription in Mr. Wise's copy is not apparently on an integral leaf of the book: so that the captious might have said (with justice) that it was really no evidence at all. The same objection applies to the evidence of the inscription on the fly-leaf of the Wrenn copy. But the inscription in Forman's copy, although dated thirty-two years after publication and not one of presentation in the proper sense at all, must certainly have been written for him by Morris, presumably after he had acquired the book. Although not very strong evidence for authenticity, it was at least something: and yet it was not produced. Why? Can it have been that Buxton Forman was not quite sure of the book himself? His description of it in his bibliography is full of negatives, and contains no positive information at all, even at second hand; and Proctor's letter, coming from such a quarter, must have been enough to raise doubts in anyone's mind.

All this, however, is speculation, and the question will be found discussed further on pp. 137, 138. That the book is a forgery is proved fact.

POSTSCRIPT

Of the numerous other pamphlets by William Morris, only one seems suspicious; namely, *The Two Sides of / the River / Hapless Love / and / the First Foray of / Aristomenes / By / William Morris / London /* 1876 / [*Not for Sale*]. The first of these poems had appeared in *The Fortnightly Review*, October, 1868, and was afterwards reprinted in *Poems by the Way*, 1891: the second had been published in *Good Words*, April, 1869, but was not republished during the author's lifetime.

The British Museum copy was not acquired till 1894, and there are no copies in the Cambridge University Library or in the Bodleian. The Ashley copy (III. 168) has the author's autograph on the half-title, and the Buxton Forman copy was described as "autograph presentation copy from the author": we have seen, however, in the case of *Sir Galahad*, that Morris' careless good-nature made him generous with his signature, and the fact that that book is a proved forgery must affect the evidence for authenticity provided by similar late or undated inscriptions by him on other books. This was one of the books in the cache, Mr. Gorfin purchasing eight copies from Mr. Wise on April 13, 1910, for the sum of £5: its auction record, apart from the Forman copy, is bad—all copies being either in original wrappers or uncut in modern binding: and it resembles the proved members of the group in its bibliographical status as well as its provenance.

Type and paper, however, provide no positive evidence against it, though the fact that it is printed in our type B[1] is disturbing; but in view of the two inscribed copies we cannot characterise it as highly suspicious, even though its provenance in quantity and its auction record are by no means reassuring.

[1] See above, p. 67.

Dante Gabriel Rossetti

THE authorities for the bibliography of Rossetti are (i) the bibliography by his brother, W. M. Rossetti, as published in two parts in *The Bibliographer* (New York), Vol. I. pp. 420–430 (1902), Vol. II. pp. 34–44 (1903) [Rossetti A]. (ii) *Additions* to this, by Colonel W. F. Prideaux, in *The Bibliographer*, Vol. II. pp. 243–247 [Prideaux]. (iii) *A Bibliography* . . . by W. M. Rossetti, London, Ellis, 1905 [Rossetti B]. This is a revised and corrected version of (i).

SISTER HELEN

Sister Helen ; / a ballad / by / Dante G. Rossetti. / Oxford : / Printed for Private Circulation. / 1857.

Small 8vo, uncut ; folded, unstitched, no wrappers (two copies known with undescribed wrappers, see below).

No imprint. Printed on cream wove paper, in a Small Pica modern style.

The poem is preceded by a *Prefatory Note.*

First printed in *The Dusseldorf Artist's Annual*, 1853, a publication edited by Mrs. William Howitt ; subsequently, with a number of revisions, in the *Poems* of 1870.

Unknown to Slater (1894) : mentioned by Mr. Wise in his review of Slater in *The Bookman :* Rossetti A (1902), I. 423 : "There was also, in 1857, a separate print of the poem, with the imprint, 'Oxford, For Private Circulation.' The person concerned in this reissue is not named : it was, in fact, the Rev. William Fulford, who had edited the Oxford and Cambridge Magazine." Rossetti B (1905), p. 11 : the same note is reprinted word for word.

No copy in the British Museum or Bodleian. The copy in the Cambridge University Library (Syn. 6.91.21[18]) was presented by Mr. Wise on September 1, 1916. Ashley IV. 112, two copies ; one bearing W. M. Rossetti's signature (undated) on the title-page ; the other described as having previously belonged to Swinburne ; both are in modern bindings, uncut. Wrenn IV. 31 (morocco, uncut).

The first copy to appear at auction sold for £19 10*s*. (with MS.) at Sotheby's on June 10, 1903 (The Library of a Gentleman, lot 415), and twenty-one copies in all are recorded. The highest price for an ordinary copy was $80 in 1926 (November 29, Anderson Galleries, A. E. Newton sale, lot 155[a] ; sheets, uncut) ; the lowest, 26*s*. in 1932 (May 25, Sotheby, Miscellaneous, lot 130, morocco). Normal prices have ranged between £4 and £7. Of these copies, thirteen were in sheets, folded, uncut: six in morocco, uncut, without wrappers: the two Buxton Forman copies (1920, Anderson Galleries, March 15, lot 587,[1] and April 26, lot 879), both in morocco, uncut, "with wrappers bound in." These wrappers seem to be the only ones recorded. No copies contained inscriptions, though several had pieces of MS. inserted.

Mr. Gorfin purchased one copy from Mr. Wise on August 15, 1910, for £3, but he had sold others on commission.

The paper is composed of esparto, with a trace of rag: it cannot have been manufactured until after 1861.

The text type (E in our schedule) is identical with that used for *Geist's Grave*, 1881.

Conclusion.—There was no copy of this pamphlet in the Rossetti sale in 1882, which contained copies of all his other books (except *Verses*, 1881; see below), including *The Düsseldorf Artist's Annual*. The first reference to its existence seems to be in Mr. Wise's review of Slater in 1894. Swinburne, who is reported by Mr. Wise to have possessed a copy, wrote to the author when reading the proofs of the *Poems* of 1870 in words which definitely imply that he had never seen the poem before;[2] which looks as if he acquired his copy subsequently to that date. There was no particular reason why W. M. Rossetti should have been more sceptical about a reputed specimen of his brother's work, of this early date, than Browning had been about his wife's, or Swinburne about his own, and his undated signature on the title-page of Mr. Wise's copy implies no more than acceptance of any

[1] This copy contained "on one of the fly-leaves a MS. verse in the hand of Rossetti." Since, however, fly-leaves have no integral connection with the books to which they are attached, within a modern binding, the value of this MS. verse as evidence for authenticity is nil.

[2] *Letters*, edd. Hake and Rickett, 1918, p. 35.

book in such distinguished hands. The Fulford story, which is plausible enough, was presumably already attached to the book when it was first brought to his attention.

Whatever was the depth of W. M. Rossetti's conviction of the book's authenticity, it is conclusively proved a forgery by its paper; and it resembles in every respect of format, auction record and bibliographical status the other forgeries in the group.

VERSES

Verses / By / Dante Gabriel Rossetti. / London: Privately Printed: / 1881.

8vo, pink printed wrappers, uncut.

No printer's imprint. Printed on Van Gelder hand-made paper, and three copies on vellum, in a Small Pica old style type.

Contents. *At the Fall of the Leaf*, and *After the French Liberation of Italy*.

The first poem was published in *Love Lily and Other Songs by Dante Gabriel Rossetti, set to music by Edward Dannreuther*, 1884. The second poem had been printed as a fly-sheet [? 1869]: it was subsequently published in the *Poems* of 1904.

Unknown to Slater (1894): mentioned by Mr. Wise in his review of Slater in *The Bookman:* Rossetti A (1902–3) I. 427, II. 38: Prideaux (1903), p. 247: Rossetti B (1905), pp. 17, 28 (see below).

The British Museum copy (C.59.g.8) was purchased from Cornish for 3 guineas on November 12, 1894. No copy in the Cambridge University Library. No copy in the Bodleian. Ashley IV. 144, one of the three copies on vellum. Wrenn IV. 37 (original wrappers).

The first copy to appear at auction fetched £2 12*s.* at Sotheby's on July 31, 1896 (condition not stated). Ten copies in all are recorded, of which seven were in original wrappers, uncut; the condition of the remaining three not given. The highest price was $55 in 1931 (January 28, American Arts, Ulizio sale, lot 811), the lowest 27*s.* in 1904 (April 26, Sotheby), both in original wrappers. No inscriptions of any kind are recorded, though a copy sold in 1929 (June 3, Sotheby, Miscellaneous, lot 318) contained a letter from Mr. Wise referring to the scarcity of the book.

Mr. Gorfin purchased one copy on August 15, 1910, for 30*s.*, but he had sold others on commission.

In 1902, W. M. Rossetti (in *The Bibliographer*) added to his description of the fly-sheet printing of *After the French Liberation of Italy* the words: "Neither has it ever been published—not, at any rate, with authority." With reference to *Autumn Song* (= *At the Fall of the Leaf*) he says: "This lyric, a very early production, was for the first time published in this form. [*Love Lily*, etc., as described above.] It reappears in the Collected Works." Later, in 1903, Prideaux, in his *Additions* in *The Bibliographer*, describes the present pamphlet in full as his final item; and in his prefatory note we read: "For the collation and description of the very rare pamphlet which concludes the list, I am indebted to my friend, Mr. Thomas J. Wise." In W. M. Rossetti's *Bibliography* in 1905, which presents the two *Bibliographer* articles revised and corrected, we find the following emended references. (1) To *After the French Liberation of Italy* (p. 17), "Neither had it ever been published with authority until, in 1904, it was included in the book (No. 54) [*Poems*, 1904]. There was, however, a reprint of it, with the song At the Fall of the Leaf . . . under the title of, 'Verses, Privately Printed, 1881.' 8vo." (2) To *Autumn Song* (p. 28), "This lyric, a very early production, was for the first time published with authority in this form [*Love Lily*, etc.], along with five other songs previously published. It had previously been printed, under the title At the Fall of the Leaf, in 1881."

The paper is a hand-made, watermarked *Van Gelder*, which is unlike that of any other member of the group.

The text type (F in our schedule) is identical with that used for the two Kipling pamphlets discussed above. Various sizes of a gothic fount are used for the title and headings throughout; and *SONNETS* on p. 11 is set in the same size of this fount as is used for *CLEOPATRA* on the cancelled title-page of the proofs of that highly suspicious pamphlet in the Wrenn Library (see below, p. 280).

Conclusion.—There is no evidence that this pamphlet was known to the author, who died in 1882, and there was no copy in the sale of his books in the same year. It is probable that W. M. Rossetti was aware of its existence by 1902, if we may judge by the first sentence quoted above from *The Bibliographer*. When, in his *Additions*, Prideaux brought it into the limelight, sponsored by an authority as eminent as Mr. Wise, Rossetti's position was a difficult one. He could no longer ignore it: and although he obviously realised that it was at any rate unauthorised, if not falsely dated, he hardly liked to say so bluntly in the *Bibliography* of 1905. He contented himself with the two quite definite negative statements quoted above.

There is no positive evidence from type or paper to prove the book a forgery in the full sense of the word. But since we have some authority for its being piratical; and since in its auction record, bibliographical status and earliest ascertainable provenance—in everything, in fact, except its paper—it is precisely similar to the numerous proved forgeries on our list; there seems to be the strongest possible evidence, short of the conclusive, for assigning to it the higher degree of culpability. The general lay-out and expensive hand-made paper, no less than the existence of the copies printed on vellum, shows that, if differing in this respect from the other books in the group, it was clearly a *de luxe* production for the avowed book-collector: and the ownership of the vellum copies (Wise, Buxton Forman, H. E. Widener) sufficiently indicates the market to which it was intended to appeal—a market hardly existing in 1881. The forger must have set up the second poem from the fly-sheet (of which Mr. Wise records (Ashley IV, 124) that " a handful of copies " were printed), and the first from *Love Lily* (1884).

John Ruskin

WE include no less than eight pamphlets by Ruskin, of which all but two are conclusively proved to be forgeries. No doubt Mr. Wise's preoccupation with his *Bibliography of Ruskin* in the years 1889–93 provided an easy victim for the forger's wares; and all of them appear in that *Bibliography*, although some are among the addenda.

There are three bibliographies of Ruskin: (i) The *Bibliography of Ruskin* by Richard Herne Shepherd, London, 1878. A fifth edition "revised and enlarged" appeared in 1882 [Shepherd]. Ruskin was presented with a copy of the first edition and wrote in reply: ". . . I can't find a single thing to correct or add—glancing through, at least."[1] (ii) *A Bibliography of the Writings in Prose and Verse of John Ruskin*. Edited by Thomas J. Wise. This was issued to subscribers in nineteen parts from September 1889 to 1893 [Wise]. Although a copy of each part was sent to Ruskin, his health did not allow him critically to examine them.[2] (iii) The bibliographical notes prefixed to each book in *The Collected Works of John Ruskin*, edited by E. T. Cook and Alexander Wedderburn, 39 volumes, London, 1903–1912 [Cook & Wedderburn]. For this work the editors collated the text of all important editions of Ruskin's books, and their scrupulous care first detected two of these forgeries, as well as providing negative evidence

[1] *Arrows of the Chace*, 1880, Vol. I. p. 276.
[2] Cook & Wedderburn, Vol. I. p. 288. See also above, pp. 114, 133.

against two more. These discoveries were announced in small type notes in a 39-volume edition; and for that reason they have not become generally known. Indeed the pamphlets in question are displayed in the Ashley Library Catalogue twenty years later with no indication of the fact that they are forgeries.

THE SCYTHIAN GUEST

The Scythian Guest; / A Poem. / by / John Ruskin. / MDCCCXLIX / (Printed for the Author.)

Small quarto, light brown paper wrappers, with the lettering of the title-page reproduced within a single rule border on the front. Edges uncut.

There is no printer's or publisher's name anywhere on the pamphlet. The text of the poem is set in a Small Pica modern face, and the first line of the title-page in a 30-point condensed roman. The paper is a cream wove.

First printed in *Friendship's Offering*, 1840, pp. 52–60. Reprinted in *Poems*, 1850, pp. 121–130.

Not in Shepherd (1882). Wise, no. 1141, Vol. II. p. 227 (pt. 16, December, 1892). Not mentioned by Slater (1894). Indicated by Mr. Wise as one of Slater's omissions in his review in *The Bookman*, May, 1894, p. 49. Cook & Wedderburn, Vol. II. pp. 101–2, note (1903).

No copies in the British Museum, the Bodleian, or the Cambridge University Library. The copy in the John Rylands Library at Manchester was purchased together with one of four copies on vellum of Mr. Wise's private edition of Ruskin's *Two Letters concerning Notes on the Construction of Sheepfolds*, 1890, for £63 in 1892. Ashley IV. 179–180. Wrenn IV. 48.

The pamphlet's first appearance in the auction room was as lot 606 at Sotheby's on June 10, 1903, when it was bought for £10 5*s*. No further copy occurred until 1929, when three copies came into the market, fetching £1 5*s*., £1 18*s*. and £3 10*s*. Another copy in 1930 fetched £2. The 1903 copy was bound in morocco, but the others were all in original state. No inscriptions are recorded. We have been unable to trace the sale of " a washed copy for £42," mentioned by Mr. Wise in his review in *The Bookman*, unless he is referring to Mrs. Rylands's purchase mentioned above.

Mr. Gorfin bought fourteen copies of *The Scythian Guest* from Mr. Wise on May 14th, 1910, at a guinea each. On April 30, 1912, he bought two more copies for £2.

When it became evident that Ruskin was permanently turning his attention to prose and art criticism, his father, whose ambition it had been that his son should be a poet, decided to print a collection of his poems privately. From 1847 to 1850, when the volume appeared, he made meticulous notes of the appearances of all Ruskin's poems; and these notes were preserved at Brantwood and were consulted by Cook and Wedderburn. There is no mention of the present pamphlet among them (Cook & Wedderburn, *loc. cit.*).

The paper when analysed showed traces of rag, but was mainly esparto fibre; as esparto was not used for the manufacture of paper until at least twelve years after 1849, the pamphlet must be a forgery.

The text is set in the fount we have scheduled as B: five other forgeries and five suspects are also printed with this fount. The 30-point condensed roman capitals used on the title-page, and also for the title-page of Matthew Arnold's *Geist's Grave*, 1881, strike us as very suspicious for 1849, but we have not been able to identify them.

Conclusion.—The suspicion engendered by the absence of this pamphlet from the notes of Ruskin's father is amply confirmed by the analysis of the paper. This forgery should have appeared in the first part of Mr. Wise's *Bibliography*, published in September, 1889; but it was included among the "Omissions" in Part 16, issued in December, 1892: so that it is not unreasonable to suppose that it came to light between those dates.

THE NATIONAL GALLERY

The National Gallery. / Two Letters / to the Editor of / The Times. / By / The Author of "Modern Painters." / London : / 1852.

8vo, stitched, no wrappers, uncut.

This pamphlet bears no publisher's name: at the foot of the last page is "London: Printed by Stewart & Murray, Old Bailey." The text is set in Small Pica old style, and the first line on the title-page in 30-point heavy capitals which have slightly cupped and full-bracketed serifs: the R has a double curved tail. The paper is a rather coarse cream wove.

The first letter was printed in *The Times* on January 7, 1847, and reprinted in *The Abuses of the National Gallery* by Verax [*i.e.* Morris Moore], 1847, pp. 44–58. It was first collected in *Arrows of the Chace*, 1880, Vol. I. pp. 53–66.

The second letter was first printed in *The Times* on December 29, 1852; it was reprinted in *Arrows of the Chace*, 1880, Vol. I. pp. 67–77.

Not in Shepherd (1882) nor Slater (1894). Wise, no. 29, Vol. I. pp. 43–4 (Part 2, November, 1889), where it is stated that these letters "were afterwards reprinted (without alteration) in *Arrows of the Chace*." A footnote adds, "This pamphlet appears to be of extreme scarcity. It was probably printed only for private distribution, as Messrs. Smith, Elder & Co. have no record of any copies having offered for sale by them" [*sic*]. Cook & Wedderburn, Vol. XII. p. 396.

The copy in the British Museum (7855.cc.46) was purchased June 16, 1890, from Otto P. Rubeck of 315 Brixton Road, London, S.W., for two guineas. No copies in the Bodleian or the Cambridge University Library. Ashley IV. 181. Wrenn IV. 48.

This pamphlet first appeared in the auction room in New York (Bangs & Co.) as lot 453*a*, on March 31, 1898, and fetched $12.50 in original state. We can trace no other separate sale, but others have appeared in bundles. There was one in lot 399 at Hodgson's on June 20, 1929.

Mr. Gorfin bought forty-one copies of this pamphlet from Mr. Wise for thirty shillings on April 12, 1910.

A detailed collation of the three texts of these two letters is given by Cook & Wedderburn (*loc. cit.*), from which the following table has been compiled: the references in column 1 are to that edition.

Reference.	*The Times*, 1847–1852.	"1852" edition.	*Arrows of the Chace*, 1880.
Letter One.			
§ 3, line 5	upon the frames [1]	upon the panes	upon the panes
§ 8, line 41	not to	not only to	not only to
§ 9, lines 4–5	acted upon in the various purchases made in the last five years	acted upon in the last five years	acted upon in the last five years
§ 9, line 7	artistical utility of	artistical ability of	artistical ability of
§ 9, line 38	genuine or untouched	genuine and untouched	genuine and untouched
Letter Two.			
§ 2, line 25	chill [2]	dirt	dirt

The two footnotes to the second letter which originally appeared in *The Times*, were reprinted in *Arrows of the Chace* at the foot of the page together with the notes added by the editor of those two volumes, which was Mr. Wedderburn himself. They are omitted altogether in the "1852" edition.

[1] Ruskin's MS. draft reads "frames": Wedderburn's emendation "panes" would make nonsense, as in paragraph 8 of the same letter Ruskin suggests that the more important pictures should be put under glass.

[2] Ruskin's MS. draft reads "damp"; but compare the last sentence of paragraph 6 in this letter, "all secure from damp, cold, impurity of atmosphere. . . ." The emendation of "chill" to "dirt" was made by Mr. Wedderburn in 1880.

There are numerous minute differences of punctuation between the version in *The Times* and the other two, but they all point to the conclusion indicated by the table set out above, that *Arrows of the Chace* must have been set up from the 1852 pamphlet or *vice versa*. As we have Mr. Wedderburn's categorical assurance[1] that the text of *Arrows of the Chace* was set up directly from *The Times*, it follows that the "1852" pamphlet must have been set up from *Arrows of the Chace*, 1880. This conclusion is entirely confirmed by the pamphlet's omission of the footnotes and its inclusion of Mr. Wedderburn's emendations.

The paper upon which the pamphlet is printed is composed of esparto and rag fibres. As esparto was not used for paper-making until after 1861, it follows that the pamphlet could not have been printed until at least nine years after the date on its title-page.

The old style type used is not the original Caslon design, and it must, therefore, be one of the Phemister family, the first of which was not cut until 1852.

Conclusion.—The text, the paper and the type of this pamphlet all prove it to be a forgery. As it was set up from *Arrows of the Chace*, it must have been produced after 1880.

[1] *Arrows of the Chace*, Vol. I. pp. xvii–xviii.

CATALOGUE OF THE TURNER SKETCHES IN THE NATIONAL GALLERY

Catalogue / of the / Turner Sketches / in the / National Gallery. / Part I. / For Private Circulation. [*This line in Gothic*] / London: / Printed by Spottiswoode and Co. / New-Street Square. / 1857.

8vo, no wrappers, uncut. The copies that we have examined had never been stitched.

The imprint of Spottiswoode and Co. is on the title-page and at the foot of the last page. Set in a Pica modern style. Printed on cream wove paper.

Besides the "Prefatory" this pamphlet contains the descriptions of only 25 sketches as against 100 in the later edition described below. Some minor additional differences were first noted by Herne Shepherd and reproduced by Mr. Wise.

There are three different pamphlets the title-pages of which conform to the transcription given above. A, which contains only 25 descriptions: B, the present pamphlet, which is a line for line reprint of A: and C, which contains descriptions of 100 sketches. The title-pages of A and C are absolutely identical, and they must have been printed from the same setting of type, which had presumably been kept standing. B follows A so closely that we enumerate four small differences by which it may be distinguished: (i) In A the colon following *London* in the imprint is immediately above the space between the *w* and the second *o* in *Spottiswoode* in the line below, whereas in B it is above the centre of the *w*. (ii) In A the *N* of *New-Street* is almost beneath the first *S* of *Spottiswoode*, whereas in B it is beneath the *Y* of *BY*. (iii) In A the full-point after *Square* is below the space between the second and third *o*'s in *Spottiswoode*, whereas in B it is directly beneath the second *o*. (iv) The figure 7 in the date is quite different. In A its cross-stroke has a slightly marked double curve, and the serif at the end extends only downwards, while the main stem is straight: in B the cross-stroke is straight, and the serif at the end extends both up and down, while the main stem is slightly curved.

None of the bibliographies distinguish A and B. Shepherd [1882], No. 53, pp. 22–3, gives A and C. Wise, Nos. 62 and 63, Vol. I. pp. 72–3 (Part 3, January, 1890), gives A and C. A footnote to No. 62 reads: "This pamphlet is extremely scarce, the only copies known to me being those in the possession of Mr. Alexander Wedderburn, of Cadogan Place, S.W.; and Mr. William Ward, of Richmond.—T. J. W." Cook & Wedderburn, Vol. XIII. p. 186, 1904.

No copies in the British Museum, the Bodleian or the Cambridge University Library. The Victoria and Albert Museum, South Kensington, has A and C. Their A has no reception date: C was received November 30, 1875. Viscount Esher (B). Wrenn IV. 50 [B ?].

The fact that A and B have not previously been differentiated makes it impossible to say to which issue belonged the only copies which have appeared as separate lots in the auction room. The first formed lot 742 at Sotheby's on May 12, 1897, when it fetched £2 12*s*., in a sale which contained a number of the pamphlets under investigation: the second was sold on June 10, 1903, in the same rooms. There was, however, a copy of B in a bundle sold as lot 399 at Hodgson's on June 20, 1929 (now Viscount Esher's).

Mr. Gorfin bought an unspecified number of B from Mr. Wise for ten shillings on April 12, 1910.

The paper of B is composed of a mixture of straw and esparto with traces of chemical wood. Apart from the minute but highly suspicious presence of the chemical wood, it is condemned by the esparto, which was not used for paper-making until four years later than the alleged date of printing. A and C are both printed on pure rag papers.

Conclusion.—The fact that the title-page of B has been reset, while in the later form of the pamphlet (C) it was printed from the same setting of type as A, would alone suggest that B was a later reprint. But, as it is printed on paper that could not have been made until at least four years afterwards, there can be no doubt that it is a forgery.

THE QUEEN'S GARDENS

The / Queen's Gardens / A Lecture / delivered at the Town Hall, Manchester, / On Wednesday, December 14, 1864 / by / John Ruskin, M.A. / Manchester: / Printed in Aid of the St. Andrews Schools Fund / 1864 / Price One Shilling.

8vo, uncut. According to Mr. Wise it was issued stitched, but the copies that we have examined had not even been stitched. No wrappers.

At the foot of the last page is this imprint: "Manchester: R. Charleston and Sons, Ardwick Green." The text is set in a Long Primer modern style. The paper is a cream wove.

This pamphlet is substantially the second lecture, *Of Queens Gardens*, in *Sesame and Lilies.*

This lecture was delivered by Ruskin at the time and place specified on the title-page given above. It was reported in *The Manchester Examiner and Times*, Dec. 16, 1864. It first appeared in book form in *Sesame and Lilies*, 1866.

Not in Shepherd (1882) nor Slater (1894).

Wise, no. 1143, II. 220 (*Omissions*, part 16, Dec. 1892). "The pamphlet doubtless had but a small and merely local circulation, and is now extremely rare. A full account of the only copy at present known to exist will be found in the *Bookman* for *February*, 1893."

The Bookman, February, 1893, p. 145, col. 1, in an article signed "W," but in fact written by Mr. Wise himself (see his *Bibliography*, II. 203): "The text varies considerably from that contained in 'Sesame and Lilies' and may be taken to be the text of the lecture as it was actually delivered. It is this that lends unusual interest to the slender volume, and causes its recovery to be a matter for mutual congratulation by the student and the bibliographer. It displays the great care bestowed by Mr. Ruskin upon one portion at least of 'Sesame and Lilies,' and gives an insight into the endless labour he expended in the elaboration of this most popular of his books. The most cursory glance suffices to discover revisions upon every page, but only by a close comparison of texts can it be ascertained how systematic and minute these revisions are—every change a certain improvement, and calculated to enhance the force, the vigour and the beauty of the prose."

Cook & Wedderburn XVIII. 13–15 (1905).

No copies in the British Museum, the Bodleian Library or the Cambridge University Library. Ashley IV. 182. Wrenn IV. 52.

Mr. Gorfin bought seven copies of *The Queen's Gardens* for £5 from Mr. Wise on April 14, 1910.

We have only been able to find four separate occurrences of this pamphlet in the auction room:

1894, Aug. 3. Sotheby's, Miscellaneous Sale, lot 374. Bought in at £4 by the anonymous owner.
1906, June 27. Sotheby's, Miscellaneous Sale, lot 250, uncut, £2 10*s*.
1908, March 25. Sotheby's, The Library of John Morgan, lot 394, bound in morocco by Zaehnsdorf, £4 6*s*.
1910, June 15. Sotheby's, Miscellaneous Sale, lot 113, uncut, £3 3*s*.

There was also a copy in a bundle, lot 420, at Sotheby's on June 10, 1903.

No mention of any such firm as *R. Charleston and Sons*, or any printers in Ardwick Green, can be found in the Manchester Directories of 1858 and 1869, which are all that we have been able to examine.

The paper is composed of esparto with a trace of chemical wood; while this is not absolutely impossible for 1864, it is much more likely that it was manufactured after 1883.

Cook and Wedderburn made a detailed collation of the text of the various editions of *Sesame and Lilies* for their standard edition (*loc. cit.*). The first four editions in book form (1865, 1865, 1866, 1867) have identical texts, but Ruskin made a number of minor alterations when the work was issued as the first volume of his *Collected Works* in 1871. The text of the pamphlet differs from both: it omits a number of passages, which were undoubtedly delivered by Ruskin in the actual lecture, as they appear in the report given in *The Manchester Examiner and Times:* but what the pamphlet contains is even more striking than what it omits. We have here summarised in tabular form a number of differences first pointed out by Cook and Wedderburn. The line references in the first column are to their edition.

Reference.	"1864."	1865.	1871.
§ 58, end	as a gentle angel, bringing courage and safety by her presence, and defeating the worst malignities of crime by what women are fancied most to fail in—precision and accuracy of thought.	as a gentle angel, to save merely by her presence, and defeat the worst intensities of crime by her smile?	as a gentle angel, bringing courage and safety by her presence, and defeating the worst malignities of crime by what women are fancied most to fail in—precision and accuracy of thought.
§ 59, l. 29	infallible sense	infallible and inevitable sense	infallible sense
§ 73, l. 4	one which they must	one which let them	one which they must
§ 73, l. 17	crawling	scrambling	crawling
§ 73, l. 18	strangest	most strange	strangest
§ 78, l. 3	not for their freedom from evil, but for their possession of good	not for what is out of them, but what is in them	not for their freedom from evil, but for their possession of good

Thus in each case where Ruskin had altered the text for the 1871 edition, this "1864" pamphlet reproduces those alterations; and the conclusion that it must have been set up from the 1871 text becomes inevitable.

The pamphlet is printed in Clay's Long Primer No. 3, some letters of which were not cut until after 1880. This is the same type that was used for Mrs. Browning's *Sonnets* and fourteen other forgeries described in these pages.

Conclusion.—It seems unlikely that the printer who is supposed to have printed this pamphlet ever existed: but the facts that it was set up from a text of 1871 and printed by R. Clay and Sons in a much later fount clearly condemn it as a forgery.

LEONI

Leoni ; / A Legend of Italy. / By / J. R. / London : / 1868.

Small 8vo, mottled grey printed wrappers, uncut.

At the foot of the last page is the imprint " London : / Strangeways & Walden, Printers, / Castle St., Leicester Sq." Set up in a Long Primer old style. Printed on a cream wove paper.

First printed in *Friendship's Offering*, 1837, pp. 217–226. It was not reprinted until 1903, in the first volume of the *Collected Works*.

Not in Shepherd (1882). Slater (1894), p. 219 : " Sells readily for £5." Wise, no. 139, I. 147–8 (part 5, May, 1890) : " The copies of the separate—1868—issue, described above, were reserved for private distribution only." Cook & Wedderburn, I. 288 (1903).

There is no copy in the British Museum or the Bodleian Library. The Cambridge University Library copy was presented by Mr. Wise in 1916. Ashley IV. 185 (2 copies). Wrenn IV. 53 (2 copies).

The first appearance of this pamphlet in the auction room was as lot 741 in a miscellaneous sale at Sotheby's on May 12, 1897, when it was bought for £6 15*s.* ; and this remains the highest price that has been paid for it. Since then we have traced twelve sales in England, all of which were anonymous. Prices varied between £1 and £3 until March 7, 1932, when a copy only fetched eight shillings at Sotheby's. The only copy sold in America appears to have been in the Brayton Ives sale, which fetched 25 dollars as lot 850 at the Anderson Galleries on April 8, 1915. In two of these cases the condition of the pamphlet is not stated ; in one case it had been bound in morocco by Rivière with the wrappers ; in all the remaining eleven cases it was in its original state.

Mr. Gorfin bought thirteen copies from Mr. Wise for £2 12*s.* on April 13, 1910, and another copy for 4*s.* on April 30, 1912.

Cook and Wedderburn brought two kinds of negative evidence against this pamphlet. They could find no trace of Ruskin's having owned a copy, and no reference to it among his papers; nor have we been able to find any trace of a presentation copy. Furthermore, on stylistic grounds—and no one was better qualified for such a judgment—they did not believe that the prefatory note was written by Ruskin. On the other hand, Mr. George Allen "had some recollection of having seen a copy at Denmark Hill."

More damning was the evidence which they discovered from the printers. The successors of Strangeways and Walden, J. Strangeways & Co., still had in 1903 their old ledgers for the year 1868; and though these recorded Ruskin's *Notes on the Employment of the Destitute and Criminal Classes* printed by them in that year, there was no trace of *Leoni*.

The pamphlet is printed in an old style Long Primer fount (C in our schedule), identical with that used for two other forgeries and seven suspects.

The paper proves on analysis to be a mixture of rag, esparto and chemical wood. The fact that it contains a substantial proportion of rag fibre rules out any of the possible explanations for the presence of small quantities of chemical wood advanced on p. 49; and in any case the amount of chemical wood here found could hardly be explained by any of those hypotheses. The paper was undoubtedly manufactured after 1874.

Conclusion.—The negative evidence was sufficient for Cook and Wedderburn to condemn this pamphlet as a forgery. The analysis of the paper puts the matter beyond all doubt.

THE FUTURE OF ENGLAND

The Future of England / A Paper Read at the R.A. Institution / By / John Ruskin, L.L.D. / 14th December, 1869. [*This is the heading to page* 1 *of the text.*]

8vo, dull green wrappers, printed on the front, within an ornamental border; " A Paper read at / The Royal Artillery Institution, / Woolwich. / By / John Ruskin, L.L.D. December 14, 1869. / Woolwich : / Printed at the Royal Artillery Institution. / M.DCCC.LXX." Edges uncut.

Apart from that on the front wrapper, there is no publisher's or printer's imprint. The text is set in Clay's Long Primer No. 3. The paper is a white wove.

There is an alleged reprint, which does not have the wrappers, and has " (*reprint*) " above the title on the first page of text. Otherwise it is exactly identical, and from the same setting of type.

First printed in *The Crown of Wild Olive* (Fourth edition), 1873, pp. 146–174.

Wise, no. 133, I. 138–9 (part 5, May, 1890) : " The pamphlet was printed solely for private distribution, and has now become of very considerable scarcity." Cook & Wedderburn, XVIII. 377 (1905).

No copies in the British Museum, the Bodleian Library or the Cambridge University Library. Ashley IV. 186. Wrenn IV. 53.

This pamphlet only appears five times in the records of the sale room. In a miscellaneous sale together with some of the other forgeries at Sotheby's in 1897 (lot 743, May 12, £1 18*s.*) : at Puttick & Simpson's in the following year (lot 261, July 20, £2 6*s.*) ; and there were three copies in " The valuable Library of a Gentleman living in Yorkshire " sold at Sotheby's on June 10, 1903.

Mr. Gorfin bought " from 30 to 40 " copies from Mr. Wise about 1910 ; but these apparently included some copies of the reprint.

The paper is composed of chemical wood and esparto fibres. Chemical wood is not a possibility at this date.

The text of this pamphlet is set in Clay's Long Primer No. 3, certain letters of which were not cut until after 1880. This is the identical type used for the Reading *Sonnets* and fourteen other forgeries.

Conclusion.—Both paper and type condemn this as a forgery.

SAMUEL PROUT

Samuel Prout. / By / John Ruskin, M.A. / Honorary Student of Christ Church / and / Slade Professor of Fine Art. / Oxford: / Printed for Private Circulation only. / MDCCCLXX

Small 8vo, bright blue paper wrappers, with the title-page reproduced on the front cover, edges unopened and uncut.

On the reverse of the title-page is the imprint "T. & G. Shrimpton, Oxford." The text is set in a Small Pica modern style. Printed on a cream wove paper.

On the leaf following the title-page is this note: "It is more than twenty years since these admirable remarks appeared in the *Art Journal.* Their author leaves them in silent neglect. They are therefore here revived in print for the benefit of a few friends who are at once hearty admirers of Prout and reverent listeners to Professor Ruskin on this as on all other subjects. Oxford, 1870."

This essay first appeared in *The Art Journal*, March, 1849, pp. 76–77. It was first collected in *On the Old Road*, 1885, Vol. I. pp. 206–220.

Not in Shepherd (1882) or Slater (1894). Wise, no. 148, I. 154 (part 5, May, 1890). Cook & Wedderburn, XII. 304 (1904).

No copies in the British Museum or the Cambridge University Library. The copy in the Bodleian Library was bought from Mr. Gorfin in 1925. Ashley IV. 86. Wrenn IV. 54.

This pamphlet first appeared in the auction room as lot 745 at Sotheby's on May 12, 1897, in a sale which contained a number of the forgeries here described. It was bought for £2 10*s*. Four other sales are recorded—Puttick's, June 14, 1897, lot 226; Puttick's, Feb. 13, 1901, lot 215; Sotheby's, March 25, 1907, John Morgan's Library, lot 396; Sotheby's, June 15, 1910, lot 115. None of these sold for more than one guinea.

Mr. Gorfin bought twenty-six copies from Mr. Wise for £1 6s. on April 13, 1910, and another copy for one shilling on April 30, 1912.

The paper is composed of esparto fibres with traces of rag: this is a perfectly normal content for a paper in 1870.

The type (B in our schedule) is the same as that used for four other suspects and six convicted forgeries.

Conclusion.—There is no proof that this is a forgery. Nevertheless, it is clear from the prefatory note that Ruskin was in no way connected with its printing, and we suspect that it was printed at a date much later than that given on its title-page.

R

THE NATURE AND AUTHORITY OF MIRACLE

The Nature and Authority / of / Miracle / By / John Ruskin / 1873. / (For private distribution.)

Small 8vo, stitched, no wrappers, uncut.

There is no publisher's or printer's name on this pamphlet. The text is set in Small Pica old style (D); the third line of the title-page is set in the same unusual fount of capitals that was used for the first line of the title-page of *The National Gallery*. Printed on a somewhat thick wove paper.

The leaf following the title-page has the following note set in italics: "On behalf of a small knot of earnest 'Christians,' I have sought and obtained permission to print a few copies of the following essay, which appeared a short time ago in the 'Contemporary Review.' Our desire was to have so weighty an argument in support of the Christian Verity in a handy and permanent form. J. B. H. Christmas, 1873."

The real first edition of this essay was anonymous: its title read: "Metaphysical Society's Papers, no. xxxii. / The Nature and Authority of Miracle. / Anon." It is headed at the top of the first page "To be read on Tuesday, Feb. 11, 1873. At the Grosvenor Hotel, at 8.30 p.m. Private." It was reprinted in *The Contemporary Review*, March, 1873, pp. 627–634, and first appeared in book form in *On the Old Road*, 1885, Vol. II. pp. 353–356.

Shepherd (1882) only gives the article in *The Contemporary Review*, p. 54. Wise, no. 197, I. 211 (part 7, October, 1890). The Metaphysical Society edition is recorded among the "Omissions" as no. 1144, II. 229 (part 17, April, 1893). Cook & Wedderburn, XXXIV. 114 (1908).

The British Museum copy (4376.aa.1) was purchased June 16, 1890, from Otto P. Rubeck of 315 Brixton Road, London, S.W., for £2 2*s*. No copies in the Bodleian Library or the Cambridge University Library. Ashley IV. 87. Wrenn IV. 54.

The first copy to appear in the auction room was part of "The Property of a Collector" sold at Puttick & Simpson's as lot 225*a* on June 14, 1897. This collector appears to have had a number of the forgeries on our list. The lot was bought for £1 18*s*. The copy belonging to John Morgan, who also had a number of these forgeries, was bound in morocco by Zaehnsdorf, and was bought for £4 4*s*. as lot 400 at Sotheby's on March 25, 1908. The only other sales recorded, both of copies in original state, were at Sotheby's in 1910 (lot 116, June 15, Maggs Bros., £1 1*s*.) and at the Anderson Galleries in 1922 (lot 210, January 18, $2.50). A number of the forgeries were in each of these sales. Other copies have been included in bundles in some of Mr. Gorfin's more recent anonymous sales at Hodgson's.

Mr. Gorfin bought thirty-six copies of this pamphlet from Mr. Wise for £1 7*s*. on April 12, 1910. He also states that he had a bundle of reprints of this essay, which appeared to him identical but for the word "reprint" in italics within brackets above the first line of the title. He unfortunately destroyed these as valueless.

The paper is composed of esparto with traces of chemical wood. The presence of chemical wood is unlikely but not impossible at this date.

The type both of the text and of the title-page is identical with that used in *The National Gallery*, which has been trebly proved a forgery. It is practically certain, not only from the unusual type, but from the similarity with which it is "displayed," that both pamphlets were printed by the same printer, probably about the same time.

Conclusion.—In this case there is no absolute proof of forgery, but there is a deal of suspicion. Not only does it appear to have the same origin as a proved forgery, but it was acquired by the British Museum from the same source at the same time and the same price as that forgery. This was the earliest noted record of both pamphlets, and its subsequent appearances are in no better company.

Robert Louis Stevenson

THE authorities for Stevenson's Bibliography quoted below are as follows. (i) *A Bibliography of the Works* of R. L. S., by Colonel W. F. Prideaux, C.S.I., London, Hollings, 1903 [Prideaux]. (ii) *Catalogue of the Books and Manuscripts* of R. L. S. in the Library of the late Harry Elkins Widener, Philadelphia, 1913 [Widener]. (iii) *First Editions of the Works* of R. L. S. A Check List. New York, The Grolier Club, 1914 [Grolier]. (iv) Prideaux's Bibliography, "A New and Revised Edition, Edited and Supplemented by Mrs. Luther S. Livingston," London, Hollings, 1918 [Prideaux–Livingston]. This is the standard bibliography.

Reference is also made to the Catalogue of Books from Stevenson's Library, sold by Mrs. Isobel Strong, who had inherited them from her mother, Mrs. R. L. Stevenson. These books came up at the Anderson Galleries, New York, November 23–25, 1914, and January 25–27, 1915; and the virtual completeness of the range of the author's own and other copies of his first editions renders the absence of any particular volume conspicuous.

On April 24–28, 1899, a number of rare Stevenson pamphlets (some in duplicate) were included in a sale at Sotheby's by order of the executors of the author's mother: none of the books discussed below figured in this property. In Sotheby's sale of July 28–29 of the same year, a second collection appeared (lots 406–460).

These were consigned anonymously,[1] but were stated in *Book Prices Current* (presumably following the Catalogue) to have been "until recently in the possession of a cousin of the Author, to whom they were given by him; many of them bear her autograph." This collection is roughly similar in constitution to the previous one, *except* that all the books we are about to consider appear in it. Since the catalogue does not state which of the books bear the author's cousin's autograph, it is impossible to tell how many, and which, had been added by the subsequent owner who now consigned them: but the inclusion of *On the Thermal Influence of Forests*, which is a proved forgery, shows that the superficially imposing provenance was being used to cover some "salting," and consequently presence in this sale is no authentication.

[1] Messrs. Sotheby are unable, in the absence of any records, to establish the identity of this consignor.

THE THERMAL INFLUENCE OF FORESTS

On the / Thermal Influence of Forests. / By / Robert Louis Stevenson, Esq. / Edinburgh: / Printed by Neill and Company. / MDCCCLXXIII.

8vo, pale blue printed wrappers, uncut.

There is no imprint beyond that on the title-page. Printed on cream wove paper in Clay's Long Primer No. 3.

This is not to be confused with what is usually known as "the *second* separate impression," which was issued in dark blue plain wrappers and has on the title-page the words "From the Proceedings of the Royal Society of Edinburgh, vol. viii, 1872–1873." The two are otherwise very similar, having the same collation and being page for page the same in lay-out.

This paper was read before the Royal Society on May 19, 1873: it was first printed in the *Proceedings, etc.* (as above), pp. 114–125: and subsequently in the *Appendix* volume of the Edinburgh edition, 1898.

Not in Slater (1894): Prideaux (1903), p. 115: Widener (1913), No. 7: Grolier (1914), No. 7: Prideaux–Livingston (1918), pp. 134–136.

No copy in the British Museum, Bodleian or the Cambridge University Library. Wrenn IV. 196 (two copies in original wrappers). Ashley VI. 2 (wrappers). No copy in the Isobel Strong sale of Stevenson's library 1914–15.

The first copy to appear at auction fetched £14 in 1897 (May 15, Sotheby, Miscellaneous, lot 834, half morocco with the wrappers preserved), and practically every year since then has produced two or three copies in the original wrappers. The price dropped to 4 guineas in 1900, but rose again to £12 in 1902, reached $102.50 in the Forman sale in 1920, and during 1928–30 ranged between £16 and the highest recorded, $125 (Kern sale, January 21, 1929, Anderson Galleries, lot 1143). No copy bore any inscription of any kind.[1]

Mr. Gorfin purchased twenty-seven copies from Mr. Wise on April 18, 1910, at 5*s.* each.

Prideaux (1903) says, " It is generally supposed that the issue without this addition [*From the Proceedings*, etc., on the title-page] is the earlier and that only 26 or 27 copies were printed." On his applying to the printers, Messrs. Neill & Co., the following reply was received (January 16, 1902): " We have to state that we printed the article by R. L. Stevenson on *The Thermal Influence of Forests*. We find that Mr. Stevenson ordered 50 extra copies of his article. . . . The copy to which you refer as having a special title-page is probably one of these 50 copies. . . . It is at the author's option to order any extra copies for his own private use, for which he pays, and he may, if he so desires it, have the pagination altered,[2] and a title-page and cover set specially for himself." This note and Neill's letter were reprinted unaltered in Prideaux–Livingston (1918). Grolier describes this pamphlet as " first separate edition," putting the " Proceedings " edition as " second separate edition." Mr. Wise (Ashley, 1925) calls it " first edition " and does not mention the other.

Now the fact that Stevenson ordered fifty copies of *a* separate offprint is vouched for by the printer's ledgers; and that it was the edition with the words " From the Proceedings, etc." on the title-page is rendered absolutely certain by the presence among his own books and papers after his death of no less

[1] Prideaux (1903) stated that the copy sold at Sotheby's in 1897 had a presentation inscription. There is no mention of this in the entry in *Book Prices Current*, which there certainly would have been had it been there; and the statement is omitted in Prideaux–Livingston (1918) in tacit acknowledgment of the error.

[2] Both pamphlets have the altered pagination.

than six copies out of that 50.[1] These formed lots 626–628 in Part I, and lots 501–503 in Part II, of the Isobel Strong sales in 1914–15 (see above, p. 245), and were duly described (after Prideaux, Widener and Grolier) as "second separate edition" by the auctioneers. There were no copies of the present pamphlet in either of these sales.

The validity of Prideaux' suggestion that "only 26 or 27 copies" of the present pamphlet were printed might well have been impugned in 1918, if anyone had cared to look up the auction records. We now know that besides the fifty or more copies which have appeared in the sale room since 1897, a stock of twenty-seven was still in the possession of Mr. Wise in 1909. Prideaux' reported estimate of the number originally printed is therefore exposed as ridiculously misleading, and one wonders whether the "general suppositions" as to the priority and as to the number came from the same source; and if so, what that source was.[2]

The paper on which this book is printed is composed of chemical wood, esparto and rag. The presence of the first in any quantity, as here, proves that the paper could not have been manufactured before 1874, and it is highly unlikely before 1883.

Certain letters of the text type, Clay's Long Primer No. 3, were not cut for that firm until after 1880, which proves the book falsely dated. The fact that this version of the type is peculiar to Clay proves that the imprint is fictitious. Its identity with that used for the Reading *Sonnets* and a number of other proved forgeries establishes this book as a member of the group.

[1] There was also a presentation copy in the John Morgan sale in 1902 (lot 265).

[2] See above, p. 129, for a possible explanation.

Conclusion.—This pamphlet is proved a forgery by its type and its paper, and the negative evidence in support of these two positive condemnations is satisfactorily strong and detailed. It is remarkable both for the unusually large number which must have been printed; also for the success with which it ousted the genuine article from the position of priority and, by means of a "supposition" in the standard bibliography, was credited with a degree of scarcity very far beyond its deserts.

THE STORY OF A LIE

The Story of a Lie. / By / Robert Louis Stevenson. / London: / Hayley & Jackson, Little Queen St., W.C. / 1882.

8vo, stitched or folded, uncut, without wrappers.

Imprint on verso of title—"James Goodwich & Sons, Printers, London." Printed in a Small Pica modern style on a rough cream wove paper.

First published in *The New Quarterly Magazine*, New Series, No. 25, October 1879, pp. 307–355: afterwards in Vol. II of the Edinburgh Edition, 1895, pp. 293–374.

Prideaux (1903), p. 15: "*The Story of a Lie* was prepared for issue in 1882, but, in consequence of a dispute which arose with the proposed publishers upon the question of copyright, the project was abandoned, and the book withdrawn before publication. The work was never 'made up' for issue, and the few copies that have survived are merely such sets of the sheets as chanced to have been preserved by the publishers and printers." Prideaux–Livingston (1917), pp. 15–16 reprints this note.

No copy in the British Museum, Bodleian, or Cambridge University Library. Ashley VI. 3 (morocco, uncut). Wrenn IV. 198 (morocco, uncut). No copy in the Isobel Strong sale.

The first copy to appear at auction fetched £30 10*s*. in 1899 (July 28, Sotheby, lot 451, calf, uncut). This was in the property discussed above, p. 246, and the catalogue note stated that "only some half-dozen copies are believed to have been preserved." Twenty-five copies in all are recorded in the rooms; five uncut in modern bindings, two in grey wrappers, one in watered silk, ten unbound uncut; the condition of the remainder is not given. The highest price was $275 in the Kern sale (January 21, 1929, Anderson Galleries, lot 1150);

the lowest *22s.* in 1907 (December 10, Hodgson, Miscellaneous, lot 506). Normal prices have ranged between £7 and £20 in London, and between $50 and $100 in New York. No inscriptions of any kind are recorded, though a copy was sold in 1918 (March 19, Puttick, Miscellaneous, lot 411, £18) with a letter from Mr. Wise referring to the book.

Mr. Gorfin purchased twenty copies from Mr. Wise at £1 each on August 24, 1910, and one further copy at the same price on April 30, 1912.

Both the publisher's and printer's imprints struck us as unfamiliar. On investigation we could discover no other books published by Hayley & Jackson in *The English Catalogue* for 1881–90, and they do not appear in *Kelly's Post Office Directory* during the years 1881–83. Moreover, the occupants of all the premises in Little Queen Street, W.C., are given, as usual, and the only empty house in the street remained untenanted all through those years—a fact which makes an otherwise possible transient establishment of Hayley & Jackson in it rather unlikely. On referring to *Kelly* for James Goodwich, we found one saddler and one cheesemonger of that name; but no printer.

The type employed is the one we have scheduled as B. It is the same as that in which six proved forgeries and four other suspects are printed.

Conclusion.—There may have been such firms as Hayley & Jackson and Goodwich. There may be some authenticated copy of the book in existence. Its typographical identity with six proved forgeries may be an accident. There may be some explanation of the large number of copies, over and above those sold at auction, which were still in one place in 1910. Its common provenance with the rest of the group may have no significance. There may be some reason why no copy appeared in the rooms until 1899. Its absence from the Isobel Strong sale may have some simple explanation.

Confirmatory evidence on any of these points has, however, eluded our researches; and in default of it, this book must be considered extremely suspicious.

SOME COLLEGE MEMORIES

Some College Memories / By / Robert Louis Stevenson / [*vignette portrait*] / Edinburgh: / Printed for Members of the / University Union Committee / 1886.

Small 8vo, thick grey printed wrappers, uncut.

There is no imprint. Printed on cream wove paper in a Pica old style.

First printed in *The New Amphion* (by various authors) 1886: afterwards in *Memories and Portraits*, 1887.

Unknown to Slater (1894): Prideaux (1903), p. 47: Widener (1913), No. 85: Grolier (1914), No. 82: Prideaux–Livingston (1918), pp. 49–51.

There is no copy in the British Museum, the Bodleian or the Cambridge University Library. No copy in the Isobel Strong sales. Ashley VI. 6 (original wrappers). Wrenn IV. 200, two copies (original wrappers).

The first copy recorded at auction appeared in 1897 in a miscellaneous sale at Puttick's which contained a large number of the forgeries (June 14, lot 247). It fetched £12. Like eleven others of the thirteen which have since appeared, this was in the original wrappers, uncut. The condition of the thirteenth copy is not given. During the next twenty years much lower prices ruled: £2 1*s.* in November of the same year, £1 (the lowest point) in 1907, £5 5*s.* in the Prideaux sale in 1917. Since 1921, however, English prices have ranged from £7 to £11, American from $37.50 to $70. No copy is recorded as having borne any inscription whatever.

Mr. Gorfin purchased five copies from Mr. Wise at 10*s.* each on April 29, 1910, and two more on May 2, 1910.

The text type (G in our schedule) is identical with that used for *The Sailor Boy*, 1861, a proved forgery, and the *Ode on the Opening of the Colonial and Indian Exhibition*, 1886. The display type in the heading to the opening of the text (which contains a very noticeable spurred capital G) is identical with that used for the first two lines of the title of the *Ode*, 1886, and for the half title of the Shelley Society's *Rosalind and Helen* (printed by Clay, 1887).

Prideaux (*loc. cit.*) has the following note: "It has been stated that this *brochure* was printed at the instance and at the cost, of Mr. W. H. Hepworth, Examiner in Art at South Kensington, and that it was produced with its author's consent and approval. On the other hand, doubts have been thrown on its authenticity. The curious reader may consult the correspondence on this subject that took place in *The Athenæum*, Jan. 8, Jan. 22, Feb. 5, Feb. 26, 1898."

That there had been a fair number of curious readers of the correspondence at the time may or may not be reflected in the low prices which the pamphlet continued for a number of years afterwards to fetch in the rooms. But as the much higher prices of the last decade seem to show that people no longer look up Prideaux' references, we are reprinting this entertaining correspondence in full.

From *The Athenæum*, Jan. 8, 1898.

"SOME COLLEGE MEMORIES

"Messrs. T. & A. Constable write from the University Press, Edinburgh:—

"'Application has been made to us from two sources for information about a pamphlet, at present being offered for sale at extraordinary prices, entitled 'Some College Memories,' by Robert Louis Stevenson. It contains eighteen pages, and is stitched in a purple-grey wrapper, which is ornamented with a vignette of the late Prof. Kelland, pirated from an etching by Mr. Hole. The pamphlet has neither publisher's nor printer's imprint, but it is stated on the title-page that it has been printed for members of the Edinburgh University Union Committee. 'Some College Memories' was first contributed by Mr. Stevenson to a little volume called 'The New Amphion,' which was printed by us for the Edinburgh University Union in November 1886. This paper was reprinted in 'Memories and Portraits' (Chatto & Windus, 1887), and in the first volume of the Edinburgh edition of Mr. Stevenson's works. The origin of the grey pamphlet is unknown to us as well as to Mr. Colvin and Mr. Baxter. Its existence was also unknown to the editors of 'The New Amphion,' who were the secretaries of the University Union Committee. It appears to have been printed to catch the collector of first editions and can doubtless be multiplied indefinitely. But it is not a first edition—merely a pirated reprint, of which the sale is illegal'."

"Messrs. Constable are, we fancy, in error. Stevenson, if we mistake not, had some copies printed off in 1886 for distribution among his friends connected with the University. We are informed by a bibliographer of note that he has seen one copy of the grey pamphlet bearing an inscription of some length in Stevenson's handwriting, which he is persuaded is quite genuine."

From *The Athenæum*, Jan. 22.

'SOME COLLEGE MEMORIES

University Press, Edinburgh, Jan. 11. 1898.

" The authenticity of the grey pamphlet is but a small matter to continue a correspondence about, yet we think it a duty to collectors to reply to your remarks on our former letter.

" We have compared the text of 'Some College Memories' as printed in 'The New Amphion' with Mr. Stevenson's original manuscript. We find that the printed text differs in several places from the manuscript from which it was set up, showing that Mr. Stevenson had revised the proofs of 'The New Amphion' and had made alterations on them. The text of the grey pamphlet is exactly the same as that of the 'Amphion,' showing that it is a reprint from that little book.

" We must repeat our conviction that the grey pamphlet is merely a pirated reprint, and was not printed for Mr. Stevenson, for the following reasons, among others :—

" 1. It is difficult for us to believe that between November 30th (the date of issuing 'The New Amphion') and December 31st, 1886, Mr. Stevenson would, unknown to Mr. Colvin and Mr. Baxter, have commissioned any Edinburgh printer other than ourselves to reprint his article.

" 2. It is impossible to believe that Mr. Stevenson would have stated that the pamphlet was printed for the University Union Committee when, on the authority of the secretaries, it was not printed for that Committee, and until now its existence was unknown to them.

"3. It seems preposterous to believe that Mr. Stevenson would have secretly photographed and reproduced a portrait which was the work of one friend and the property of another, if for no higher reason than that he could have had the original plate if he had wanted it.

T. & A. Constable."

From *The Athenæum*, Feb. 5.

"SOME COLLEGE MEMORIES

15 St. George's Rd. N.W. Jan. 31, 1898.

"It might have been supposed that the editorial note appended to Messrs. Constable's first communication would have sufficed to settle the question of the position in Stevenson bibliography to which the separate print of 'Some College Memories' was to be assigned. But since Messrs. Constable have thought proper to reopen the question, it may be as well to state clearly what was the genesis of the little book.

"After having made its first appearance in 'The New Amphion,' 'Some College Memories' was reprinted in Edinburgh at Christmas 1886. It was produced under the distinct direction—or permission—of Robert Louis Stevenson, and was seen through the press by Mr. W. H. Hepworth,[1] Examiner in

[1] We have been unable to find out very much about this Mr. Hepworth. The Director of Establishments at the Board of Education states that "a Mr. W. Hepworth was employed from March, 1881, and regularly to June, 1896, as an occasional Examiner in Art at South Kensington. The Board have no knowledge of him after 1896." He is not mentioned in that very comprehensive work, Boase's *Modern English Biography* (4 vols., 1892, etc., and several supplements), nor *a fortiori* in any of the Supplements to *The Dictionary of National Biography*. He does not appear in Palmer's Index to *The Times*, so

Art at South Kensington, and—outside that inner circle of close companions which included Mr. Edmund Gosse, Mr. Sidney Colvin, Mr. Charles Baxter and others—one of Stevenson's most valued friends and correspondents. That the distribution of the little book was never carried out to the extent its author had intended was no doubt due to Mr. Hepworth's very indifferent health; added to which in 1886 there were probably not more than a dozen persons who would have troubled to preserve it, even had it reached their hands. Possibly, also, the festivities of the season may have served to interfere with the despatch or receipt of copies of the tract.

"Briefly, the book is no 'piracy,' as it was printed under its author's direct instructions; neither is it in any way a 'spurious print,' as it was printed in 1886, as duly set forth upon its title-page.

"Messrs. Constable's suggestion that because the pamphlet of 1886 was not printed by themselves, therefore it must be spurious, can hardly be serious, although, of course, had it been printed by direction of the Committee of the University Union, no doubt Messrs. Constable would have been employed to produce it. But it was not printed by direction of the Committee. It was printed by Stevenson himself, in conjunction with Mr. Hepworth, for distribution among members of that Committee

that he apparently received no obituary notice there. More relevant, perhaps, to our present inquiry, is the fact that he is nowhere mentioned in *The Letters of Robert Louis Stevenson* (enlarged edition, edited by Sidney Colvin, 4 vols., Methuen, 1911). The absence of any contribution by him, either personally or as directly quoted by Mr. Wise, to the present correspondence, suggests that he probably died between 1896 and 1898: otherwise he would surely have been called in evidence by one side or the other.

and other friends, and it was open to Mr. Hepworth to have the work executed at any printing house he chose. The most natural course for him to pursue would be to commission, not Messrs. Constable, but the printers who in 1886 and the surrounding years were producing the majority of Stevenson's books.

" Messrs. Constable's further remark—that because the text of the separate print agrees with that contained in 'The New Amphion' and does not follow the original 'copy,' therefore the separate print was unauthorised—is also difficult to follow. Had the pamphlet been printed by Messrs. Constable themselves, they would naturally have set up its pages from the revised text as contained in 'The New Amphion' and would never have gone out of their way to revive the cancelled readings of the manuscript. It cannot, therefore, be conceived as possible that Stevenson, when arranging with Mr. Hepworth to issue the private print, would have instructed him to go to Messrs. Constable and obtain the original (and discarded) copy of a text which he had already sufficiently revised. Unquestionably the only reasonable plan to adopt would be to work from a copy of 'The New Amphion.' Messrs. Constable's collation of the original manuscript is of considerable value to the bibliographer, as showing that Stevenson was given the opportunity of revising the text of his essay during the passage of 'The New Amphion' through the press, and that he availed himself of the opportunity afforded. To myself, as the bibliographer of Robert Louis Stevenson, this fact is of peculiar interest; I had always regarded these 'Memories,' delightful as they are, as entirely lacking revision. But the result of such collation can have no bearing whatever upon the genuineness of the privately printed booklet. Fortunately the position of that book is unassailable, and its validity is beyond dispute.

THOMAS J. WISE."

From *The Athenæum*, Feb. 26.

"SOME COLLEGE MEMORIES

"Could Stevenson, forsaking awhile the fellowship of the immortals, revisit a world he has so much delighted, would it be fair for Bibliography (while strewing flowers in his path) to ask a simple question or two?

"'Did you in December, 1886, the month following the copyright publication of "Some College Memories" by Messrs. Constable & Co. (in "The New Amphion"), direct Mr. Hepworth to print a separate issue, with the following words on the title-page and cover: "Edinburgh: printed for Members of the University Union Committee, 1886"?'

"Stevenson: 'My object in producing this private issue, without informing any of my Edinburgh friends, or taking any notice of Messrs. Constable's copyright interest, must remain an undiscoverable secret. I might easily have obtained Messrs. Constable's consent to reprint the "Memories"; I might also have borrowed their block for the portrait; but I did neither of these things. You may observe that the printing is anonymous—that it is inferior to the work of the better houses. That no copies ever reached the members of the University Union Committee, for whom the booklet was professedly printed, is not to be wondered at. I took precautions to prevent it! Purposely avoiding everything that was easy, natural, and inexpensive, I have entirely succeeded in the attainment of my object—to create a mystery and confuse and puzzle everybody.'

" 'Can you state who did the printing for Mr. Hepworth; how many copies were done; and if any copy has ever been in your own possession?' These are questions I leave to be answered by the wiseacre bibliographers.

FRANK T. SABIN."

It will be observed that the editorial comment to the first letter seems to rest entirely on the "bibliographer of note" and the copy with the long presentation inscription. Whether this bibliographer was in fact Mr. Wise, or not—and his description of himself in the third letter as "the bibliographer of Robert Louis Stevenson" and his vigorous defence of the pamphlet both seem to point to him—it is a very odd thing that no more is heard of that presentation copy. Mr. Wise's case for the defence was not so strong that he could afford to neglect such a powerful witness to the pamphlet's authenticity, if it existed. As he makes no reference to it, we may reasonably conclude that it does not: and, in fact, no presentation copy has ever been recorded elsewhere.

Then, it cannot but be felt that Mr. Wise's defence as a whole is curiously unsatisfactory. Quite apart from the absence of any supporting authority, independent confirmation, external evidence and so forth, which might be expected from "the bibliographer of Stevenson" to establish the authenticity of the pamphlet beyond the cavilling of Messrs. Constable, Mr. Wise is reticent on several interesting points. He seems to be fully informed about Mr. Hepworth's instrumentality in the printing, but we are not told who the printer was. He refers to "the printers who in 1886 and the surrounding years were producing the majority of Stevenson's books," as if these were all done at one printing house with whose name his readers would be immediately familiar. In point of fact, Stevenson's books between 1885 and 1888 inclusive were printed by the following, in chronological order: Spottiswoode, Spottiswoode, Spottiswoode, R. & R. Clark, Spottiswoode, James Henderson, Cassell, Spottiswoode, R. & R. Clark, R. & R. Clark, R. & R. Clark, Cassell, Cassell. Even if, therefore, Mr. Hepworth had "pursued the natural course," he would have found Stevenson with three regular printers; and it would have been interesting to know to which of them Mr. Wise was referring.

Again, he leaves us uncertain of Stevenson's exact part in the printing. "It was produced under the distinct direction—or permission—of R. L. S. . . . it was printed under its author's direct instructions. . . . It was printed by Stevenson himself . . . it was open to Mr. Hepworth to have the work executed at any printing house he chose . . . when arranging with Mr. Hepworth to issue the private print." The fact of Stevenson's connection with it is reiterated, but the nature of that connection remains obscure.

Constable's three tabulated arguments are very inadequately dealt with: Mr. Wise answers half of each of the first two, and ignores the third entirely—that damning charge of the copied block. And he makes no attempt to explain the extensive ignorance of all the people who were most likely to know about, and possess, copies of the pamphlet, beyond an unconvincing reference to Mr. Hepworth's health and the Christmas season, and a more than unconvincing suggestion that there were "probably not more than a dozen persons who would have troubled to preserve it"—this in 1886!

Mr. Wise, in short, evaded all the really awkward questions, made considerable play with several red herrings, and at bottom did very little but proclaim dogmatically the authenticity of the pamphlet.

Sabin's ironical pleasantries evoked no further reply at the time. Perhaps this is not surprising.

Mr. Wise, however, had the last word. In 1925, after all the controversy had been forgotten, he appended the following bland note to the description of his copy in the Ashley Catalogue (*loc. cit.*): "The First Edition. . . . *Some College Memories* originally appeared in *The New Amphion*, published in Edinburgh in November, 1886. It was immediately reprinted (with the Author's consent and approval) in pamphlet form, as described above, for Private Circulation, by W. H. Hepworth, Examiner in Art at South Kensington."

Conclusion.—The late date of this piece puts it outside any positive tests from its type or paper: but it is impossible to avoid the conclusion that the two last sentences of Constable's first letter describe it accurately. The fact that the Secretaries of the University Union Committee knew nothing of it makes it probable that its imprint is false, and its typographical affinities are in these circumstances distinctly unfortunate. It may have been printed in 1886, as Mr. Wise insisted, but it seems certain that this pirated reprint was aimed at the collector, and its similarity in bibliographical status, bad auction record and earliest ascertainable provenance, to the large number of proved forgeries, inclines us to place it in the group.

POSTSCRIPT

Stevenson's bibliography is rich in pamphlets, leaflets and privately printed pieces of various kinds; but beyond the three books discussed above there are only two others which seem to lack any authentication. Presentation or amply provenanced copies exist of all the rest and the Davos–Platz leaflets are fully pedigreed; but *Thomas Stevenson*, 1887, and *War in Samoa*, 1893, which require investigation because of their presence in company with the forgeries, do not appear to have any evidence to support them.

Thomas Stevenson (Prideaux–Livingston, p. 53), which we have had no opportunity of examining,[1] has no imprint, and from its description, the wrapper seems to be somewhat similar to that of *Geist's Grave*. It had appeared in *The Contemporary Review* for June, 1887, and was afterwards included in *Memories and Portraits* later in the same year. No copies are found in the copyright libraries, which is not perhaps remarkable, but its absence from the Isobel Strong sale is not in its favour. No presentation copies are recorded, and all the fourteen which have passed through the sale rooms were in original wrappers, uncut. Mr. Gorfin purchased the residue of Mr. Wise's stock about 1910, to the number of "six or eight" (exact details are unfortunately not available). Between 1899, the first auction record, and 1912, the price ran between £3 12*s*. and £5 15*s*.; but from 1922 to 1932, £20 to £25 was the rule. The Gosse copy, however, with an autograph letter, reached £80 in 1929.

[1] But see Stop Press, p. 379.

War in Samoa (Prideaux–Livingston, p. 85) has no imprint, and it also is described as having been reserved for private circulation. It had appeared in *The Pall Mall Gazette* of September 4, 1893. No copies appear in the copyright libraries, nor in the Isobel Strong sale. There are, however, three copies in the Wrenn Library. Mr. Wise had a stock of copies, and Mr. Gorfin purchased "ten or so" about 1910. It is probably a piracy.

Ticonderoga, 1887 (Prideaux–Livingston, p. 60), was present in Mr. Wise's stock, Mr. Gorfin purchasing three copies at 15*s*. on April 26, 1910. Investigation, however, proved it to be perfectly genuine. It was printed for copyright purposes, and although the author "never saw it,"[1] Mr. William Maxwell (of Messrs. R. & R. Clark) confirms it as an undoubted production of the firm, and indeed a typical example of Robert Clark's style in lay-out. It is not known to us who supervised or gave instructions for the printing. Stevenson himself was in London in December, 1886, and in Edinburgh in May, 1887, but his explicit denial of even seeing a copy makes it clear that he was not responsible. Yet the fact that the format of the book was changed at the last moment from foolscap 4to to post 4to is clear evidence of some official care. Since, however, one of the three surviving "trial" foolscap 4to copies is in the Ashley Library, while another was in Mr. Wise's possession until 1916,[2] there seems good reason to suppose that he was in touch with the production, and his possession of these copies of the regular edition is therefore quite natural.

[1] Letter to C. B. Foote, quoted in *Book Prices Current*, 1915, pp. 502, 503.

[2] See McCutcheon sale catalogue (April 20, 1925, American Arts, lot 609).

Algernon Charles Swinburne

SWINBURNE'S first bibliographer was Richard Herne Shepherd, who issued the first edition of his work in July, 1883; the fourth and revised edition appeared in 1887 [Shepherd]. Mr. T. J. Wise has produced three bibliographies of Swinburne. He contributed the first to *Literary Anecdotes of the Nineteenth Century*, Vol. II. pp. 291–374, 1896 [Wise A]. The second and most elaborate was privately printed in an edition of 125 copies in 1918 [Wise B]. The third, called *A Swinburne Library*, 1925, is a reprint of the relevant portions of Mr. Wise's catalogue of his own Ashley Library. He enjoyed peculiar advantages for the work; for more than twenty years he was an acquaintance of the poet, and when Swinburne died in 1909, his literary executor, Theodore Watts-Dunton, gave Mr. Wise the opportunity to acquire whatever he wanted, whether in print or manuscript, from the poet's library.

DEAD LOVE

Dead Love. / By / Algernon C. Swinburne. / London / John W. Parker / and Son, West Strand. / 1864.

Small 8vo, red wrappers printed in black, uncut. It is to be noted that in the only copy in mint state examined by us, which was a personal gift from Mr. Wise to its present owner, the wrappers had not even been pierced for sewing, although the rest of the pamphlet was sewn.

The imprint at the foot of the title-page is John W. Parker and Son, West Strand, and the printer's imprint on the reverse of the leaf is " London : / Savill and Edwards, Printers, Chandos Street, / Covent Garden." Set up in a heavily leaded Small Pica old style. Printed on cream wove paper.

There is a facsimile of this pamphlet, the production of which, according to Mr. Wise, " can hardly have been other than fraudulent " (Wise B, I. 65). Mr. Wise gives a number of tests for distinguishing the facsimile : one which he does not mention is that the imprint in the original is set in 11 point, while in the facsimile it is in 10 point. It should also be noted that the reproduction of the title-page of the facsimile which he gives in his Bibliography is not quite accurate in omitting the full-point after " Love." The facsimile was manufactured before 1904.

This prose story was originally printed in *Once a Week* for October, 1862, Vol. VII. pp. 432–4, to accompany a drawing by M. J. Lawless. It was not subsequently included in any of the author's books issued in his lifetime.

Not in Shepherd (1887), although the magazine appearance is noted on p. 17. Slater (1894), p. 291 : " This is a very scarce piece." Wise A (1896), II. 300. Wise B (1918), I. 62–73.

The copy in the British Museum (C.59.c.25) was presented by Mr. T. J. Wise, 12 April, 1890. No copies in the Bodleian Library or the Cambridge University Library.

Ashley, VI, 51–54, three copies, one of which has an undated inscription from William Morris to Dr. Westland Marston.[1] Wrenn, IV. 247.

This pamphlet seems to have occurred for sale at auction seventeen times, in every case either in original state or a modern binding. Its first appearance was as lot 299 at Sotheby's on 17 July, 1907, when it was bought for £3 15*s.* There was a copy in the Lapham sale (New York, Dec. 1908, lot 1268) which sold for $50. The next two copies in 1912 and 1914 fetched £9 15*s.* each. After that its price in the English auction rooms has sunk until Mr. Gorfin bought in a copy in one of his anonymous sales at thirty shillings. In America the Jerome Kern copy fetched sixty dollars in January, 1929; copies at the American Art Galleries in February and April of the same year fetched five dollars and twenty dollars respectively, and the highest price of all, $120, was given for it in the same rooms on 11 March, 1930. No early inscriptions are recorded.

Mr. Gorfin bought " about 20 " copies from Mr. Wise.

The type of this pamphlet (D in our schedule) is the same as that used for one other forgery and two suspects.

The paper is composed mainly of esparto, and there are minute and very suspicious traces of chemical wood; but these are hardly conclusive in themselves.

The imprint, however, is remarkable. The firm of John W. Parker and Son changed its style to that of Parker, Son and Bourn. After considerable search we can find no books with the earlier imprint dated later than 1860; and no examples of the later imprint before 1861. The earlier imprint is used up to December, 1860, on *Fraser's Magazine*, and from January, 1861, onwards the later imprint takes its place: this is also the case with the advertisements in *The Publishers' Circular*; so that there can be no doubt that the style of the firm was changed from

[1] See above, p. 115.

"John W. Parker and Son" to "Parker, Son and Bourn" on January 1, 1861. But the firm itself did not survive the change for long. By the end of April, 1863, Parker had already made arrangements for liquidation.[1] "A change," stated *The Publishers' Circular* of October 15, 1863 (p. 508), "almost unparalleled in the history of publishing houses, which has for some time been rumoured, is at length officially announced. We allude to the sudden retirement of the firm of Parker, Son and Bourn, and the transfer of the whole of their copyrights to Messrs. Longman & Co." The November issue of *Fraser's Magazine* is the first to bear Longman's imprint; but the transfer of stock as well as of copyrights must have taken place about this month, as some of them, notably the works of Charles Kingsley and Charlotte Yonge, had been re-transferred to Macmillan's before the end of 1863. It is clear, therefore, that the imprint of this pamphlet is not only one which had been abandoned four years earlier, but also that of a firm which had become wholly extinct the year before.

Conclusion.—The paper of the original pamphlet is suspicious, and the imprint shows clearly that it must be a forgery. It is evidence of the influence that these forgeries have had upon the book market that one of them should itself have been copied: and it is ironical that it should be of this "rare book" and its facsimile that Mr. Wise wrote the remark which we have quoted at the beginning of our book: "The whole thing proves once more that, easy as it appears to be to fabricate reprints of rare books, it is in actual practice absolutely impossible to do so in such a manner that detection cannot follow the result" (Wise B, I. 73).

[1] A letter of his to this effect is printed in Edward Bell's *George Bell, Publisher*, 1924, pp. 72–3.

LAUS VENERIS

Laus Veneris. / By / Algernon Charles Swinburne. / London: / Edward Moxon & Co., Dover Street. / 1866.

8vo, plain wrappers of various colours, uncut.

On the reverse of the title-page is: "London: / Bradbury, Evans, and Co., Printers, Whitefriars." Set in a Small Pica modern style. Printed on a cream wove paper.

Printed in *Poems and Ballads*, 1866, pp. 11–30.

Not in Shepherd (1887). Slater (1894), 289–290. Wise A (1896), II. 304–5. Wise B (1919), I. 96–104.

There is a copy in the British Museum (C.57.d.27), presented 12 April, 1890, by Mr. T. J. Wise. No copies in the Bodleian Library or Cambridge University Library. Ashley, VI. 57–58. Wrenn, IV. 249.

This pamphlet first appeared in the auction room at Sotheby's as lot 1248 on 22 Feb., 1897, when it fetched £23 10*s*. Its next highest price was $95 in the Kern sale in 1929, and its lowest six dollars at the American Art Galleries, New York, on 1 April, 1931. In four of the thirty-one recorded sales the condition of the pamphlet is not stated; seven copies were in modern binding, and the remaining twenty in original condition. No inscriptions are recorded.

Mr. Gorfin purchased "about 15" copies from Mr. Wise.

The paper, which is pure esparto, is not unlikely in a book of this date.

The Small Pica modern style (B in our schedule) in which the pamphlet is printed is the identical fount used for six proved forgeries and four other suspects. We have not been able to find it in any books which Bradbury, Evans and Co. printed about this time.

The origin of this pamphlet is extremely puzzling; and we therefore transcribe from Sir Edmund Gosse's *Life of Swinburne*, 1917, pp. 141–2, the fullest account that has been given:

"In January, 1866, it was decided to make a beginning by issuing, as a test, a small privately printed edition of what was, oddly enough, looked upon by the friends as the most dangerous of the pieces, namely *Laus Veneris*. Accordingly, Moxon issued a very few copies of this poem as a little book by itself. Of the genesis of this interesting pamphlet, Swinburne gave an account in later years. 'It was,' he wrote, 'more an experiment to ascertain the public taste—and forbearance!—than anything else. Moxon, I well remember, was terribly nervous in those days.'" [This is cited without any reference from Mr. Wise's note in *Literary Anecdotes*, 1896, Vol. II. p. 304, where, however, it is introduced by the phrase "Swinburne said."] "The reference is to the firm, since Moxon himself was dead, but his business was continued by a certain J. Bertram Payne, who, no doubt, represented 'Moxon' to the poet's consciousness.

"In spite, however, of the imprint on *Laus Veneris*, there certainly had been a proposal that the ancient firm of Murray should publish the complete collection and Lord Houghton, rather prematurely, submitted the manuscript to Albemarle Street. Swinburne was not quite pleased; 'I do not,' he wrote to Joseph Knight, 'overmuch like my poems sent as it were for approval like those of a novice.' This anxiety was well grounded, for Mr. Murray at once refused them (March 4), and in terms which stung the poet to fury. He said he would permit no more interference, and 'Moxon' finally deciding to take it, the thick volume now entitled *Poems and Ballads* was in the hands of the printers by March, 1866. On the 19th of April Swinburne was correcting proofs of this and of a prose book on Blake of which he had sent part to press before the close of 1865." Sir Edmund Gosse then tells us of the careful preparations made by Lord Houghton to prepare the public for the appearance of the volume. The narrative then proceeds (p. 149): "The labour of preparing for the reception of *Poems and Ballads* was complete. The banquet was ready, the company assembled, but the principal guest failed to arrive. The volume had been announced to appear early in May; by the middle of July it had still not made its appearance. All the reasons for this delay are not quite defined, but it seems that an early copy of the bound volume being sent to the author in May, he immediately detected in it between twenty and thirty serious misprints, which had escaped him in the revise. How it had been possible for Swinburne to overlook so large a number of faults in his proofs it is not easy to conjecture, but the fact is certain. He returned the copy to Moxon forthwith, insisting that the errors might all be rectified as completely as possible. This involved a great deal of expense and delay. Mr. T. J. Wise, who discovered this fact, and who has carefully compared the original corrections in the poet's handwriting with the final text, tells me that 'to effect this revision some of the sheets had to be reprinted *in toto*; in certain cases portions only of the sheets were reprinted; in other instances, where punctuation only was involved, the missing stops were inserted by hand.' At any rate, it was an exasperating business, which delayed the final appearance of the book until late in the summer."

It is unfortunately not now possible to determine how much of this whole account is due to oral tradition, how much to Mr. Wise's ingenious reconstruction, and how much to Sir Edmund's own delicate intuition. But two dates can be definitely established from independent sources: (*a*) That *Poems and Ballads* in its corrected form was ready by July 24, 1866, because the British Museum received its copy on that date. (*b*) That *Laus Veneris* cannot have been printed until after May 7, 1866, because on that date its printers, Bradbury and Evans, changed the style of the firm to "Bradbury, Evans, & Co." and the pamphlet bears the imprint in its later form. (Information kindly supplied by their successors, The Whitefriars Press Ltd.)

The last fact seems to destroy the whole *raison d'être* of the separate form of *Laus Veneris* as Mr. Wise reports Swinburne to have explained it. Indeed from Gosse's account (p. 138) it would appear that the consultations about the propriety of publishing the poem took place early in December, 1865; but the printed date 1866 on the pamphlet did not allow him to postulate a date of production earlier than January of that year. But, if *Laus Veneris* was produced as late as May, 1866, what relation does it bear to *Poems and Ballads*? It is not printed from the same setting of type, as Mr. Wise implies (Wise B, I. 99); and it is hardly conceivable that the same printers should have reset this single poem in separate form when the completion of the whole collection was already overdue.

Now the delay from May to July in the appearance of *Poems and Ballads* is explained by Swinburne's detection of numerous misprints in an advance copy of the book. This identical copy is now in the Turnbull Library at Wellington, New Zealand, and it contains three "misprints" in the course of this poem: "eust" for "eut" p. 12, line 12; "péché" for "pesché" p. 12, line 16; and "word's" for "words" p. 17, line 5 from foot. It will be noticed that the first two, which occur in Swinburne's fictitious quotation in old French at the beginning of the poem, would more properly be described as alterations than as misprints. If *Laus Veneris* had been set up early in May, or at any time before Swinburne's final correction of the advance copy, it would surely have followed the uncorrected text; but actually it corresponds with the text in its finally revised form as published late in July.

The fact that both texts were printed by the same firm makes it extremely probable that one was set up from the other; but the presence of the "misprints" shows that *Poems and Ballads* was not set up from *Laus Veneris*, and the only explanation left is that the separate pamphlet was set up from the second and corrected form of the whole collection later than July, 1866.

If this is so, Swinburne's carelessness in omitting to correct the misprints in proof, which puzzled Sir Edmund Gosse, can now be simply explained. Mr. Wise has inserted in his copy of *Laus Veneris* this letter to J. B. Payne:

"Dear Sir,

"I send the proof, which of course was here, and turned up at once. I hope you will get it in time to avoid any inconvenience.

"Yours truly,

"A. C. Swinburne.

"P.S.—I have only glanced at the proof. If there are any errors, please correct them."

In the first place it is to be noticed that this letter is not dated nor does it mention *Laus Veneris* by name, and so it might refer to any of the other books undertaken for Swinburne by E. Moxon & Co. These were *Atalanta in Calydon*, *Chastelard*, *Poems and Ballads*, and *William Blake*. If it referred to *Poems and Ballads*, it would at least explain the presence in that volume of so many misprints on the eve of publication.

Against this explanation must be set the fact that Mr. Wise published his version of what Swinburne said thirteen years before he died, and Swinburne is not known to have contradicted it. But as he would not expose a wrong attribution in Herne Shepherd's Bibliography, how much greater must have been his scruples against publicly contradicting an acquaintance from whom he had accepted such generous gifts as Brontë manuscripts, and his own *Cleopatra* costing seven guineas. (*Correspondence*, edd. Gosse and Wise, 1918, II. 191, 188, 193, 250.)

Conclusion.—All this is not conclusive: but it would seem that Mr. Wise must have misunderstood, and consequently misreported, what Swinburne actually said. In any case there can be no doubt that *Laus Veneris* was printed after 7 May, 1866; and almost certainly set up from *Poems and Ballads*. It has, therefore, no status as a first edition; and its typography and provenance associate it with the other forgeries.

CLEOPATRA

Cleopatra [*in black letter*] / by / Algernon Charles Swinburne. / [*rule*] / London : / John Camden Hotten, Piccadilly. / 1866.

Small square 8vo. The wrappers are plain, and Mr. Wise distinguishes two varieties, one of a thick, pale buff paper, and the other of a thin pale brown. Edges uncut.

The printer's imprint at the foot of the last page is "Printed by J. Andrews, Clements Lane, E.C." Set up in Long Primer old style. Printed on a cream wove paper.

This poem was first printed in *The Cornhill Magazine*, September 1866, Vol. XIV. pp. 331–3, to accompany a drawing by Frederick Sandys. It was not reprinted during Swinburne's lifetime.

Not in Shepherd (1887), though he notices the magazine publication on p. 10. Slater (1894), 292 : "This is one of the scarcest of Swinburne's publications." Wise A (1896), II. 314–316. Wise B (1918), I. 139–144.

The British Museum copy (C.59.b.15) was purchased of Otto P. Rubeck of 315 Brixton Road, S.W. on May 13, 1890, for five guineas (see above, p. 145). No copies in the Bodleian Library or the Cambridge University Library. Ashley, VI. 62, 63 (two copies, one with a note by Swinburne on the fly-leaf). Wrenn, IV. 248–9 (two copies and the proof sheets).

This pamphlet has appeared in the auction room twenty-seven times. On three occasions its condition was not specified ; in all the other sales it was either in original state or separately bound in a modern binding. The first copy to appear was lot 1561 at Sotheby's on 4 December, 1891, and was bought for £9. Thereafter its price has fluctuated between £2 and £7, but a copy was sold for only 14*s*. in 1919. A presentation copy *from* T. J. Wise *to* Swinburne fetched £5 at his sale on June 19, 1916, and was resold in the Gosse sale on

February 25, 1929, for £8. Another association copy with a letter from T. J. Wise fetched £12 10s. as lot 329 at Sotheby's on 3 June, 1929; this is the highest price recorded.

Mr. Gorfin bought "about 6" copies from Mr. Wise.

The statements about this pamphlet are so conflicting and the problems which they raise so numerous that it will be necessary to quote them at length before trying to provide any solution.

A. C. Swinburne to T. J. Wise, 27 April, 1888.[1]

"DEAR MR. WISE,

"I am almost equally distressed and gratified by the extravagance of your kindness in sending me the little *Cleopatra*. I do not like to deprive you of what you thought worth—as you mentioned in your previous letter—a somewhat considerable price; considering that the most ardent bibliomaniac, if not a most outrageous egoist, draws the line at his own works. On the other hand, I cannot but value very highly such an evidence of good will, and such an example of generosity.

"I am quite certain, quite positive, that I never set eyes on the booklet before, nor heard of its existence."

On May 2 of the same year, Swinburne again wrote to T. J. Wise. ". . . About modern rarities—unless the rare impression contains something unprocurable—I am so indifferent that it would be a sin and a shame for me to deprive you of your *Cleopatra*. Seven guineas! Heaven and Earth! It would have been dear at as many shillings and not cheap at as many pence. . . . I need hardly say that I know nothing,

[1] *The Letters of Algernon Charles Swinburne*, edd. E. Gosse and T. J. Wise (1918) II. 188–9.

and never heard of it till now, or any such volume as you mention published or printed by Hotten under my name" (*ibid.*, pp. 193–4).

In his *Bibliography of Swinburne* (1918, I. 143) Mr. Wise writes:—" In both instances the reading of the pamphlet [' Shred ' for ' Shed ' in stanza II, line 5; and ' hand ' for ' heart ' in stanza IX, line 1] is obviously superior to that of the magazine, and disposes of Swinburne's suggestion, made in a letter addressed to myself, that Hotten had produced the former [*i.e.* the pamphlet] without the authority of the author. Clearly Swinburne did authorise the issue of the pamphlet, and revised the text of the poem for that purpose. This statement is supported by the fact that among the papers preserved at The Pines, and acquired by me from Watts-Dunton, was a set of proof-sheets of *Cleopatra*. These were pierced through the centre of the leaves, having apparently been thrust upon the point of an old-fashioned file. But Swinburne's memory was not always to be relied upon where the history of his own writings was concerned; witness, for example, his emphatic repudiation of the authorship of *Dolorida*."

In the *Catalogue of the Wrenn Library* (IV. 248) Mr. Wise has something further to say, referring to " The original proof-sheets of the first edition," which are preserved in the library. " There are many differences to be observed between this proof and a copy of the completed pamphlet. For example, the types (which were evidently rejected by the author) employed for the half-title and title are larger and bolder than those finally adopted. The volume was purchased by Mr. Wrenn from the late Dr. Underwood, who stated that these proof-sheets, and also the proof-sheets of *The Jubilee*, by which they were accompanied, were formerly in the possession of, and were acquired by him from, Richard Herne Shepherd, who informed him that those of *Cleopatra* had been obtained by him from the publisher, John Camden Hotten. Their pedigree is therefore complete."

These various statements show that there are at least four questions to be answered: (i) Did Swinburne have anything to do with the production of the pamphlet? (ii) Did Hotten? (iii) Is it a forgery of later date? (iv) Did Shepherd forge it?

(i) Against Swinburne's explicit and twice repeated denial of any knowledge of this pamphlet, Mr. Wise advances three points: (*a*) that the difference in text between the two versions postulates the author's own revision; (*b*) that the discovery of a set of proofs at The Pines after Swinburne's death proves that he originally published the pamphlet; (*c*) that his denial is of no value because he denied the authorship of *Dolorida*.

(*a*) Of the two alterations, "shred" for "shed" may be considered an improvement, but "hand" for "heart" is palpably not. The second of these corrections was already incorporated in the text of the Wrenn Library proofs; but the first is corrected in the margin, and this, at any rate, was not done by Swinburne himself. In any case it is altogether too extravagant to claim that these two alterations are so "obviously superior" that they must be due to Swinburne himself and no one else.

(*b*) The discovery of a set of the proofs at The Pines is odd; but its implications are hardly enough to set against Swinburne's own statement: and what has happened to these proofs now? Mr. Wise says that he bought them from Watts-Dunton, but they are not to be found in *The Ashley Library Catalogue* or *A Swinburne Library*; and one would think that Mr. Wise would have found a particular satisfaction in preserving them, no less for their sentimental than for their evidential value.

(*c*) Mr. Wise thinks that Swinburne's denial of the authorship of *Dolorida* was due to lack of memory (cf. also *Bibliography*, Vol. I. p. 336); but, whether he wrote it or not,[1] there were obvious reasons for denying it. Swinburne was at any rate a gentleman; Ada Isaacs Menken had been his mistress; and, whatever he might write in her album, he would hardly acknowledge in public verses which were tantamount to an admission of that fact. Altogether Mr. Wise's grounds for putting aside Swinburne's denial of any knowledge of *Cleopatra* seem hardly sufficient. Swinburne did not deny writing the poem, so why should he deny publishing it?

(ii) The printer's imprint at the end of the pamphlet is "J. Andrews, Clements Lane, E.C." No such name, either as a printer or as dwelling in Clements Lane, is to be found in *Kelly's Post Office Directory* for the years 1865, 1866, or 1867; and this suggests that the imprint is false. If Hotten had it printed in 1866 without Swinburne's consent and with a false imprint, why did he put his own name on it? Presumably because he thought there was a market for it. But the sale of Swinburne's books at this date was by no means brisk; and copies of the first editions of all the books which he published (with the exception

[1] Mr. Wise produces no conclusive evidence to show that Swinburne wrote *Dolorida*. For Swinburne's own explanation of the circumstances under which he copied it into Ada Isaacs Menken's album see his letter to MacGeorge of January 10, 1884 (printed in the MacGeorge sale catalogue, Sotheby, July 1, 1924, lot 1288).

of *Siena*, see below, p. 287) were taken over by Chatto & Windus in 1873.[1] Why were there no copies of *Cleopatra*?

(iii) But what evidence is there that it was published in 1866 at all? If the printer's imprint is false, why not the date as well? In actual fact the first indisputable evidence that we have of the pamphlet's existence is Swinburne's letter to Mr. Wise of April 27, 1888. The simplest explanation of the false imprint and Swinburne's ignorance is that the whole pamphlet is a forgery.

(iv) But if it is a forgery, the existence of proof-sheets takes on a fresh importance. Mr. Wise says that Shepherd bought them from Hotten. If he did, it must have been before Hotten's death in 1873. If Shepherd had the proof-sheets by that date, why did he not include the book in his bibliographies issued in 1883 and 1887? If he had forged it himself, he would have been still more likely to have included the pamphlet in his bibliographies, because there could be no better way both of advertising and authenticating his wares. But the fact remains that he did not; and the only evidence against him is Mr. Wise's statement about the provenance of the Wrenn set of proofs.

The more the origins of this pamphlet are probed, the more disquieting become the questions which arise. The provenance of the proof-sheets as given by Mr. Wise can hardly be maintained in view of its total omission by Shepherd; but it transpires from a letter which we have received from the Librarian of the Wrenn Library that Mr. Wise himself conducted the negotiations which led to Wrenn's acquisition of the proof-sheets.

[1] See their full-page advertisement in *The Bookseller*, 2 May, 1874, p. 405.

Mr. Wise seems to have acquired three copies of the pamphlet before 1890, his own copy, the copy which he gave to Swinburne, and the copy which Mr. Rubeck sold to the British Museum. He had "about six" copies in 1909; and about the same date he sold the proof-sheets as well. All these facts rest upon independent evidence.

Mr. Wise thinks that the pamphlet is genuine because of the difference of the two readings and his own discovery of a set of proofs at The Pines; and he sets aside Swinburne's denials on the ground that his evidence is unreliable. None of these arguments are convincing evidence of the authenticity of the pamphlet; and the fact that Mr. Wise, who edited Swinburne's Letters in 1918, could write in 1920 a note in the Wrenn Library Catalogue suggesting that the types of the earlier title-page were *evidently* rejected *by the author*, shows that he cannot have considered the problem with proper care, and that his conclusions should not be taken as trustworthy.

The paper is composed of esparto and rag, which would be a normal content for 1866.

The type is the one we have scheduled as C. It is identical with that used for three proved forgeries and six other suspects in the group.

Conclusion.—The pamphlet remained unknown for more than twenty years after its supposed date of publication: now more than thirty copies are recorded. Swinburne twice emphatically denied any knowledge of it; and its imprint is apparently false. Nevertheless, it is, in theory, possible that it is not a forgery.

DOLORES

Dolores. / By / Algernon Charles Swinburne. / London: / John Camden Hotten, Piccadilly. / 1867.

Small 8vo, issued, according to Mr. Wise, " in plain paper wrappers, of various colours, without lettering or ornament." Edges uncut.

There is no printer's imprint. Set up in Clay's Long Primer No. 3. Printed on a cream wove paper.

This poem had been previously published in *Poems and Ballads*, 1866, pp. 178–195.

Not in Shepherd (1887); Wise A (1896), II. 316–317; Wise B (1918), I. 158–162.

The British Museum copy (C.57.e.57) was presented by Mr. T. J. Wise on 14 June, 1919. No copies in the Bodleian Library or the Cambridge University Library. Ashley VI. 71. Wrenn IV. 250 (two copies).

We have traced the appearance of this pamphlet in the auction room sixteen times. On the first occasion as lot 1267 at Sotheby's on 27 June, 1898, it fetched £2 12*s.*; its next appearance was in the Crampton sale at Sotheby's on May 12, 1904 (lot 409), when it reached £7 5*s.* Thereafter the price has varied between £4 and £6 with one exception in 1919 when a copy was sold for ten shillings. The sale catalogue gives no description of one copy which was sold in 1909, and an unbound and imperfect copy was sold in one lot with a copy of *Cleopatra* at Hodgson's on 12 January, 1921; but with these exceptions all the copies were either unbound and uncut or in a modern binding.

Mr. Wise writes (*Bibliography*, I. 161): " Some years ago a small ' remainder ' of *Dolores* came to light. The copies of which this ' remainder ' consisted were in the original unfolded sheets, and were, of course, without wrappers."

Mr. Gorfin bought " about 20 " copies from Mr. Wise.

According to Mr. Wise (*loc. cit.*), "Swinburne himself, upon being appealed to for information upon the subject, declared that he had no recollection of the circumstances in which it was produced."

The paper is composed of esparto and straw, with minute traces of chemical wood. The chemical wood is decidedly suspicious for 1867.

The type is Clay's Long Primer No. 3 with the distinguishing characteristics which were not manufactured before 1880. Fifteen other forgeries are printed in this type. The capitals used for "Dolores" on the title-page are identical with those in the fifth line of the title-page of *The Nature and Authority of Miracle* by Ruskin, and with those used for the first line of the first title-page of the edition of *Rosalind and Helen* printed by Clay for the Shelley Society in 1888.

Conclusion.—This pamphlet is clearly a forgery; but the object of forging it when it does not even pretend to be a first edition is difficult to understand. Nevertheless, it has always commanded a substantial price in the auction room.

SIENA

Siena. / By / Algernon Charles Swinburne. / London: / John Camden Hotten, Piccadilly / 1868. / (All Rights Reserved.)

Small 8vo, edges trimmed, issued in plain orange wrappers.

There is no printer's imprint. Set up in Clay's Long Primer No. 3. Printed on a cream wove paper.

This poem was first published in *Lippincott's Magazine* (New York), June 1868, pp. 622–629. To secure the copyright in England an edition of six copies was printed for Hotten (Wise B. *loc. cit.*) and these are now, we believe, all accounted for. The British Museum copy was received on May 27, 1868. The present pamphlet is an attempted facsimile of this copyright edition; there is a full point after "Piccadilly" on the title-page of the original, which is absent in the facsimile.

Shepherd (1887) mentions the copyright edition only. A single proof page from a projected edition of the Ashley Library Catalogue inserted in the British Museum copy of the facsimile, and with the Museum stamp "9 Dec. 1893" on the reverse, calls it the first published edition, and says: "Mr. Swinburne states that Hotten sold copies readily at five or ten shillings apiece."

Slater (1894), p. 294: "A pirated reprint is occasionally met with and, having been very carefully executed, it is almost impossible to detect it from the original. . . . There is no doubt that many of these forged copies are on the market."

Mr. Wise, reviewing Slater's book in *The Bookman*, May 1894, p. 50: "The 'masterly pirated reprint' of 'Siena' described on p. 294 is a creation of the author's fancy, these 'forged copies' being none other than examples of the first published edition of the pamphlet, Hotten, 1868."

Wise A (1896), II. 321–322. "Second—or spurious—edition." "Hotten is known to have sold copies readily at five or ten shillings apiece." Wise B (1918), I. 174–8.

The British Museum copy (C.59.g.5.) was presented by Mr. Wise on 9 December 1893. No copies in the Bodleian or Cambridge University Libraries. Ashley VI. 75, 76. Wrenn IV. 125.

It is difficult to separate these two very similar editions in the records of the auction room. Altogether there appear to have been twenty-eight sales of both editions; and six of these were probably the genuine copyright edition. (i) Alfred Crampon sale, Sotheby's 3 June, 1896, lot 417. (ii) Sotheby's, 20 April, 1899, lot 990. (iii) Sotheby's, 29 June, 1916, lot 26 was Andrew Chatto's copy, and was sold together with the original manuscript. He had apparently acquired both when taking over Hotten's business; the lot fetched £134. (iv) Anderson Galleries, New York, March, 1920, lot 829 in the Buxton Forman sale was a presentation copy to F. G. Waugh; it realised $107.50. (v) Sotheby's, 5 April, 1921, lot 236; this copy without wrappers was bound with a number of other pamphlets in limp roan, and had on the title-page "W. M. Rossetti from the Author, 1868," in the recipient's handwriting. (vi) Hodgson's, 20 June 1929, lot 330.

The first of the remaining twenty-two copies was lot 508 at Sotheby's on 11 December, 1889, which fetched three guineas; another copy fetched £6 5*s*. in 1891; thereafter its price has varied between £1 and £5, but most copies have been sold at between £1 and £2.

Mr. Gorfin bought thirteen copies from Mr. Wise on 11 April, 1910, for £5.

The pamphlet is printed in Clay's Long Primer No. 3, of which the distinguishing letters were not manufactured until after 1880. It is therefore clear that Hotten can have had nothing to do with it, as he died on 15 June, 1873. The imprint and the date are both false.

It is interesting to contrast Mr. Wise's reaction to the discovery of this forgery with his indignation at the attempt to facsimile *Dead Love* (see p. 269). In December, 1893, he presented a copy to the British Museum, with a signed note distinguishing it from the original edition. Inserted in that copy was a proof page of a projected edition of the Ashley

Catalogue, in which Mr. Wise stated that it was the first published edition, and that Swinburne himself had stated that Hotten had sold the booklets readily at five or ten shillings apiece. Three months later, when Slater's book came out, Mr. Wise in a review in *The Bookman* poured scorn on Slater's statement that it was a "masterly pirated reprint," which he described as "a creation of thc author's fancy." In 1896 Mr. Wise described it as "second—or spurious—edition," and the statement attributed to Swinburne in 1893 becomes "Hotten is known to have sold . . ." This is the definitive form of the story, and is repeated in subsequent works. In 1910 Mr. Wise had as many as thirteen copies to sell.

Conclusion.—There can be no doubt that this forgery is a deliberate attempt to produce a facsimile of the genuine copyright edition.

POSTSCRIPT

The discovery that these five pamphlets were probably forgeries impelled an examination of Swinburne's other books; and it is necessary to pass them in brief review in order that any further suspicion may be kept within proper limits.

There is not the slightest reason to impugn any of the cloth-bound books or any of the posthumous pamphlets printed for Mr. Wise. Of the various pamphlets sponsored by Shepherd (*A Word for the Navy*, 1887; *The Question*, 1887; *The Jubilee*, 1887; *Gathered Songs*, 1887), by Mr. Wise (*Note on Epipsychidion*, 1886; *Grace Darling*, 1893; *The Ballad of Bulgarie*, 1893; *Robert Burns*, 1896), and by others (*The Bride's Tragedy*, 1889; *The Ballad of Dead Men's Bay*, 1889; *The Brothers*, 1889; *A Sequence of Sonnets on the Death of Robert Browning*, 1891; *Music: An Ode*, 1892), some may at the worst have been piracies, but there is no ground whatever for supposing them to be forgeries.

Five pamphlets, *Notes on Poems and Reviews*, 1866 (first issue); *Notes on the Royal Academy Exhibition*, 1868; *Ode on the Proclamation of the French Republic*, 1870; *Under the Microscope*, 1872; and *Note of an English Republican on the Muscovite Crusade*, 1876, are attested by contemporary reception dates in the British Museum[1] copies, and *Euthanatos*, 1881, by an inscription in March of that year by Frederick Locker-Lampson in his copy.

[1] None of these are printed in any of our scheduled types.

The three books which exist only in the form of proof-sheets (Act I of *Bothwell*, 1871; *Lesbia Brandon*, 1877; and *Russia: An Ode*, 1890), as well as the two broadsides (*An Appeal to England*, 1867; and *The Commonweal*, 1886) present an appearance so totally different from any of the forgeries that we have had under examination, that even if two of these were not fully authenticated, there would be no reason to suspect them. The second issue of *Notes on Poems and Reviews*, 1866, while not so completely different, does not really resemble any of the proved forgeries, and we have found no traces of its survival in any large quantity. The British Museum copy was not acquired until 1890.

Four items remain: *An Appeal to England*, 1867 (the octavo pamphlet), *The Devil's Due*, 1875, and two undated leaflets, *Dolorida* and *Unpublished Verses*, assigned by Mr. Wise to 1883 and 1888. *Dolorida* is listed in the fourth (1887) edition of Herne Shepherd's Bibliography and *Unpublished Verses* was catalogued for sale by Mr. W. T. Spencer in 1890 at 1*s*. Mr. Wise attributes both these piracies to Herne Shepherd; furthermore, neither of them is dated, and both are printed on a laid paper. These two points differentiate their technique from that of the proved forgeries, and there does not seem to be any serious reason to question the account of their respective origins given by Mr. Wise (*Bibliography*, I. 133–4 and 335–6).

There is no independent record of the existence of the pamphlet *The Devil's Due*, 1875, before 1897, when Mr. Wise acquired a copy from Watts-Dunton, and he secured " some fifteen more " three years later (*op. cit.*, p. 250). Twelve copies have been sold at auction between 1907 and 1932, and we can trace another four copies in existence. The type and paper tests yield entirely negative results, so that, although the absence of an early pedigree is unsatisfactory, it is hardly sufficient to justify suspicion.

The pamphlet issue of *An Appeal to England against the Condemned Fenians*, 1867, is a more serious matter. Paper and type tests are negative, but there seems to be nothing to authenticate it except Swinburne's autograph on Mr. Wise's copy. The British Museum copy was presented by Mr. Wise on 12 April, 1890, and the catalogue states that it was printed for distribution gratis by the Manchester Committee for the Release of the Condemned Fenians. But *The Irishman* and *The Flag of Ireland*, both Dublin papers, which devoted much attention to the doings of this committee, make no mention of the pamphlet. It differs notably from Le Fanu's *Shamus O'Brien*, which was printed in Manchester at this time for a similar purpose; and indeed the old style type, the generous spacing and the careful presswork all suggest the requirements of a bibliophile market rather than the needs or resources of popular propaganda. It is printed in a Clay fount (C) used for three forgeries and six other suspects. The earliest record of its existence is Mr. Wise's gift to the British Museum in 1890; and the discovery of the real first edition, which is a broadside, was not made by Mr. Wise until after 1897. Mr. Wise sold two dozen copies of this pamphlet at five shillings each to Mr. Gorfin on 12 April, 1910: it has come up for sale in the auction room sixteen times since 1897. Although we cannot prove this pamphlet to be a forgery, its authenticity seems open to very serious doubt.

Alfred, Lord Tennyson

THE principal authorities for the bibliography of Tennyson, as cited below, are as follows. (i) *A Bibliography . . . of the published and privately printed writings . . .* by the Author of *Tennysoniana* [= Richard Herne Shepherd] London, 1896 [Shepherd]. (ii) An article entitled *The Building of the Idylls*, by Mr. Wise, in Vol. II of *Literary Anecdotes of the Nineteenth Century*, London, 1896, pp. 219–272 [Literary Anecdotes]. (iii) *Bibliography of the First Editions in Book form*, etc., New York, 1901. The preface is signed L. S. L. (= Luther S. Livingston). This is a very full and scholarly description[1] of a set collected by Messrs. Dodd, Mead (and afterwards purchased by J. P. Morgan) with notes of the few missing items [Livingston]. (iv) *A Bibliography of the Writings*, etc., London, 2 vols., 1908. The preface is signed T. J. W. (= Thomas J. Wise). This is the only comprehensive bibliography [Wise]. Reference is also made to Hallam Tennyson's *Memoir*, 2 vols., London, 1897 [Memoir].

[1] For the relation of this to Mr. Wise's *Bibliography*, see above, p. 129.

MORTE D'ARTHUR, etc.

Morte D'Arthur; / Dora; / and other Idyls. / By / Alfred Tennyson. / London: / Edward Moxon, Dover Street. / MDCCCXLII.

Small 8vo, uncut; the only copies recorded in original state were folded, without wrappers; "stitched," according to Mr. Wise.

Imprint on verso of title—"London: / Bradbury and Evans, Printers, Whitefriars." This is repeated on the verso of the last leaf. Printed on a cream wove paper in Clay's Long Primer No. 3.

Published in the *Poems* of 1842 (2 vols., Moxon).

Unknown to Slater (1894). *Literary Anecdotes* (1896), II. 222–224: "One of the rarest of what we may call the Tennysonian essays or trial books." Unknown to Shepherd (1896), who, however, remarks *à propos* of the *Poems*, 1842 (p. 16): "It seems probable that before the actual publication of these two long-awaited and eagerly expected volumes, early copies of the proof-sheets were handed about among the author's literary friends with the view of eliciting their suggestions." He then quotes two stanzas transcribed by Mrs. B. W. Procter for Samuel Rogers in a letter dated 1842, as from *Locksley Hall*. These do not appear in the published version of 1842, but they were included in *Locksley Hall Sixty Years After*, as published in 1886. "From whence," he continues, "could these two stanzas be derived if not from an early set of proofs or small privately printed issue, communicated to the Procters before publication?" Hallam Tennyson, *Memoir* (1897), I. 189: "In 1842 he had eight of the blank verse poems printed for his private use, because he always liked to see his poems in print some months and sometimes years before publication." Wise (1908), I. 76: "This extremely valuable little volume."

Unless, as is unlikely, Hallam Tennyson was reconstructing events from the existence of copies of the present volume, it seems clear from his statement that proof copies of a selection of the *Poems* of 1842 were printed for Tennyson's own use; and Shepherd's deduction of the existence of such a thing—which conforms perfectly to the author's known practice—seems to rest on very satisfactory evidence. He had copied the two stanzas direct from Mrs. Procter's original letter. This independent confirmation is impressive; but its value in our present quest for authentication is annihilated by one unfortunate fact: namely, that *Locksley Hall* is not one of the pieces included in the volume we are considering. Hallam Tennyson says the proof selection contained eight poems: the present volume contains eight poems. But if we accept Shepherd's evidence, and there seems no reason to doubt it, the proof volume sent by Tennyson to the Procters [1] contained a different selection. No copy of this seems to be recorded: but this is not remarkable, when we consider that whenever a batch of Tennyson proof volumes turns up—as in the Knowles sale in 1928—the majority usually are unrecorded. If the genuine original proof selection of 1842 contained *Locksley Hall* and the present book does not, we are reduced either to postulating the printing of two different selections during that year or to seeking in some other direction for the origins of *Morte D'Arthur*.

There are no copies in the British Museum, the Bodleian, or the Cambridge University Library. Ashley VII. 110 (modern morocco, uncut). Wrenn V. 29 (modern morocco, uncut).

This book first appears in the auction records in 1902, when the John Morgan copy fetched $490 (New York, Bangs, April 1, lot 357). This, like four others of the eight recorded, was in morocco, uncut. The next copy sold fetched only £10 (Sotheby, March 22, 1907, Van Antwerp sale, lot 225, sheets, folded), but two further copies in morocco uncut, made £16 and £20 in July 1907 and June 1908 respectively.

---

[1] Bryan Waller Procter is better known by his pen name of Barry Cornwall. As one of the best-known poets of his day, and the friend of Shelley, Lamb and Beddoes, no one was a more likely recipient of one of these proof copies.

In 1919 a fine copy in sheets fell at £1 in a miscellaneous sale at Sotheby's (February 17, lot 361). In the following year, however, the first of Buxton Forman's two copies (morocco, uncut) reached $130 at the Anderson Galleries (March 15, lot 851), and the latest record is $120 at the Amelia sale in 1930 (American Arts, October 27, lot 171, morocco, uncut).

The paper on which this book is printed is composed of esparto and chemical wood, a content inconsistent with its alleged date by more than three decades.

The type is Clay's Long Primer No. 3, of which the distinguishing sorts were not cut until after 1880. The date is therefore proved false by about forty years. This is the type in which the Reading *Sonnets* and fourteen of the other forgeries are printed.

Conclusion.—Whatever the format and contents of the proof volume mentioned by Hallam Tennyson, the paper content and the type of the present book decisively confirm the inference from Shepherd's evidence that this is not it. If no copies of the genuine book are extant now, it is reasonable to suppose that none were known at the date when this forgery was manufactured, and it is likely that the forger took advantage of the tradition, afterwards officially confirmed in the *Memoir*, to produce something which would fit the case. It must have been fabricated before 1896, when *Literary Anecdotes* first recorded its existence, and presumably after Tennyson's death in 1892.

THE SAILOR BOY

The Sailor Boy. / By / Alfred Tennyson, D.C.L. / Poet Laureate / [*Printer's Device*] / London: / Emily Faithfull & Co., Victoria Press. 1861.

8vo, stiff cream wrappers, edges trimmed. The title is reproduced on the front wrapper surrounded by a border, below which are the words "25 Copies for the Author's Use." The back wrapper carries within a similar border the imprint, "The Victoria Press."

Imprint as above. Printed on cream wove paper in a Pica old style type.

This poem was first printed in *The Victoria Regia, A Christmas Miscellany*, 1861. It was subsequently included, revised, in *Enoch Arden*, 1864.

Unknown to Shepherd (1896), who merely lists *The Victoria Regia*. Livingston (1901), p. 37. Wise (1908), I. 164–167, gives a list of the variants between this and the *Enoch Arden* text, adding, "The *brochure* is now of extreme rarity and commands a considerable price."

The British Museum copy (C.58.b.26) was received on July, 8, 1899. It was presented by Mr. Wise. No copy in the Cambridge University Library. No copy in the Bodleian. Ashley VII. 123, morocco, uncut, original wrappers bound in. Wrenn V. 34, morocco, uncut, wrappers bound in.

The first copy to appear at auction made $275 in 1902 (April 1, Bangs, John Morgan sale, lot 426, morocco, uncut). Eleven copies in all are recorded, of which four were in original wrappers, uncut, the remainder in modern bindings uncut, two having the wrappers preserved. The highest price was £62 in the Gosse sale (May 13, 1929, Sotheby, lot 132, wrappers), the lowest $40 in the Forman sale (March 15, 1920, Anderson, lot 856, wrappers). The Poor copy made $305 in 1908; the Pittar copies £23 and £20 in 1918 and 1919 respectively, but more recent prices have usually been lower. No inscriptions are recorded in any of these copies.

This was one of the books sold by Mr. Gorfin on commission for Mr. Wise.

Since this pamphlet purports to have originated in circumstances which suggest an offprint, one would expect it at least to be set up in the same type as *The Victoria Regia.* It is, in fact, entirely reset, and divided into stanzas. Much more peculiar, however, is the fact that the device on the title page is clearly a process engraved reproduction of that used on *The Victoria Regia.* Reference to Plate IV (facing p. 76) will show a number of differences in the copied block used for *A Sailor Boy.* Typical instances are: (i) The thick line on the left hand of the shield is much less regular, and appears to have been touched up by the block-maker. (ii) The *s* which occurs twice in the motto at the top of the shield has reproduced badly in both places. (iii) The top of the main stem of the F in the monogram on the shield is noticeably more ragged. (iv) On the left hand side the space between the lowest ivy leaf and the edge of the shield has filled up. (v) The lowest trail of ivy is obviously coarser.

The border on the wrappers is identical with that used on the wrapper of *Carmen Sæculare,* 1887.

The paper on which this pamphlet is printed is composed of a mixture of rag and chemical wood. It could not, therefore, have been manufactured until after 1874 at the earliest, and it is unlikely before 1883.

Conclusion.—The dark suspicions aroused by the copied block [1] and the border are turned into a certainty by the damning evidence of the paper. The pamphlet is clearly a forgery.

[1] Cf. Stevenson's *Some College Memories,* above, p. 254, and Thackeray's *A Leaf from a Sketch Book,* below, p. 350.

ODE FOR THE OPENING OF THE INTERNATIONAL EXHIBITION

Ode / For the Opening of / The International Exhibition. / By / Alfred Tennyson, P.L., D.C.L. / London: / Edward Moxon & Co., / Dover Street. / 1862.

Small 8vo, uncut; folded, without wrappers, according to Mr. Wise, but see below for the auction records.

Imprint on verso of title—" London, Bradbury and Evans, Printers, Whitefriars." Printed in Clay's Long Primer No. 3, on a cream wove paper.

Previous and subsequent printings, see below, under *Collation*.

Unknown to Shepherd (1896): Livingston (1901), pp. 40–43: Wise (1908), I. 167–170, who lists a few of the variant readings, without apparently perceiving their significance, and describes the pamphlet as " now one of the scarcest of Tennyson's original editions." Not recorded in *The English Catalogue*.

No copy in the British Museum. No copy in the Cambridge University Library. No copy in the Bodleian. Ashley VII. 123–4, with a presentation inscription on the half-title from A. Strahan, undated. Wrenn V. 35 (two copies in morocco, uncut).

The first copy to appear at auction fetched £5 5*s*. in 1904 (April 18, Sotheby, Miscellaneous, lot 727, wrappers). Only three others are recorded, the Hermann copy (1909, $46, wrappers), the Wallace copy (1920, $95, wrappers) and the Gosse copy (1929, £17, half morocco, uncut). These " wrappers " are all described as " original," and in the case of the Hermann copy also as " pink." This conflicts with Mr. Wise's description (*loc. cit.*). No inscriptions of any kind are recorded.

This was one of the books sold on commission by Mr. Gorfin for Mr. Wise. He finally purchased a single copy about 1910 (exact details not available).

Collation.—Nine different versions of the text of this poem have now to be considered, as follows:—

(1) Accompanying the musical setting by J. B. Sterndale Bennett. 4 parts. The date on these was changed periodically, but the earliest recorded is April 12, 1862 (Livingston, p. 44).

(2) *The Times*, April 24, 1862, p. 9. An unauthorised version, taken from (1) with several errors.

(3) The present pamphlet. Mr. Wise states (*Bibliography*, I. 168) that this was "issued on May 1st, 1862," and that "one thousand copies were printed for sale (at the price of *One Shilling*) at the Exhibition Building." The source of this precise information is not stated (? confusion with No. 4).

(4) *Ceremonial to be observed*, [etc.] *May 1st*, 1862, pp. 22–23. The official programme, Imperial 8vo, price One Shilling. This was for sale on the opening day.

(5) *Fraser's Magazine*, June, 1862, p. 803. The poem occurs in an article on the Exhibition, and is described as the authorised version, with some sarcastic remarks at the expense of *The Times*' mistakes on April 24 (quoted without acknowledgment by Mr. Wise, p. 168).

(6) *The Times*, July 14, 1862, p. 7. Mr. Wise states that this was "reprinted correctly," but in fact only the grosser of the two misprints to which the author in a letter (April 28) had called attention, was corrected; and a number of further independent readings appear, all of a minor character.

(7) *The Works of Alfred Tennyson*, 1872, Vol. III. pp. 200–202.

(8) The 1874 edition of the *Works*, Vol. IV. pp. 100–101.

(9) Ditto, 1889, p. 223. The texts in *The Poetical Works*, 1890, *The Works*, 1894, and *The Poetical Works*, 1896, follow this in every particular.

We have been unable to discover a copy of the official programme or of the issue with music, for collation. Livingston, however, records that the latter agreed with *Fraser* with the exception of one omission which will be noted in due course. The variations disclosed by a careful comparison of the texts of the other six versions are shown in the accompanying table, and they provide evidence enough.

It will be seen that variations occur at eighteen points, of which two stand out above the rest in significance for our present purpose—which is to discover to what state of the text the pamphlet conforms. On the first of these, the variant *peace / earth* in the last line, the pamphlet agrees with the editions of 1872, 1874 and 1889–96, against *Times* A, Fraser and *Times* B; also against the music issue, according to Livingston. That is, (3) agrees with (7), (8) and (9) against [(1)], (2), (5) and (6). In the continually altered Stanza IV, the pamphlet agrees with the 1889–96 text against every single one of the others, which exhibit five differing versions among seven of them. As to the sixteen minor variant readings, whatever agreement or disagreement there may be amongst the others, the pamphlet and the 1889–96 text agree exactly throughout.

Had the pamphlet been issued on May 1st, 1862, one might reasonably expect it to conform to what the major variations establish as the earliest state of the text:

Stanza and Line.	*The Times* (A), April 24 (2).	The Pamphlet, May 11 (3).	*Fraser's Magazine*, June (5).	*The Times* (B), July 14 (6).	*Works*, 1872 (7).	*Works*, 1874 (8).	*Works*, 1889, '90, '94, '96 (9).
I. 2	inventions stored	invention stored	invention stor'd	inventions stored	invention stored	invention stored	invention stored
I. 3	th'invisible	the invisible	th'invisible	th'invisible	the invisible	the invisible	the invisible
II. 1	O, silent father	O silent father	O silent father	O! silent Father	O silent father	O silent father	O silent father
II. 3	thee	thee	thee	Thee	thee	thee	thee
III. 1	thine,	thine,—	thine,—	thine,	thine,	thine,—	thine,—
III. 6	engin'ry	enginery	engin'ry	engin'ry	enginery	enginery	enginery
III. 9	Fairy fine	fairy-fine	Fairy fine	Fairy fine	fairy-fine	fairy-fine	fairy-fine
III. 13	Part divine	Art divine	Art divine	art Divine	Art divine	Art divine	Art divine
III. last 3 lines	*omits*	*omits*	War himself . . . but strike in vain.	*omits*	*omits*	*omits*	*omits*
IV.	*omits*	Is the goal so far away? Far, how far no tongue can say, Let us dream our dream today.	And is the goal so far away? Far, how far, no tongue can say: Let us dream our dream today.	And is the goal so far away? Far, how far, no tongue can say: Let us have our dreams today.	*omits*	Is the goal so far away? Far—how far no tongue can say; Let us dream no dreams today.	Is the goal so far away? Far, how far no tongue can say, Let us dream our dream today.
V. 2	chain	chain,	chain,	chain,	chain,	chain,	chain,
V. 3	fair white-winged	fair white-wing'd	fair, white-winged	fair white-winged	fair white-wing'd	fair white-wing'd	fair white-wing'd
V. 5	hours,	hours;	hours;	hours,	hours,	hours;	hours;
V. 9	nature's	Nature's	nature's	nature's	Nature	Nature's	Nature's
V. last	peace	earth	Peace	peace	earth.	earth	earth

in fact, it conforms, and in every minutest point, to the latest, that of 1889–96. Now Tennyson, as we know, and as the changes in Stanza IV here demonstrate clearly enough, continually revised his texts and sometimes harked back to discarded readings. But there are limits to all probabilities, and one cannot but feel that to suppose the 1889 text to have been set up verbatim from the pamphlet, across all the subsequent developments, very definitely exceeds such limits. This leaves us with only one alternative; an inevitable one. The pamphlet must have been set up from the 1889 text.

The paper of this pamphlet is composed of rag and chemical wood. The presence of the latter constituent proves that it cannot have been manufactured before 1874, and it is highly unlikely before 1883.

The type (A in our schedule) is the same as that used for the Reading *Sonnets* and fourteen other forgeries in the group. It is peculiar to Clay, therefore the imprint is false: several letters of it were not cut till after 1880, so that its date is false by eighteen years at least.

Conclusion.—This pamphlet is trebly proved a forgery, on the evidence of its paper, its type and its collation. The last also makes it certain that it was fabricated later than 1889.

LUCRETIUS

Lucretius / By / Alfred Tennyson / Poet Laureate / Cambridge, Mass. / Printed for Private Circulation / 1868

Square 8vo, light brown sand-grain cloth, uncut, lettered up the spine—*Tennyson's Lucretius*, 1868—in type-set caps.

Imprint on p. 27—" University Press, Cambridge: Printed by Welch, Bigelow, and Co." Printed on cream wove paper; the text in a Small Pica modern style, the preface in Clay's Long Primer No. 3.

Pp. 5–6 carry a Prefatory Note, signed " J. T. F. November 1868."

First printed in *Macmillan's Magazine*, May, 1868, pp. 1–9: also in *Every Saturday* (New York), May 2, 1868: subsequently in *The Holy Grail*, 1870.

Unknown to Slater (1894) and Shepherd (1896). Mentioned by Mr. Wise in *The Bookman* (1894). *Literary Anecdotes* (1896), II. 245. Livingston (1901) p. 54: " It is curious that, though printed in this country, no copies seem to turn up here in the market." Wise (1908), I. 191, notes one or two textual variants, and identifies the " J. T. F." of the preface as James Ticknor Fields.

The British Museum copy (11646.ff.31) was purchased on September 13, 1892, from F. G. Aylward. No copy in the Cambridge University Library. No copy in the Bodleian. Ashley VII. 127 (original cloth). Wrenn V. 36 (original cloth).

The first copy to appear in the rooms made £12 in 1896 (June 3, Sotheby; Alfred Crampon sale, lot 451). This, like all but two (undescribed) of the twelve copies recorded in all, was in original cloth. This was the highest price; and to one of the lowest, £3, which was all the next copy brought in 1900, the editor of *Book Prices Current* appended the note, " An extremely low and apparently quite accidental price " (December 3, Sotheby, Miscellaneous, lot 1194). Prices, however, remained at £4–£6 (the Forman copy touched the lowest figure, $10, in 1920), only rising again to £9 in 1929, perhaps on the strength of the catalogue note, " Reprinted by F. J. Furnivall " (June 20, Hodgson, Miscellaneous, lot 374). No inscriptions of any kind are recorded.

This was one of the books sold on commission for Mr. Wise by Mr. Gorfin, who also purchased one copy on April 26, 1910, at 15*s*.

The paper is composed of esparto, with a trace of chemical wood. Esparto was not in use in U.S.A. for paper-making until 1907.

The contradictions of the place, date and content of the paper are resolved by the evidence of the type. For although there is no question mark, the rest of the type in the preface is the same as that used for the Reading *Sonnets* and so many of the other forgeries. Had there been a question mark, it would almost certainly be the tell-tale Clay sport: even if it were not, several letters of the type as visible were not cut until after 1880. The text type (B in our schedule) is identical with that used for five other proved forgeries and five suspects in the group.

Conclusion.—This book is proved by its paper and its type to be a forgery; and the forger must therefore be credited with the composition of the prefatory note.

It is the only book on our list which has a cloth casing, and it is worth noting that it is lettered *up* the spine, which is the usual practice in this country. In U.S.A. such lettering is almost invariably set running downwards.

THE LOVER'S TALE. 1870

The Lover's Tale / By Alfred Tennyson / With a Monograph / By the Author of "Tennysoniana." / London / Fifty Copies printed for Private Circulation / M.D.CCC. LXX.

Small 8vo, stitched, uncut, no wrappers.

There is no printer's imprint. Printed on a cream wove paper in Clay's Long Primer No. 3.

There is a six-page bibliographical preface, signed "The Author of Tennysoniana./August, 1870."

This is described by Mr. Wise as the "First Pirated Edition" and must be carefully distinguished from the five others attributed to Richard Herne Shepherd. The poem was first printed in 1832 for inclusion in the *Poems* (1833), and although it was withdrawn from that volume a few copies were provided with a title-page (dated 1833) and distributed to friends. Mr. Wise refers to a letter of Arthur Hallam's for the statement that these numbered no more than six. Four are recorded as surviving to-day.[1] In 1868 Tennyson again contemplated publication of the poem, much revised; and again the abandoned book survives in the form of proofs. Three copies are known; one given by the author to Locker-Lampson, another given by Strahan (of Strahan and Isbister, the proposed publishers) to George MacDonald, now in the Ashley Library, a third in the possession of A. H. Japp, a friend of Tennyson's, and afterwards in the Jerome Kern collection. The poem was finally

[1] See W. H. Arnold, *Ventures in Book Collecting* (1923), pp. 236–238.

published, again revised, in 1879. Shepherd's piratical reprints, discussed below, are dated (two 1870 and four[1] 1875) between the abortive printing of 1868 and the actual authorised publication in 1879.

Not in Slater (1894): Shepherd (1896), p. 14: "In the summer of 1870, and again in 1875, under the auspices of the Editor of 'Tennysoniana,' the Fragment of 'The Lover's Tale' was reprinted for private circulation, from the original edition, as it appeared in 1833. These two unauthorised reprints were rigorously suppressed and called in, and only a few copies of each were actually circulated." There is (pp. 49–50) a collation of Shepherd's 1875 edition, the arrangement of *Contents* of which differs from any of those described by Mr. Wise, and a note of the printers of both editions (see below). Livingston (1901), pp. 56–7: "This is the earliest, according to Mr. Wise,[2] of Shepherd's six pirated editions." Wise (1908) II. 8 *et seq.*

No copy in the British Museum. No copy in the Cambridge University Library. No copy in the Bodleian. Wrenn V. 37 (morocco, uncut). Ashley VII. 109 (morocco, uncut).

Mr. Gorfin purchased twenty copies from Mr. Wise at 8*s.* each on April 14, 1910, a further copy on April 22, and two more on April 30, 1912, all at the same price.

The auction record of this book is worthless as evidence, since it is impossible to distinguish it from the other piracy of the same date; but it may be noted that the Lapham copy of one of them made $51 in 1908. No authenticated copies, of course, occur in either case.

The paper is composed of 100 per cent. chemical wood, and it cannot, therefore, have been manufactured until after 1874: it is much more likely to belong to a date later than 1883.

Certain letters of the type (Clay's Long Primer No. 3) were not cut for that firm until after 1880.

Piratical though it might be, this book, as placed by Mr. Wise at the head of the six he attributes to

[1] Three of these we have not seen, and their attribution to Shepherd rests on the authority of Mr. Wise.

[2] See above, p. 130.

Shepherd, was not unimportant. The 1833 edition survives in only four examples so far recorded: sets of the 1868 proofs are even less numerous: and the first piratical edition of 1870 is the nearest to a first that most collectors can hope for. We have two questions to answer. First, is it what Mr. Wise calls it? Second, if not, what is it and by whom was it produced?

The double evidence of the paper and the type proves conclusively that it was not printed within at least ten years of the date on its title-page. It therefore has no claims whatever to the position assigned to it by Mr. Wise.

The second question might seem at first sight worth little trouble in answering: but the fact that this proved forgery is printed in our forger's favourite type necessitates disposing of its connection with Shepherd, who might otherwise be thought to qualify for identification with him; and to do this we must review these Shepherd piracies as a whole.

Mr. Wise (*loc. cit.*) attributes six spurious editions of this poem to Shepherd, two dated 1870 (the present book and another) and four dated 1875. He quotes, from "a Daily Newspaper" of January 31, 1876, an account of the case of *Tennyson v. Shepherd*, in which the facts that the defendant had printed an edition in 1870—voluntarily withdrawn under unofficial pressure—and a further one in 1875—the cause of the action—were admitted; and he states that "the injunction prayed for was made perpetual on January 29th, 1876."

Mr. Wise's explanation of the four editions not mentioned in the case is as follows. That after the suppression of the first 1870 edition (reputedly the present book), Shepherd reprinted it before the end of the year: that "by 1875 Mr. Shepherd appears to have disposed of all the copies of *The Lover's Tale* printed in 1870, for in that year he again put the poem into type, printing a third set of Fifty Copies": that "The third batch of fifty copies does not seem to have lasted long, for it was speedily followed by a Fourth Pirated Edition": that, following "the Fifth Edition of his pirated issue . . . (printed still in 1875) . . . towards the close of 1875 appeared the Sixth (and last)."

Now these are all distinct editions, with various differences fully described by Mr. Wise; but their sequence as given by him seems peculiar. If one batch of fifty copies lasted Shepherd from 1870 till 1875 (we know now that the "First" of the two need not be accounted for), what explains the sudden spate of editions in 1875? If the first 1875 edition went off rapidly, why did he not reprint in a larger number—leaving the false limitation notice nevertheless, if he was really such a rogue as Mr. Wise makes out? Instead of this we have four distinct printings. Mr. Wise makes this sound less improbable by stating that the application for the injunction was not made by Tennyson and his publishers until December 1875: in actual fact, an interim injunction was granted on July 31 and duly served on Shepherd, who wrote to Tennyson in humble apology on August 5th. The "Interrogatories for the Examination" is dated August 12; and Shepherd's "Answer to the Bill of Complaint" was sworn and filed on October 5th.[1]

Quite apart from Shepherd's apologetic professions, the keen eyes of the plaintiff's solicitors would have pre-

[1] All these facts and quotations are drawn from the official documents of the case, preserved in the Public Record Office.

vented his reprinting after the interim injunction had been served, and this leaves only seven months for four separate and distinct editions. This, if even plausible, would argue phenomenal demand: and in fact we find from the official documents that the demand was not even brisk. Shepherd swore in evidence that of his 1875 edition, printed "in the spring of this year," only 15 copies had been sold by July 31st. He had given away 36 (including a copy to Swinburne) and the remaining 55 were still in his possession, ready to be (as they ultimately were) surrendered. 100 copies had been printed by Ogden & Co., of 172 St. John's Street, Clerkenwell;[1] and his total receipts for the copies sold, at varying prices, amounted to only £14, whereas the printing had cost £7 4*s*.

There is no reason to doubt these figures: less, perhaps, because Shepherd had sworn to them than because they were so readily verifiable: and they suggest that Mr. Wise's explanation and arrangement of these editions may be something less than final.

Returning to the question of the two "1870" editions, we find that Shepherd swore as follows:—"I caused the said poem to be reprinted in August 1870. . . . The printers I employed were Strangeways and Walden of 28 Castle Street, Leicester Square.[1] I ordered 50 copies to be struck off, but I believe the actual number printed was 54 or 55; of these 25 only were delivered to me, the rest remained in the printers' hands." After explaining his ready acquiescence in the remonstrances of Basil Montagu Pickering and his withdrawal of the edition, he proceeds to account for the total number—14 copies sold to three book-

[1] These printers' names were given by Shepherd in his *Bibliography*, p. 50.

sellers at 3*s*. 6*d*., 11 given away, 28 or 29 at the printers'. The names of all recipients are given (except of one gift copy not recollected), and 11 or 12 of the 14 were recovered from the booksellers and handed over, with the stock at the printers', to Pickering.

These modest prices accord very ill with the "Price Twenty Shillings" on the verso of the title-page of the present book; and the official figures of the numbers compare very oddly with the stock in Mr. Wise's hands, amounting even in 1910 to 23 copies. But in spite of such inconsistencies he classified the book as "First Pirated Edition." Mr. Wise, it is true, credits Shepherd with knavery which presumably would not stop short of perjury: but it must be remembered that Pickering was still alive when this case was tried, and Shepherd would hardly have dared, even had he wished, to tamper seriously with the facts as they concerned him. Moreover, we know from the case of Ruskin's *Leoni* (*q.v.*) how efficiently detailed a reference was available in the ledgers of Strangeways and Walden, the printers in question.

Whether Shepherd's 1870 edition is identical with Mr. Wise's "Second Pirated Edition," or whether it remains still undescribed, we have no means of knowing. It remains only to consider the possibility that Shepherd produced the present book at some date later than 1880, for only so can he be identified with our forger, who undoubtedly did print it.

The only shadow of an argument that Shepherd produced it, is the presence of his name (or rather title) on the title-page and the presence of his preface; which presumably led Mr. Wise to attribute it to him. But this preface, the bibliographical "Monograph on the Lover's Tale," had already been printed separately by Shepherd for sale at two shillings. It is not dated, but it is placed by Mr. Wise between the so-called "first" and "second" pirated editions in 1870; and it was a simple matter to combine it with the poem, date it "August 1870," and produce a volume which fits in very plausibly at the head of the list.[1]

The arguments against Shepherd's responsibility are several. Mr. Wise states that after January 29, 1876, "Mr. Shepherd does not appear to have made any further attempt to reprint *The Lover's Tale*," though he accuses him of putting single copies, kept back in 1875, into the market from time to time. We have seen, however, that Mr. Wise's statements in connection with these books are not entirely reliable, and Shepherd's innocence rests on much securer grounds.

First, there is no evidence that Shepherd ever dated his books falsely. When, for instance, he printed his second piracy in 1875, he dated it correctly. If, like our forger, he had had his eye on the first edition market, it would have been perfectly simple to have reproduced his suppressed 1870 edition, from the preserved proofs of which the other was printed; and his failure to adopt such an easily fraudulent plan marks him clearly as a different kind of operator altogether.

Secondly, when this book was printed, the authorised edition of 1879 was already on the market, and this removed the whole motive of Shepherd's piratical printing. What he was interested in was poems which were unobtainable among their authors' current volumes, and his whole series of reprints reflects this harmless passion for "literary rag-picking." In his Defence in the "Lover's Tale" case he lays the strongest emphasis on the injustice of the suggestion that he was out to catch "collectors of rare

[1] Copies were so bound up with the 1875 edition.

and curious books," and establishes by a mass of evidence the fact that the book had been sold, as far as he was concerned, quite openly for what it was.

It had not, in fact, caught on among collectors at all, as the figures show; and it is only the complexion put on his productions by the trade in later years and the realisation by bibliographers that they had some importance, that has caused Shepherd to be connected with this kind of first edition "racketeering" at all.

Conclusion.—There is, in short, no reason for supposing that Shepherd had anything to do with this forgery. It was executed after 1880; ingeniously confected into an appearance of priority over the real 1870 Shepherd edition; and fathered on Shepherd because it suited the needs of the imposture, and because he was a somewhat discredited peg on which such a thing could be safely as well as plausibly hung.

THE LAST TOURNAMENT

The / Last Tournament / By Alfred Tennyson, D.C.L. / Poet Laureate / Strahan & Co. / 56, Ludgate Hill, London / 1871 / [All rights reserved.]

Small 8vo, stitched, uncut, without wrappers.

Imprint on verso of title and at foot of p. 54—" Printed by Virtue and Co., City Road, London." Printed in Clay's Long Primer No. 3, on cream wove paper.

Contents. Prefatory note: text of the poem.

For details of prior and subsequent printings see below under *Collation*.

Unknown to Shepherd (1896): *Literary Anecdotes* (1896), II. 252–258: Memoir (1897), II. 126: " In 1871, *The Last Tournament* was privately printed, and then published in the *Contemporary Review*": Livingston (1901), p. 60: Wise (1908), I. 194–6, " the little volume is of considerable rarity."

No copy in the British Museum. No copy in the Bodleian. The copy in the Cambridge University Library (Syn.4.91.58) was presented by Mr. Wise on August 14, 1916. Ashley VII. 129–30, two copies; one with a presentation inscription from A. Strahan, the other with the inscription " Of this private edition of The Last Tournament not more than twenty copies were printed. A. Strahan."; neither of these inscriptions is dated. Wrenn V. 37 (morocco, uncut).

The first copy to appear at auction fetched £31 10*s*. in 1900 (February 28, Sotheby, Miscellaneous, lot 1385; morocco, uncut). Nineteen copies in all are recorded, of which one was in modern morocco with gilt edges, two in undescribed condition, the remaining sixteen in modern morocco, uncut. The highest price was $300 for the Lapham copy in 1908 (December 1, Anderson, lot 1373, morocco, uncut), but since then there has been a gradual decline—£30 in 1916

(July 17, Sotheby, Miscellaneous, lot 1106), $95 in 1920 (March 22, American Arts, Wallace, lot 1299), and a drop to £3 5s. in 1931 (April 27, Sotheby, Miscellaneous, lot 404)—all these being uncut copies in morocco. No inscriptions of any kind are recorded.

Mr. Gorfin purchased one copy from Mr. Wise, but he had sold others on commission.

Collation.—There are seven different versions of the text to be considered: (1) The Locker Lampson–Wise "trial book" of [? 1868][1]: (2), (3) and (4) are successive states of the proofs for the *Contemporary Review*. These wrappered pamphlets came from the library of Sir James Knowles, the editor of the *Contemporary*, and are now in the possession of Messrs. Pickering and Chatto. (5) The *Contemporary Review* for December, 1871, pp. 1–22. (6) The present pamphlet ("Author's Private Edition"). (7) *Gareth and Lynette*, 1872, pp. 91–136.

This order may at first sight seem arbitrary, since Hallam Tennyson believed the pamphlet to have preceded the *Contemporary Review*, and Mr. Wise assigns it positively to November. But whereas 6 and 7 differ markedly from the common lay-out of 1–5, they correspond with each other line for line so closely that in spite of the six textual differences noted by Mr. Wise (*Bibliography*, pp. 195–6), one must obviously have been set up from the other. It might, indeed, seem perfectly natural that 7 should have been set up from 6; but it happens that a proof of the last leaf of 7 has survived, with corrections in Tennyson's hand.[2] Now all the alterations indicated on this proof

[1] This is described in the Rowfant Library catalogue as being endorsed "Proof," so that neither Tennyson nor Locker apparently regarded it as a "trial-book" at all. Moreover, the catalogue does not assign to it any date.

[2] This leaf is reproduced by Mr. Wise, facing p. 193 of his *Bibliography*. It is first mentioned as part of the proofs of *Gareth and*

were in the text of *Gareth and Lynette* (7) as finally published; and if 6, the pamphlet, is, as it purports to be, earlier, none of them, naturally, will be found there. In fact, however, although the *earlier* form of the *major* alteration [1] made on this leaf of proof duly

---

Lynette in the Rowfant (Locker-Lampson) Library Catalogue (Vol. II. p. 100). Mr. Wise confesses (*Bibliography*, p. 194) that he removed it from its place and added it to the unique copy of the "trial book" of [1868], which lacked the last leaf, on the assumption (for which he offers no evidence) that it was part of that book. Now whatever may be the position of the "trial book" (and Mr. Wise adduces no evidence that it was produced in 1868), this particular leaf cannot be of that date. In 2 and 3, the two earliest of Sir James Knowles' proofs, the 14th line from the end of the poem reads "He said and turn'd and flinging round her neck," while 4 and 5 read "He rose, he turn'd, etc." This alteration, then, was made between the second and third proofs of the poem for the *Contemporary Review*, and must belong to the autumn of 1871. And since the text as set up on this leaf of proof is exactly identical with 5, the final version printed in the *Contemporary*, it cannot possibly belong to 1868. Moreover, the type in which it is set is the same as that used for the published *Gareth and Lynette* volume, and differs from that employed in all the other versions under consideration. Furthermore, this leaf is paged "131" in Tennyson's hand—a number quite irreconcilable with a proof either of the *Contemporary Review* or of the "Author's Private Edition." It does, however, fit the *Gareth and Lynette* volume, although when that came to be published this page became 135 owing to the addition of two fly-titles earlier in the book. In short, this leaf belongs in its original place with the rest of the *Gareth and Lynette* proofs, and its removal and addition to the "trial book" is entirely unjustified. These Rowfant proofs are now in the Wrenn Library, and it is worth noting that they are placed in the catalogue (V. 38) *after* the "Author's Private Edition," are dated "1871" and described merely as "The Original Proof Sheets." This, of course, besides being inconsistent with Mr. Wise's dating in the *Bibliography*, gives the misleading impression that they are proofs *of* the "Author's Private Edition." This ought not to have escaped the attention of the editor of the catalogue, Mr. Wise.

[1] Lines 12 and 13 from end:

> "Claspt it, and cried 'Thine Order, O my Queen!'
> But, while he bow'd to kiss the jewelled throat,"

for

> "Claspt it; but while he bow'd himself to lay
> Warm kisses in the hollow of her throat,"

appears in the pamphlet (as with the five other changes elsewhere in the poem, whose unrevised states appear in 5), three minor alterations are found *in their corrected form.*[1] Which, as Euclid would say, is impossible.

The only possible explanation is that the pamphlet was set up from the published text: the six obvious major changes were restored to their earlier form (from the *Contemporary* text); but three minor variations at least—more might be visible if we had available more of Tennyson's corrected proof of 7—were overlooked, and they are enough to betray the true status of the pamphlet.

The paper is composed of rag and chemical wood, and the presence of the latter constituent in any quantity proves that it cannot have been manufactured until after 1874.

Certain letters of the type in which this book was printed were not cut for Clay until after 1880: it is the same as that used by them for the Reading *Sonnets* and fourteen of the other forgeries. The fact that it is peculiar to Clay proves the Virtue imprint to be fictitious.

Conclusion.—This book is condemned as a forgery by its false date and false imprint, supported by the powerful evidence of the collation. Hallam Tennyson's statement must either derive from the same source as that of *Literary Anecdotes*, or else refer to the " 1868 " proof—no authority has been quoted for this dating and it seems to be purely conjectural. As for Strahan's statement, it is no real evidence for

[1] Line 22 from end, capital O for " order "; space between lines 19 and 20; line 14, " then " for " and."

authenticity, because Mr. Wise's copy of the *Ode for the Opening of the International Exhibition*, 1862, which is equally a proved forgery, also has a presentation inscription from Strahan. Moreover, his statement in Mr. Wise's other copy about the number printed compares very oddly with the figures of the auction record, to which must be added the four copies whose location we have given above—making 23 in all. In the present case, however, Strahan may have been thinking of copies of the proofs of the poem as set up for the *Contemporary Review*, of which he was the publisher, and this would provide an alternative explanation for Hallam Tennyson's statement.

A WELCOME TO ALEXANDROVNA

A / Welcome / to / Her Royal Highness Marie Alexandrovna, / Duchess of Edinburgh. / By / Alfred Tennyson, Poet Laureate. / Henry S. King & Co. London. / 1874.

Small 8vo, stitched, without wrappers.

Imprint on p. 8—" Bradbury, Agnew & Co., Printers, Whitefriars, London." Printed on cream wove paper in a Long Primer old style.

Not in Slater (1894) : not in Shepherd (1896) : Livingston (1901) : Wise (1908), I. 225 : " Forty Copies only were printed, all for private circulation."

The British Museum copy (C.58.b.39) was presented on Jan. 9, 1904, by Mr. Wise. No copy in the Bodleian or in the Cambridge University Library. Ashley VII. 137 (morocco, uncut; presentation inscription from A. Strahan). Wrenn V. 39 (two copies, in morocco, uncut).

We can find no record of any sale of this pamphlet in the auction room. Two copies of the quarto edition fetched $170 and $112.50 in 1898 and 1902 respectively.

This was one of the books sold on commission by Mr. Gorfin for Mr. Wise.

There are five forms of this poem to be considered. (1) The present pamphlet, which Mr. Wise states (*loc. cit.*) was issued on March 6th. (2) *The Times*, March 7, p. 5. (3) The " second private edition " ; a quarto, with Henry S. King's imprint at the end and printed on paper watermarked " Towgood's / Extra Super " ; issued, according to Mr. Wise, in March. (4) The " early (probably authorised) reprint of the

Quarto" with the misprint *Alexandrowna*.[1] (5) *Works*, 1874, Vol. IV. pp. 104–106.

Apart from one or two insignificant changes of punctuation, there is only one textual variation. In the present pamphlet the fourth line of the second stanza reads *And all the sultry plains of India known*. "At the last moment," says Mr. Wise, "this reading appears to have dissatisfied the poet, for a second impression, in quarto [No. 3], was immediately struck off, in which the above line was changed to: *And all the sultry palms of India known*."

Now, as this correction was made early enough to be incorporated in *The Times* of March 7,[2] it is perhaps permissible to wonder why the issue of the 8vo pamphlet on March 6 was not suspended. It is also odd that the 4to, which was "immediately struck off" and "at the last moment," should be an elaborate, carefully printed affair, with borders and cherubs; and entirely different from the 8vo in style, when one would expect it to be from the same setting of type.

Whether, however, we accept Mr. Wise's reconstruction of the events or not, the existence of two "privately printed" pamphlets side by side has got to be accounted for somehow. Hallam Tennyson said (*Memoir*, II. 155) that it was "printed in *The Times* and on separate sheets," and in view of the autographed and pedigree copies of the 4to which have survived, there can be no doubt that it was to that—a single half-sheet, folded in two—that he was referring. It is a handsome brochure, and although it has only the publisher's imprint it can be attributed with some confidence, on stylistic grounds, to the Chiswick Press,

[1] We have been unable to find a copy of this for examination.

[2] The 1874 and 1889 texts also read *palms*.

whose characteristic lay-out and ornaments are not easily mistaken.

What, then, is the 8vo pamphlet? In its general lay-out it has a noticeable resemblance to the forger's "house style," and its type gives a more definite edge to the resemblance. The type, C in our schedule, is identical with that used for four proved forgeries and five other suspects in the group, including *The Falcon*, *The Cup* and *The Promise of May*. Such resemblance, however marked, is not, of course, anything near proof. But, as Mr. Wise's explanation of this 8vo pamphlet seems not quite adequate, we offer instead the submission that the forger produced it; gave it one unique variant reading, which should lead people to suppose it the earliest version of the text; and "uttered" it in the usual way. It has no authentication, it has no satisfactory *raison d'être*, it is found in very bad company at an early date; its type and lay-out are not in its favour. We regard it as suspicious, and presentation inscriptions from Strahan are not the best kind of authentication—witness *An Ode*, 1862, and *The Last Tournament*.

THE FALCON

The Falcon / London: Printed for the Author: 1879.

8vo, light brown wrappers, uncut.

No imprint. Printed on a cream wove paper, in a Long Primer old style type.

Printed in the "trial book" of 1882, with *The Cup*: first published in 1884, also with *The Cup*.

Unknown to Shepherd (1896): not mentioned in *Literary Anecdotes* (1896): Livingston (1901), p. 73: Wise (1908), I. 236: "Printed for Private Circulation only, probably for stage purposes."[1]

The British Museum copy (C.59.g.25) was presented by Mr. Wise on May 11, 1907. The Cambridge University Library copy (Syn.4.91.58[3]) was presented by Mr. Wise on September 8, 1916. No copy in the Bodleian. Ashley VII. 141: "The first edition, privately printed for stage purposes."[1] Wrenn V. 41 (morocco, uncut).

The first copy to appear in the auction room made £52 in 1899 (November 20, Sotheby, Miscellaneous, original wrappers, uncut). This same sale saw the first appearance of *The Cup* and *Carmen Sæculare*. Prices ruled high for several years, the W. H. Arnold copy fetching $410 in 1901 and the John Morgan copy $230 in 1902. The Hermann copy, however, only reached $140 in 1909, and by 1916 the Dunwoody copy had declined to $45. With two exceptions (Wallace, $85 and Forman, $100, both in 1920) the book has remained at about this level ever since the last record, being $42.50 in 1930. Twelve copies in all are recorded, none with inscriptions of any kind; three being in modern morocco, the Forman copy in folded sheets, the remainder in original brown wrappers, uncut.

This was one of the books sold by Mr. Gorfin on commission for Mr. Wise.

---

[1] See note to *The Cup*, below, p. 331.

Collation.—There are three forms of the text to be considered. (1) The present volume. (2) The "trial book" of *The Cup and The Falcon*, 1882, of which the only copy known is in the Ashley Library (VII. 147). This was presented by Tennyson to "his wife's niece, Miss A. G. Weld" ("his niece, Miss Lushington," as described in Mr. Wise's *Bibliography*, I. 256), and bears corrections in his hand. (3) The published edition of *The Cup and The Falcon*, 1884.

Livingston (*loc. cit.*) records that the only variations between the texts of (1) and (3) are—12 of punctuation, 2 of the spelling of past participles, and one change of *thee* to *you*.

Mr. Wise in his *Bibliography* writes of (1) (p. 237): "The text is a 'clean' and exact one, and the differences between it and the published text of 1884 are of the slightest possible description. The changes made —or suggested—in the 'trial' edition of 1882 were merely tentative, and were not adopted when the play was published in 1884." Again, of the 1882 edition he writes (p. 259): "In the case of *The Falcon* a more ambitious attempt was apparently made to revise the text of the play. A close collation of its pages discloses a number of small verbal alterations; two short passages which are in the edition of 1879 do not occur; whilst five lines are to be found which do not appear either in the private edition of 1879, or in the published edition of 1884. It is evident that in 1884, when the two plays were finally published, this copy of the edition projected two years earlier was not forthcoming, having in the meantime been given to Miss Lushington [see above]. Thus the slight changes of text exhibited by it were not consulted in the course of printing the published book, which, save for a few trifling verbal alterations, is a precise reprint of the private edition of 1879."

The second passage is reprinted in the Ashley Catalogue (VII. 147) with the change of name from *Lushington* to *Weld*.

The type (C in our schedule) is identical with that used for *The Cup*, *The Promise of May*, *A Welcome to Alexandrovna* and four proved forgeries.

Conclusion.—For information respecting the text of (2) one has to rely entirely on Mr. Wise's statements, as quoted above;[1] and as he gives no specific instances of textual differences, it is impossible to draw any definite conclusions from the collation of the three texts. In the case of *The Cup* he reproduces a page of (2) carrying some corrections, the damning inferences of which are discussed below (p. 330), and one of the most suspicious characteristics of the present book must therefore be held its exact similarity in type, format and bibliographical status to another which is almost certainly spurious.

It is, moreover, clear from what Mr. Wise says that (1) and (3) represent the established text, while (2) is substantially different; and this sequence even Mr. Wise realised to be odd. The explanation which he offers postulates that, just because only one copy of the "trial book" survives to-day, no others at all were available in 1884. It is in the last degree unlikely that Tennyson should either have given away all the copies that he had had printed, or, if he had, that he should have been unable to borrow one of them for use two years later. No explanation is offered for two equally curious circumstances. First, why, if he had already

[1] Mr. Wise did not reply to our request for permission to collate the book.

got one "privately printed edition" in hand, should Tennyson have felt any need for another in 1882? Secondly, even if (3) could not be set up from (2), why could not (2) have been set up from (1), of which plenty of copies were available? It is remarkable that whereas (2) survives in only one copy, with a first-class pedigree and notes in the author's hand, this book (1) is comparatively common and yet no copy is recorded with a pedigree of any kind whatever.

This 1879 edition, in short, is quite definitely suspicious.

THE CUP

The Cup / London: Printed for the Author: 1881.

8vo, light brown wrappers, uncut.

There is no printer's imprint. Printed on cream wove paper, in a Long Primer old style type.

The play was in 1882 printed (with *The Falcon*) as a "trial book." This edition has Kegan Paul's name on the title and was printed by Spottiswoode. It was published (also with *The Falcon*) by Macmillan in 1884.

Unknown to Shepherd (1896), who, however (p. 59; on the published edition), "hazarded the conjecture" that some such editions as the present might have been done for the actors; "but," he says, "I do not possess special information, still less did I ever see or hear of a copy of either." Not mentioned in *Literary Anecdotes* (1896). Livingston (1901), pp. 77–81. Wise (1908), I. 249–252, gives "an analysis of the text" prepared by Livingston, and based on his *Bibliography* (*loc. cit.*). This analysis covers the variants between the 1881 and 1884 texts, and Mr. Wise deals with those between 1881 and 1882 under his entry for the latter volume (*op. cit.*, pp. 256–259, with a page in facsimile).

The British Museum copy (C.58.b.25) was presented by Mr. Wise on March 11, 1899. The Cambridge University copy (Syn.4.91.58[5]) was presented by Mr. Wise on September 8, 1916. No copy in the Bodleian. Ashley VII. 145 (original wrappers, uncut). Wrenn V. 42 (morocco, uncut).

The first copy to appear at auction fetched £46 in 1899 (November 20, Sotheby, Miscellaneous, lot 1394). Three years later the John Morgan copy fetched $340 (April 1, 1902, Bangs, lot 411, morocco, uncut). The Lapham copy only reached $120 in 1908; the Wallace copy in 1920 only $70, and this figure is about the average for more recent years. The Gosse copy (£34 in 1929) had an important autograph letter inserted. Eleven copies in all are recorded; six in original wrappers, uncut, three in modern binding, uncut, the Forman copy in folded sheets, and one in undescribed condition. No inscriptions of any kind are recorded.

This book was sold by Mr. Gorfin on commission for Mr. Wise.

The text type (C in our schedule) is identical with that used for *The Falcon*, *The Promise of May*, *A Welcome to Alexandrovna* and four proved forgeries in the group.

Collation.—There are six forms of the text to be considered. (1) This pamphlet, 1881. (2) The "trial book," 1882, of which the only known copy was presented by the author to "his wife's niece, Miss A. G. Weld" (Ashley VII. 147, implicitly correcting the statement in the *Bibliography*, I. 256, "his niece, Miss Lushington"). (3) The first published text, in *The Cup and The Falcon*, 1884. (4) Volume IV of *The Dramatic Works*, 1886. (5) *The Poetical Works*, 1889. (6) Volume VIII of the *Works*, 1893.

Apart from minor changes of punctuation, corrections of misprints, etc., there are two important variant passages:—

A. The four lines at the beginning of Act II, "Artemis, Artemis, hear us," etc. (p. 26 of the pamphlet). These occur in (1), (2) and (6): they are omitted from (3), (4) and (5). Hallam Tennyson (*Memoir*, II. 336) says that his father wrote in these lines for Mary Anderson's projected production in 1887, but Mr. Wise points out that they were merely restored to their original place.

B. On p. 11 of the "trial book" (2)—reproduced facing p. 258 of Mr. Wise's *Bibliography*—we find that Tennyson made a correction in MS., and over part of this, a second correction. The original setting read :—

SYNORIX

Sinnatus ! Sinnatus ! How they shout the man.

SYNORIX

He comes, a rough, bluff, simple-looking fellow !
I'll join with him.
I may reap . . .

Tennyson deleted the second SYNORIX and substituted *looking off stage*: he also made an insertion before *I'll join with him*, of these words :—

Scarce one to keep the fealty of a wife
If craftily assail'd.

For this second line he then substituted *Assail'd by Craft and Love.*

The 1884 text incorporates these corrections, with some further ones, reading as follows :—

Looking off stage]. He comes, a rough, bluff, simple-looking fellow.
If we may judge the kernel by the husk,
Not one to keep a woman's fealty when
Assailed by Craft and Love. I'll join with him.

This version is found unchanged in 1886, 1889 and 1893 (except for a reversion to *Assail'd* in 1889). It is also the text of the 1881 pamphlet.

Now A shows a perfectly reasonable variation—reasonable, that is, in view of Tennyson's known habit of restoring discarded lines. But B is a very different matter. There are three distinct states of the text. First, the 1882 "trial book," as printed: second, the same, twice corrected: third, the 1884–1886–1889–1893 version, further corrected on the same lines, and quite clearly, from its persistence, the final text. We should expect the pamphlet to give either the first state, or an even earlier form: in fact it gives the latest, the established, form.

In view of the gradual development of this final form, visible in Tennyson's original 1882 text, the first MS. corrections, the second MS. correction, and the final corrections which give us the 1884 text, it is surely impossible that this trebly corrected version could have been printed in 1881. How could an edition of 1881 show corrections made in or after 1882, and further corrections made in 1884? Is it conceivable that Tennyson, sending the copy of the pamphlet to the printer for the "trial book," should have made no less than five corrections in it, and afterwards, on two, and perhaps three, separate occasions, gradually re-corrected to the original reading? This would be no mere harking back to a discarded line: it would be pulling down a completed house in order to rebuild it, slowly and with care, exactly the same.

The only possible explanation of this apparent inconsistency is that the pamphlet was set up from one of the later texts.

Conclusion.—It must be clearly realised that all our knowledge of (2), the unique "trial book," is derived from the collation and facsimile given by Mr. Wise in his *Bibliography*; and it is quite possible that if further details were available,[1] other evidence as damning as that submitted above would be forthcoming. This is merely the result of studying a single page.

[1] We received no reply to a request for permission to collate the volume.

There is no positive evidence of type or paper against this book: but the argument from the collation is overwhelmingly strong, and all the familiar characteristics are visible. The combination gives us a moral certainty.

Incidentally, it has never been explained why Tennyson, when he must still have had quite a number of copies of *The Cup* (and of *The Falcon*) in this pamphlet form, " printed for Private Circulation only, probably for stage purposes,"[1] should have wanted to print a " trial " edition only a year later in so small a number that only a single copy survives to-day. This single copy has an impeccable provenance, and notes in the author's hand: the fifteen copies of the pamphlet known to us have not a shadow of a provenance or inscription between them.

[1] Wise, *Bibliography*, I. 250. This suggested reason for the printing directly contradicts Mr. Wise's own statement on p. 262 of the same volume. He there says, of *The Promise of May*, 1882, " it is fairly safe to assume that the private edition of 1882 is a veritable ' trial book,' printed by the poet for his own use, as was the case with the whole of the Tennyson dramas with the two exceptions of *Harold* and *Queen Mary*. It is also noticeable that the title-page clearly states that the book was '*Printed for the Author*.' The imprint would hardly have appeared in this form had the book been a mere theatre-print."

THE PROMISE OF MAY

The / Promise of May / London: Printed for the Author: 1882

8vo, light brown wrappers, uncut.

There is no publisher's or printer's imprint. Printed on cream wove paper, in a Long Primer old style type.

The play was in 1883 printed as a "trial book," with Kegan Paul's name on the title-page and Spottiswoode's imprint. Mr. Wise records (*Bibliography*, I. 265) the reported existence of a third "trial book" of 1886, when a revival of the play was in contemplation: he suggests that the six copies reputed to have been done of this were really six sets of the relevant pages of proof from *Locksley Hall*, in which volume it was in that year first published by Macmillan.

Unknown to Shepherd (1896), who, however, hazarded a similar conjecture here as in the case of *The Cup* (*q.v.*, p. 327); in this instance with even less probability, as Mr. Wise pointed out (*Bibliography*, p. 261), since a MS. of the acting versions exists, differing in many points from all the printed texts. *Literary Anecdotes* (1896), II. 265: "It was not then published, though privately printed copies unquestionably exist." Livingston (1901), pp. 81–83. Wise (1908), I. 260–262.

The British Museum copy (C.58.b.25) was received on March 11, 1899. It was presented by Mr. Wise. The Cambridge University Library copy (Syn.4.91.58[6]) was presented by Mr. Wise on September 8, 1916. No copy in the Bodleian. Ashley VII. 148 (original wrappers, uncut). Wrenn V. 43 (original wrappers, uncut).

The first copy to appear in the rooms made $430 in the W. H. Arnold sale in 1901 (May 7, Bangs, lot 323, original wrappers). The catalogue remarked: "This is not quite so rare as *The Falcon*, yet all told, after most diligent searching, only 11 copies are known, and some of these lack the covers." The John Morgan copy made $331 the next year (April 1, Bangs, lot 414, morocco, uncut), but by 1909 the price had dropped to $75 (April 5, Anderson, Poor sale, lot 1081, morocco, uncut), and between 1916 and 1927 the normal price in England was under £5, in U.S.A. between $25 (1916) and $67.50 (1926). Twelve copies in all are recorded, of which seven were in original wrappers, uncut, three in morocco, uncut, the Forman copy in folded sheets, and one in undescribed condition. No inscriptions of any kind are recorded.

This book was sold by Mr. Gorfin on commission for Mr. Wise.

The type (C in our schedule) is identical with that used for *The Falcon*, *The Cup*, *A Welcome to Alexandrovna* and four proved forgeries in the group.

Collation.—Here again there are three forms of the play which must be considered: (1) The present pamphlet ("the first 'trial' edition"). (2) *The Promise of May A Rustic Drama in Three Acts*, London, Kegan Paul, Trench & Co., 1883 (the "second trial edition"). This has the same provenance as the 1882 edition of *The Cup and The Falcon*, and is likewise unique. (3) *Locksley Hall*, 1886, pp. 47–201.

Of (1) Mr. Wise writes (p. 262): ". . . the Text of the privately-printed edition of 1882 is a 'clean' and exact one, and . . . the differences between it and the published text of 1886 are of the slightest possible description. Considering that this text is largely composed of speeches in which the peculiarities of a provincial dialect are punctiliously observed, it is evident that the proofs of the edition of 1882 were most carefully revised by the Author."

There can be no doubt of the authenticity of (2), which is established both by its provenance and the fact that it bears Lord Tennyson's autograph in pencil upon the cover; but its text is extremely primitive. Mr. Wise describes it thus (p. 264): "A close examination of its pages affords ample evidence that the book was not set up from either the Author's

Manuscript or from a copy of the original privately-printed edition of the previous year. It was clearly set up from a manuscript copy, and it is equally clear that this copy was not transcribed directly from the Author's Manuscript or Printed Book, but was written to dictation, the writer being in total ignorance of the niceties of the Wiltshire dialect. The pages are crowded with minute errors of spelling, to a total of several hundred. These errors are entirely phonetic, the writer having written down the words as they were pronounced—in many instances words which should be in dialect are spelled after the manner of ordinary English. Here and there some small differences of text are apparent; but these are mostly by way of omission, and are apparently the result of careless copying." On the next page we find the following footnote: "It is not for a bibliographer to be fantastic; but in view of the opposition excited by the Play, and especially of the Queensberry onslaught, there is some temptation to think of the Poet as of Achilles sulking in his tent, and leaving someone else to arrange matters when the question of printing the Drama came up in 1883. . . ."

These descriptions show that whereas the differences between (1) and (3) are minute, (2) represents a very primitive form of the play. The very lack of change between 1882 and 1886 in a piece of this form and extent seems remarkable; but why, if the play had been correctly printed in 1882, should it be necessary to set it up afresh in an inferior form in 1883? And this appears still more remarkable when it is realised that there are at least ten copies of the 1882 edition still extant, none of which bears the author's autograph, whereas there is only one example of the 1883 proof, and that does bear the author's autograph. If the 1882 edition is a forgery these difficulties disappear; and the primitive state of the text of the 1883 version need cause no surprise when compared with the "trial book" of *Property*, 1864, in which the leaf facsimiled by Mr. Wise (facing p. 178) contains eight lines and no less than thirteen mistakes.

Conclusion.—This book bears a striking similarity to the "private" issues of *The Cup* and *The Falcon*. They are all printed in the same fount of type and are noticeably similar in format and lay-out. Each is supposed to have preceded an authentic "trial book." None of them has an imprint, whereas the genuine "trial books" have both publisher's and printer's names, as have all the later Macmillan private issues. Of all three quite a number of copies are extant, not one of which has a provenance to support it, while both the genuine "trial books" are unique and derive direct from Tennyson himself. They were not printed for stage purposes (Wise, I. 262), and their existence would seem in each case to do away with the reason for printing the genuine "trial books" which so closely followed them in time.

In *The Promise of May* the argument from the collation is a general one, whereas in *The Cup* it is particular: both, however, point to the same conclusion, and although this case must be summed up as not proved, the weight of the evidence is strongly against its authenticity.

CARMEN SÆCULARE

Carmen Sæculare / An Ode / By / Alfred Tennyson, D.C.L. / Poet Laureate / London / Printed for Private Distribution / 1887

8vo, stiff cream wrappers, printed in blue within a lozenge border, gilt edges.

There is no imprint. Printed in English (13 point) old style, on rough cream wove paper.

This is the "Author's Private Edition" and must not be confused with the Macmillan pamphlet of the same date (see below).

For previous and subsequent printings see under *Collation.*

Unknown to Shepherd (1896). Livingston (1901), pp. 87–8: "Mr. Wise states that only twenty copies were printed." Wise (1908), I. 278–281: "It has been asserted that only twenty copies were printed, but there appears to be no authority for the statement." Mr. Wise gives two pages of variations between the text of the pamphlet and that of *Macmillan's Magazine*, and except for a full-point which has crept in after *Ceremonial* in the penultimate line of Stanza IV, his quotation of these is accurate.

The British Museum copy (C.58.d.32) was presented by Mr. Wise on October 10, 1903. The Cambridge University Library copy (Syn. 4.91.58[8]) was presented by Mr. Wise on August 7, 1916. Ashley VII. 154, 155 (original wrappers). Wrenn V. 45 (original wrappers).

The first copy to appear in the auction room fetched £31 in 1899 (November 20, Sotheby, Miscellaneous, lot 1397). This copy, like ten others of the fourteen recorded, was in the original wrappers. The condition of the remaining three is not given. This price was exceeded in 1902, the John Morgan copy making $155 (April 1, Bangs, lot 421, original wrappers), but the Poor and Hermann copies only reached $60 and $55 in 1909. The lowest price was $7.50 in 1922 (January 18, Anderson Galleries, a miscellaneous sale), but more recent figures range from £9 in 1928 to £4 in 1932. No inscriptions of any kind are recorded.

This book was sold by Mr. Gorfin on commission for Mr. Wise.

The border on the wrapper is identical with that on *The Sailor Boy*, and Thackeray's *A Leaf out of a Sketch-Book*, both proved forgeries.

Collation.—There are five forms of printing of this poem to be considered. (1) *Macmillan's Magazine*, April, 1887, pp. 401–406. (2) *Carmen Sæculare*, Macmillan & Co., 1887. The publishers informed Mr. Wise that fifty copies were printed for private distribution. (3) The edition with music by Stanford. This is dated February 1887 on the last page, but Mr. Wise states that this is the date upon which the engraving of the music was completed. "The book was not placed upon public sale until the twenty-second of April following." (4) The present pamphlet. (5) In *Demeter and Other Poems*, 1889, pp. 6–11.

The text apparently presents two versions, the first represented by (1), (2) and (3), the second by (4) and (5). The differences between (1) and (4) are set out by Mr. Wise, as noted above, and collation of (4) and (5) reveals complete agreement between the two at all these points. Further, Mr. Wise states (p. 278) that the texts of (1) and (2) agree "in every particular," although the setting of type is different. (2) was not apparently publicly known until a copy turned up at Sotheby's on July 18, 1900.

Now Mr. Wise states that although the *text* of (2), *i.e.* pp. 1–8, "was put into type at a date anterior to the composition of the *Magazine*" (1), the outside sheet "was provided at a later date, *i.e.* in May, 1887": whereas (4), the present pamphlet, was "issued in April." He gives no authority for either statement, but presumably his information on the first point, like the rest of his information about (2), was derived from Messrs. Macmillan (p. 278). Referring to the changes in the text which differentiate the two versions, Mr. Wise says (p. 279): "It was in order that these revisions, made after the April number of *Macmillan's Magazine* had gone to press, might be introduced, that the poet caused a few corrected copies of the *Ode* to be struck off in pamphlet form." But this explanation of the *raison d'être* of the "private" pamphlet conflicts with the probabilities inherent in the dates which Mr. Wise himself has given for the issue of the two pamphlets. He is at pains to make (4), "the Author's Private Edition," the earlier of the two: but if it really was issued in April, what would have been the point of completing (2), the Macmillan pamphlet, with uncorrected text, in the following month? If (2) had been issued earlier, then there is a conceivable reason for the existence of (4), which has the revised text: if (4) was, as Mr. Wise says, issued earlier, its printing would surely have carried with it an order for the destruction of the uncompleted (2). If the poet was so anxious to put the revised text before twenty (?) of his friends in April, what induced him to complete and put out fifty pamphlets with the uncorrected text in May? The sequence of events is, to say the least, highly improbable.

Moreover, why was (4) not produced by Messrs. Macmillan, who handled the poem in all its other forms (except, of course, the edition with music, for which, however, they gave their express formal permission) and all the rest of Tennyson's work at this date?

Conclusion.—The situation revealed above is very odd indeed. So odd, in fact, that one casts round for some hypothesis to explain the inconsistencies; and the only one which explains them all is that the "Author's Private Edition" is a forgery. Since it conforms to the proved majority of the group in its bibliographical status, provenance, bad auction record,[1] innocence of inscribed copies and so forth, this is perhaps no great stretch of imagination; and when we remember that the existence of the Macmillan pamphlet was not apparently known until 1900, we can see that its selection is true to the forger's formula.

The appearance of the genuine article afterwards was confusing; and Mr. Wise added to the confusion in 1908 when he placed the Macmillan edition as the later of the two. Our pamphlet had the revised text, and to assign to it the priority as well involved Mr. Wise in an inconsistency of which he seems to have been unaware. Nevertheless, it is a serious one; and when to it are added the various items of negative evidence with which we are now so familiar, not to mention that highly damaging border, it becomes difficult—not impossible, for there is no proof, but difficult—to regard this as anything but a very suspicious affair indeed.

[1] It should be noted that there are at least eighteen copies of this pamphlet recorded, out of perhaps twenty, whereas we can only trace four out of the fifty copies of the Macmillan edition.

POSTSCRIPT

The "private" editions of Tennyson's writings fall into four distinct categories. (*a*) The privately circulated proofs, described by Mr. Wise as "trial books." (*b*) Pamphlets which were only technically published. (*c*) Pamphlets "printed for the author" or printed for private distribution. (*d*) The Canford Manor volumes, which form a group by themselves.

(*a*) It is known[1] that Tennyson was in the habit of having his poems set up in type before giving them their final revision. These proofs, or "trial books," with the exceptions of *The Cup and The Falcon*, 1882, and *The Promise of May*, 1883, have no title-pages.[2] With the exception of two examples of *The Lover's Tale*, 1868, all recorded survivors seem to derive from the poet's family, or Frederick Locker-Lampson, or Sir James Knowles.[3] Several, like *The Holy Grail*, 1869, and *Idylls of the King*, 1869, went through several trial versions or were even reset, and the pencilled instructions on the Knowles copies indicate that usually only four or six of each were printed. All these proofs differ materially in text from the published versions and show, as might be expected, little sign of careful production.

[1] Cf. e.g. *Memoir*, I. 179.

[2] *Morte d'Arthur* hardly counts as another exception, being a proved forgery.

[3] Sold at Sotheby's, April 30, 1928.

(*b*) It was necessary, in order to secure copyright, that poems contributed to American periodicals should be technically published in England. *Early Spring*, 1883, and *The Throstle*, 1889, are instances of this. Examination of the letter books and publication records of Messrs. Macmillan & Co. has shown that all the privately printed pamphlets which bear their imprint—the two mentioned above, *Carmen Sæculare*, 1887, and *The Silent Voices*, 1892—are perfectly genuine; and this need for technical publication might also account for *England and America*, Strahan, 1872, and *Child Songs*, Kegan Paul, 1880 (but see p. 379).

(*c*) The third group falls into two subdivisions. The first includes the "author's private editions" of *The Falcon*, 1879, *The Cup*, 1881, and *The Promise of May*, 1882, which have been discussed in detail above. All these exhibit a text remarkably similar to the finally published form, and present a careful and well-printed appearance in marked contrast to the proofs of group (*a*); while their imprints, "Printed for the Author" and the number of surviving copies seem altogether foreign to Tennyson's attitude towards his work in its pre-publication state.

The second subdivision includes *Carmen Sæculare*, 1887, "Printed for Private Distribution," *To H.R.H. Princess Beatrice*, 1885 (two editions), *Ode on the Opening of the Colonial and Indian Exhibition*, 1886, and *On the Death of the Duke of Clarence and Avondale* [1892]. The first of these has been discussed above. The first edition of the second is undoubtedly genuine, being attested, for instance, by Tennyson's presentation copy to Palgrave, now in the British Museum. The others, however, having been present among the books sold by Mr. Gorfin on commission for Mr. Wise, invite examination.

We have been unable to find a copy of the second edition of *To H.R.H. Princess Beatrice*, 1885, of which Mr. Wise states[1] that "fifty copies only were struck off . . . immediately after the first edition [100 copies] . . . and printed from the same type."

Ode on the Opening of the Colonial and Indian Exhibition, 1886.

Unknown to Shepherd or Livingston. Wise, I. 274–5: "Issued (on Tuesday, May 4th, 1886) as a single half sheet, folded in two. The leaves measure $10\frac{7}{8} \times 8\frac{5}{8}$ inches. This handsome *brochure* was produced solely for official purposes, or for the use of the Court, at the Opening Ceremony of the Exhibition, and is now of extremest rarity, very few copies having apparently been printed, and fewer still preserved. As much as £40 has been paid for a fine copy in original state" (1908). Mr. Gorfin purchased "about five copies" from Mr. Wise in 1910 (exact details not available). There are copies in the British Museum (C.58.g.8, presented by Mr. Wise on October 10, 1903), in the Cambridge University Library (Syn. 4.91.58[7], presented by Mr. Wise in 1916), in the Ashley Library (VII. 153) and in the Wrenn Library (V. 44).

The pamphlet, which bears the imprint of William Clowes & Son on the title-page, is printed on a cream wove paper; the text being set in a Pica old style identical with that used for *Some College Memories*, 1886, at least a piracy, and *The Sailor Boy*, 1861, a proved forgery. The first two lines of the title-page are set in the same display fount as that used for the heading to the opening of the text of *Some College Memories*, 1886, and for the half-title of the Shelley Society *Rosalind and Helen*, printed by Clay in 1887.

[1] *Bibliography*, I. 270.

These facts are hardly sufficient to brand the *Ode* as highly suspicious, but they do little to remove the uneasiness engendered by its presence in the cache. A copy fetched $205 at the Walpole Galleries in 1917 (February 16, lot 263).

The Death of the Duke of Clarence and Avondale [1892].

Unknown to Shepherd or Livingston. Wise, I. 285–6: "This slight *brochure* [2 leaves, the last three pages blank] was printed solely for private distribution, and has now become of extraordinary rarity." Copies were sold by Mr. Gorfin on commission for Mr. Wise. There are copies in the British Museum (C.58.f.16, presented by Mr. Wise on February 9, 1908), in the Cambridge University Library (Syn. 4.91.58[9], presented by Mr. Wise in 1916), in the Ashley Library (VII. 156–7, described as having come from Mr. Hutt of Macmillans[1]), and in the Wrenn Library (V. 46).

The pamphlet has no imprint. It is printed on a cream wove paper, in a Small Pica old style (D in our schedule) identical with that used for *The National Gallery*, *The Nature and Authority of Miracle*, and *Dead Love*, all proved forgeries.

The evidence is not full enough for more than a tentative verdict, but such facts about the pamphlet as we have been able to assemble seem to make its authenticity distinctly dubious. The Buxton Forman copy fetched $135 in 1920 (lot 1091).

[1] There is no trace of the pamphlet in the Macmillan records.

W. M. Thackeray

AN INTERESTING EVENT

An Interesting Event. / By / M. A. Titmarsh. / London: / David Bogue, 86 Fleet Street; / [*rule*] / 1849.

Small 8vo, plain pink wrappers, uncut.

There is no publisher's imprint. The printer's imprint at the foot of p. 16 is "London: George Barclay, Castle Street, Leicester Square." Set up in a Long Primer old style. Printed on cream wove paper.

Originally appeared in *The Keepsake* for 1849, pp. 207–215.

This pamphlet is not mentioned in C. P. Johnson's *Hints to Collectors . . . of Thackeray*, 1885, or in the last edition of R. H. Shepherd's Bibliography, which was appended to his edition of Thackeray's *Sultan Stork and other stories*, 1887, although its appearance in *The Keepsake* is there noted.

It was first mentioned in a letter from C. P. Johnson to the *Athenæum*, no. 3270, June 28, 1890. After stating that he had never before heard of the pamphlet, "which has just come into my possession," and that it appeared to be in Thackeray's style, he proceeds, "How could it profit anybody to forge it? This copy was bought on a bookstall for a trifle three or four years ago, [it should be noted that he does not say that he himself bought it off a bookstall for a trifle] and I have never heard of another. . . . It may be a unique copy of a contemplated production." In the next number of *The Athenæum* he and another correspondent write to point out where the story originally appeared.

Slater (1894), p. 334: "One of the rarest of Thackeray's separate pieces is entitled 'An Interesting Event'; only one copy with the wrappers is known, but examples without have been sold on several occasions. On one occasion £21 was paid for a copy in this condition." *Grolier Club Catalogue* (1912), pp. 28–29. Henry S. Van Duzer, *A Thackeray Library* (1919), no. 94, p. 60.

No copy in the British Museum, the Bodleian Library, or the Cambridge University Library. Ashley VII. 168 (this and *A Leaf out of a Sketch-Book* are the only early editions of Thackeray in that catalogue). Wrenn V. 64. Viscount Esher's copy has inserted at the end a letter from Otto P. Rubeck (see p. 145) dated from 315 Brixton Road, London, S.W., on December 8, 1892, offering that copy to Messrs. B. F. Stevens and Brown. The price has been erased from the letter, but it was probably considerable, as he is at pains to state that it is one of only two known extant copies, and he encloses cuttings of the letters in the *Athenæum*.

The first sale by auction that we can trace was lot 1859 at Sotheby's on February 27, 1899, and it did not occur again in England until 1912 (lot 204, Sotheby's May 9). In America the copy in the Lapham Sale (New York, Dec. 1908, lot 1393) fetched $121; and that in the Hinckley sale (New York, Feb. 1912, lot 885) $95. There have been ten auction sales since 1918, and there was a copy in a bundle in the Smart sale at Hodgson's on July 27, 1933. Of the thirteen copies sold, the condition of one was not given, three were in modern morocco bindings and the remaining nine were in original state, though without the wrappers. Indeed none of the copies in mint state that we have examined showed any trace of ever having had wrappers. No inscribed copies have been recorded. The price in 1899 was £7 10*s*., which rose in 1912 to £10 10*s*. and has since remained between £9 10*s*. and £12. In America it has varied from $90 in the Buxton Forman sale in 1920 to $35 in 1929.

Mr. Gorfin bought "about four" copies from Mr. Wise, but he sold others for him on commission.

This pamphlet is printed in the same Long Primer old style (C) that is used for two other forgeries and seven suspects. The use of a non-Caslon old style type at this date is an anachronism by at least three years.

The analysis of the paper shows that it is almost

entirely composed of esparto, which was not introduced into the manufacture of paper until 1861, twelve years later than the alleged date of this pamphlet.

Conclusion.—The evidence of the paper and the type clearly prove it a forgery. It resembles Dickens's *To be Read at Dusk*, 1852 (see p. 185) in its selection and the method in which it was established on the market.

A LEAF OUT OF A SKETCH-BOOK

A / Leaf out of a / Sketch-Book. / By William Makepeace Thackeray. / [*Vignette*] / London : / Emily Faithfull & Co., Victoria Press. / 1861.

Small 8vo, green printed wrappers on which the setting of the title-page is exactly reproduced within an ornamental frame, below which is the statement "Only 25 Copies printed for the Author's Use." Edges trimmed.

Set in a Small Pica modern style. Printed on a cream wove paper. Two sketches by Thackeray occupy pp. [16] and [20].

This piece first appeared in *The Victoria Regia*, 1861, pp. 118–125.

This pamphlet does not appear in C. P. Johnson's *Hints to Collectors of . . . Thackeray*, 1885, or in the last edition of R. H. Shepherd's Bibliography which he appended to the edition which he published of Thackeray's early work under the title of *Sultan Stork and other stories*, 1887, although he notes the appearance in *The Victoria Regia*.

The first record of it that we can find is in a footnote to Mr. Wise's *Bibliography of Tennyson* (1908), I. 165, where he introduces an account of it with the words, "This little booklet is one of the very scarcest of Thackeray's separate pieces. . . ."

The *Grolier Club Catalogue* (1912), pp. 66, Henry S. Van Duzer, *A Thackeray Library* (1919), no. 114, p. 66.

The British Museum copy (C.58.b.29) was presented by Mr. T. J. Wise on July 8, 1899. No copies in the Bodleian Library or the Cambridge University Library. Ashley VII. 168, 169. Wrenn V. 58.

We have been able to trace eight sales of this pamphlet in the auction room : July 28, 1903, Sotheby's, lot 411, £45 10*s*.; November 1916, Anderson Galleries, New York, H. V. Jones sale, lot 542, $180; November 4, 1918, Sotheby's, lot 666, £30; December 17, 1919,

Sotheby's, lot 250, £25; November 29, 1920, Anderson Galleries, New York, J. L. Clawson sale, lot 502, $155; November 8, 1922, Hodgson's, lot 690, £21; February 17, 1926, American Art Galleries, New York, lot 570, $145; December 17, 1928, Sotheby's, lot 97, £27. All these copies were in their original printed wrappers, and had not been bound. None of them had any inscriptions.

Mr. Gorfin states that he sold about six copies on commission for Mr. Wise.

The vignette on the title-page is identical with that on the title-page of Tennyson's *The Sailor Boy*, which has been fully dealt with on pp. 75, 299. The two sketches drawn by Thackeray, however, present an analogous problem. When compared with the same drawings on pp. 124 and 125 of *The Victoria Regia*, a distinct loss of tone is noticeable on the more heavily shaded portions, particularly the faces of the nigger boys and the shadows behind them. Anyone at all familiar with process engraving knows that it is exactly in such places that it is difficult to avoid a coarsening and breaking of the lines of shading. A more detailed examination leaves little doubt that the illustrations in this pamphlet were not made from the original blocks, but from blocks photographically reproduced from the impressions in *The Victoria Regia* (see Plate IVa).

The pamphlet is printed in the same Small Pica modern style type (B in our schedule) that was used for five other forgeries and five suspects.

The paper is a mixture of rag and chemical wood; such a combination cannot be covered by the explanation possible for esparto and chemical wood. This paper must have been manufactured after 1874 and probably later than 1883.

Conclusion.—It was strange that with half of the twenty-five copies printed for the author's use still extant, none should show any signs of that use. But the evidence of the vignette and the illustrations is amply confirmed by the analysis of the paper; and there can no longer be any doubt that the pamphlet is a forgery.

William Wordsworth

TO THE QUEEN

To / the Queen: / Dedicatory verses addressed / to Her Majesty with the / author's poems / by / William Wordsworth, / Poet Laureate. / Printed for the Author / by R. Branthwaite and Son, / Kendal, 1846.

Small 8vo, a single half-sheet folded in four, without wrappers or stitching. Half-title, title, and text on two leaves. Edges trimmed.

The printer's imprint on the title-page is repeated at the foot of the recto of the last leaf. The text of the poem is printed in Clay's Long Primer No. 3.

This poem was first printed in William Knight's *Life of Wordsworth*, Vol. III. p. 470, 1889; and acknowledgments are there made to Queen Victoria for permission to reproduce the poem from Wordsworth's autograph on the fly-leaf of the copy of his *Poems*, 1845, at Windsor Castle. The poem was not included in Prof. Knight's elaborate edition of Wordsworth's *Poems* in 8 vols., 1882–6, but occurs in Prof. Dowden's edition in 1893.

The pamphlet's appearance is not mentioned in the bibliographies by J. R. Tutin (appended to *The Complete Poetical Works of William Wordsworth*, 1888), by Prof. Dowden (Vol. VII of his edition of *The Poetical Works*, 1893) or by William Knight (*Poetical Works of Wordsworth*, revised edition, Vol. VIII, 1896).

Mr. T. J. Wise records it in his *Bibliography of Wordsworth* (1916), p. 167, with the following note:

"It was at one time believed that only two examples had survived. But a few years ago a tiny 'remainder' consisting of some half-dozen copies was unearthed, but even with these the pamphlet remains one of the most uncommon of the First Editions of Wordsworth."

No copies in the British Museum, the Bodleian Library or the Cambridge University Library. Ashley VIII. 33, with a facsimile. Wrenn V. 174.

The only copy to appear at auction was in the Library of H. Buxton Forman and was sold for $165 as lot 991 in his sale at the Anderson

Galleries, New York, in March, 1920. The only other copy that we can trace belonged to John Drinkwater in 1922 and is now in the library of Viscount Esher.

Mr. Gorfin bought no copies of this pamphlet, nor can he recall having sold any on commission.

It is the only pamphlet in the series printed on a pure rag paper, which is the normal content for a paper of 1846.

The text, however, is printed in Clay's Long Primer No. 3, with the broken-backed 'f,' button-hook 'j' and the peculiar question mark. As these were not manufactured before 1880 the pamphlet is clearly a forgery. As the poem was not published until 1889, and the type was not in use after 1893, it follows that the pamphlet must have been manufactured between those dates.

—

Edmund Yates

MR. THACKERAY, MR. YATES AND THE GARRICK CLUB

Mr. Thackeray, Mr. Yates, / and / the Garrick Club. / The / correspondence and facts. / Stated by / Edmund Yates. / Printed for private circulation. / 1859.

8vo, no wrappers, edges trimmed.

The printer's imprint on the reverse of the title-page is: " London :/ Printed by Taylor and Greening, Graystoke Place, / Fetter Lane, Holborn." This is repeated in a slightly different form at the foot of p. 15. Set in Long Primer modern style. Printed on two different sorts of paper; variant X on a thick and rather rough cream wove; variant Y on a thin and coarse paper which foxes rapidly on exposure to the light.

There are at least three forms of the printing of this pamphlet apart from the differences in paper noted above. They were first put on record by Luther S. Livingston in *The Evening Post* (New York), March 31, 1906. Issue A has the name " Dickens " misspelt " Dickes " on p. 14, line 34; issue B has the name spelt correctly, but differs slightly in punctuation. C is a reprint, which has in italics below the imprint on p. 15: " Reprinted in facsimile. MDCCCXCV." It has the misprint, but follows the punctuation of B in some cases. The present pamphlet is probably identical with B.

The pamphlet has long been known to Dickens and Thackeray collectors. Slater (1894), p. 331, said that it was " worth about £10 by auction." Luther S. Livingston first distinguished the two issues in 1906, and that information was included in *The Catalogue of the Grolier Club Exhibition of the Works of W. M. Thackeray* (1912) under nos. 55, 55*a* and 55*b*, pp. 58–59. Henry S. Van Duzer, *A Thackeray Library* (1919), pp. 119–120. John C. Eckel, *The Bibliography of Charles Dickens* (1932), pp. 228–9.

The British Museum has A only. The Bodleian Library has C only. No copy in the Cambridge University Library. Ashley VIII. 47 [B ?]. Wrenn V. 59.

The auction record is obviously impossible to disentangle, but the early sales are sufficiently instructive to be noted:

1889, March 11, Sotheby's, lot 639, with relevant A. L. S. from Dickens to Thackeray, £40.
1895, Jan. 21, Sotheby's, the Library of the late Edmund Yates, lot 394, morocco, £6.
1895, Jan. 30, Sotheby's, lot 828, title torn, £4 10*s*.
1895, April 22, Sotheby's, lot 1161, undescribed, £4 4*s*.
1897, June 14, Puttick's, lot 263, the library of a collector (who had many of the other forgeries), £4 10*s*.
1897, July 19, Sotheby's, lot 5, half calf in a volume with other pamphlets, £4 4*s*.

The second sale here is probably issue A, and the fifth probably the present pamphlet, while the first, third and fourth are more likely to have been A; but it is impossible to be certain, and further records are still less helpful.

Mr. Gorfin bought fifteen copies of the present pamphlet from Mr. Wise for £3 15*s*. on April 12, 1910.

The paper of issue X is a mixture of chemical wood and rag; that of issue Y a mixture of chemical and mechanical wood. Neither combination is possible before 1874, or likely before 1883. So that the paper of both issues was manufactured at least fifteen years later than its alleged date of publication.

The type used in the present pamphlet is Clay's Long Primer No. 3, which was used for printing the Reading *Sonnets* and fourteen other of these forgeries.

Conclusion.—The present pamphlet is obviously a type facsimile of issue A, the authenticity of which is plentifully attested. We cannot say whether Livingston's issue B was contemporary with A or identical with the one here examined: but both type and paper prove the two variants of this pamphlet forgeries of later date, possibly inspired by the high price realised in 1889.

Appendix I

Census of Copies of The Reading *Sonnets*

NOTE

Reference is made to three previous censuses:—

1910. A tentative list made out by Harry Elkins Widener, communicated to us by Mrs. Livingston.

1920. A list included in the catalogue note to the W. T. Wallace copy, sold at the American Art Galleries, March 22, lot 103.

1921. A list given by de Ricci in his *Book Collector's Guide*.

GROUP I

Present or recent location known.

1. C. C. Auchincloss. New York.

   Red levant, g.t. uncut, by Rivière.

   W. T. Wallace copy (with bookplate); afterwards Carl Pforzheimer.

2. The Folsom copy (sold in New York, December, 1932).

   Morocco, g.t. uncut, by Rivière.

   Holden sale, 1920: bought by Holden from Mr. Gorfin.

3. The Chapin Library, Williams College, Massachusetts.

   Citron morocco, g.t. uncut, by Rivière.

   Clement Shorter copy: bought by Alfred C. Chapin from a New York dealer in 1915.

4. W. A. Clark. Pasadena.

   Blue levant, uncut, by Rivière.

   W. K. Bixby copy (with bookplate).

5. W. T. H. Howe. New York.

   Unstitched, uncut.

6. Mrs. Sherman Hoyt. New York.

   Red levant, g.t. uncut, by Rivière.

   George D. Smith sale, 1921.

7. Huntington Library, San Marino, California.
   Brown levant, uncut, by Zaehnsdorf.
   Purchased in 1915 from F. R. Halsey, who bought it from Messrs. Dodd, Mead in 1899.

8. Amy Lowell Collection at Harvard University, Cambridge, Mass.
   Stitched, uncut.

9. Morgan Library, New York.
   Blue levant, uncut, by Rivière.
   Van Antwerp copy (sale 1907): bought by Mr. Van Antwerp from Dodd, Mead between 1904 and 1906.

10. A. Van Sinderen. New York.
    Crimson morocco, by Rivière.

11. The late J. A. Spoor.
    Condition unknown. Now in vaults in Chicago.
    In his possession before 1910 (Widener census).

12. The late S. S. Terry.
    Brown morocco, uncut, by Rivière.
    Bought at auction in 1926 (Anderson Galleries, May 5, lot 10), consigned by a New York dealer. Now in storage.

13. Wellesley College, Massachusetts.
    Blue morocco, uncut, by the Club Bindery.
    The Axon–Arnold–Palmer copy (see above, p. 22).

14. Widener Collection, at Harvard University, Cambridge, Mass.

Morocco, uncut.

The Lapham copy (sold in 1908); bought by Lapham from Mr. Gorfin.

15. Thomas J. Wise. London.

Levant, g.t. uncut, by Rivière, rebound from "old half calf."

Purchased from Dr. Bennett in 1886.

16. Thomas J. Wise. London.

Stitched, uncut.

Purchased from Dr. Bennett in 1886.

17. J. H. Wrenn Library, Austin, Texas.

Morocco, uncut, by Rivière.

"Provenance unknown, save that it came to Mr. Wrenn from Mrs. Dykes Campbell, through Mr. T. J. Wise." (The Librarian.)

This copy was in Mr. Wrenn's possession before 1910 (Widener census): wrongly described by de Ricci as the Lapham copy.

GROUP II

Present location unknown.

18. The William W. Allis copy.

Morocco, uncut, by Zaehnsdorf.

This was sold at the Anderson Galleries, March 25, 1912 (lot 126).

19. The Mrs. R. W. Bliss copy.

Condition unknown.

Widener census, 1910: Wallace census, 1920.

20. The Stopford Brooke copy.
    Condition unknown.
    Purchased from Bennett, 1886 (Wise): sold to a London bookseller (Wise).

21. The Butcher copy.
    Condition unknown.
    Widener census, 1910: Wallace census, 1920 (misprinted B*a*tcher).

22. The Edward K. Butler copy.
    Morocco, uncut, by Rivière.
    Sold at the American Art Association, April 10, 1922 (lot 21).

23. The H. T. Butler copy.
    Condition unknown.
    Widener census, 1910.

24. The John Caldwell copy.
    Condition unknown.
    Wallace census, 1920.

25. The John L. Clawson copy.
    Stitched, uncut, traces of wrappers.
    Clawson sale, 1920; afterwards W. van R. Whitall (sale Feb. 14, 1927, American Art Association). Possibly now Lowell–Harvard (No. 8)?

26. The Denham–Dix–Wallis copy.
    Condition unknown.
    Wallace census, 1920.

27. The Buxton Forman copy.

Morocco, g.t. uncut, by Rivière.

Bought from Bennett in 1886 (Wise): Widener census, 1910: Wallace census, 1920; sold Anderson Galleries, March 15, 1920: bought then by William Campbell of Philadelphia: present location unknown.

28. The Edmund Gosse copy.

Condition unknown.

Bought from Bennett in 1886 (Wise): "Some years afterwards sold for £50. It went, I believe, to Charles B. Foote, of New York" (Wise). This was not in the Foote sale (1895), though there were many other Browning items.

29. The Brayton Ives copy.

Sewn, uncut, wrappers of a later period.

Bought by George D. Smith at the Ives sale in 1915. Possibly identical with No. 6?

30. The Lockhouse copy.

Morocco extra, uncut.

Bought by Lockhouse at Sotheby's (miscellaneous sale), March 21, 1905.

31. The MacGeorge copy.

Red morocco by Rivière.

Bought by Messrs. Quaritch at the MacGeorge sale in 1924: sold by them in 1926 to Messrs. Stevens and Brown, who are unable to trace the subsequent purchaser's name.

32. The John Morgan copy.

Red morocco, g.t. by Rivière.

Bought from Bennett in 1886 (Wise): sold in New York, April, 1902: sold at the American Art Association, Feb. 19, 1930 (lot 20), in a miscellaneous sale, for the highest recorded price, $1250.

33. The P. M. Pittar copy.

Morocco extra, by Rivière.

Sold at Sotheby's, Nov. 4, 1918 (lot 116): bought by Messrs. Stevens & Brown, who are unable to trace subsequent purchaser's name.

34. The Robert Alfred Potts copy.

Condition unknown.

Bought from Bennett in 1886 (Wise).

35. The Walter Brindley Slater copy.

Condition unknown.

Bought from Bennett in 1886 (Wise): Widener census, 1910: Wallace census, 1920.

36. The W. A. White copy.

Condition unknown.

Widener census, 1910: Wallace census, 1920: de Ricci census, 1921. The book is not in the card catalogue of the library, and Mr. White's executors suggest that he may have sold it some time before he died.

Appendix II

Mr. Gorfin's Purchases

MR. GORFIN'S PURCHASES

THIS appendix records two series of transactions; first, those purchases from Mr. Wise which Mr. Gorfin made for his stock when he was preparing to set up as a bookseller, and secondly some of the sales made by Mr. Gorfin as an agent for Mr. Wise on a commission basis.

The first list is taken from a notebook of Mr. Gorfin's, but, as he has preserved the stubs of all his cheque books and noted thereon the details of each transaction, we have been able to verify a sufficient number of entries to give us complete confidence in the accuracy of the list as a whole. It is printed *litteratim*.

				£	s.
23 Nov.	1909	19 copies	Ode on the Proc. of French Republic [1]	5	0
7 Feb.	1910	2 copies	Gathered Songs [2]	9	0
		2 copies	Home Rule for Ireland [3]		
11 April	1910	13 copies	Siena [4]	5	0
		15 copies	Unpublished Verses [5]		15
		1 copy	Ruskin's Romance [6]	1	5
12 April	1910	15 copies	Thackeray, and the G. C.[7]	3	15
		A bundle	Turner Sketches [8]		10
		24 copies	An Appeal [9]	6	0
		16 copies	St. Brandan [10]	2	8
		36 copies	Nature and A. of Miracle [11]	1	7
		41 copies	National Gallery [12]	1	10

[1] The identification and references of all these pamphlets are given at the end of the list.

Date	Year	Quantity	Title	£	*s.*
13 April	1910	26 copies	Samuel Prout [13]	1	6
		4 copies	Adv. Ernest Alembert [14]	2	0
		4 copies	Self Communion [15]	1	10
		4 copies	E. B. B. and her Scarcer Books [16]	1	0
		8 copies	Hapless Love [17]	5	0
		13 copies	Leoni [18]	2	12
14 April	1910	20 copies	Lover's Tale [19] at 8*s.*		
		45 copies	Artist and Author [20] at 4½*d.*		
		7 copies	Queen's Gardens [21] for £5	19	17
		A bundle	of Shelley Soc. Publns.[22] for £6		
15 April	1910	29 copies	Geist's Grave [23] at 5*s.*		
		10 copies	Scarcer Books [16] at 4*s.*		
		11 copies	Religious Opinions [24] at 4*s.*	17	0
		11 copies	Ernest Alembert [14] at 9*s.*		
		6 copies	Ruskin and Maurice [25] at 2*s.*		
18 April	1910	2 copies	Gold Hair [26]	2	0
		2 copies	Statue and Bust [27]	2	0
		2 copies	Cleon [28]	2	0
		27 copies	Thermal Influence [29]	6	15
		14 copies	Geist's Grave [23]	3	10
20 April	1910	12 copies	Cleon [28]	12	0
21 April	1910	16 copies	Sir Galahad [30]	7	10
		A bundle	Pauline reprint [31]	2	0
22 April	1910	16 copies	Statue and Bust [27]	16	0
		1 copy	Lover's Tale [19]		8
26 April	1910	17 copies	Gold Hair [26]	17	0
		1 copy	Lucretius [32]		15
		3 copies	Ticonderoga [33]	2	5
29 April	1910	5 copies	Some College Memories [34]	2	10
2 May	1910	2 copies	To be Read at Dusk [35] at 30*s.*	6	10
		2 copies	Some College Memories,[34] etc.		
14 May	1910	14 copies	Scythian Guest [36] at 21*s.*		
		14 copies	Dusk [35] at 30*s.*	35	14
21 May	1910	12 copies	Dusk [35]	18	0
11 August	1910	21 copies	Dusk [35]	20	0
15 August	1910	1 copy	Sister Helen [37]	3	0
		1 copy	Verses [38]	1	10
24 August	1910	20 copies	Story of a Lie [39]	20	0
27 April	1911	2 copies	Gathered Songs [2]		
		1 copy	Ballad Bulgaric [40]	9	0
		1 copy	Robert Burns [41]		
6 March	1912	2 copies	Ballad Bulgarie [40]	6	0
		1 copy	Sequence Sonnets [42]	4	0
15 March	1912	19 copies	Agatha [43]	15	0

Date	Year	Copies	Title	£	s.
30 April	1912	2 copies	Scythian Guest [36]	2	0
		1 copy	Sir Galahad [30]		10
		2 copies	Lover's Tale [19]		16
		1 copy	Samuel Prout [13]		1
		1 copy	Story of a Lie [39]	1	0
		1 copy	Brother and Sister [44]		18
		1 copy	Leoni [18]		4
		1 copy	Dusk [35]	1	10
10 May	1912	30 copies	White Man's Burden [45]	8	10
		57 copies	White Horses [46]		
Undated but	1910	23 copies	Brother and Sister [44]	20	0

[1] A. C. Swinburne, *Ode on the Proclamation of the French Republic*, 1870. This is perfectly genuine, and there is another and larger "remainder" still in existence.

[2] A. C. Swinburne, *Gathered Songs*, Ottley, Landon & Co., 1887. The imprint was an alias of R. H. Shepherd, but there is no reason to doubt the authenticity of the date. See above, p. 289.

[3] Matthew Arnold, *On Home Rule for Ireland*, 1891. This was edited by T. B. Smart, who was a friend of Mr. Wise. See above, p. 129.

[4] A. C. Swinburne, *Siena*, 1868. There can be no doubt that all these thirteen copies were of the forged reproduction of the original edition. See above, pp. 287–9.

[5] A. C. Swinburne, *Unpublished Verses* (1866). This is a quarter sheet folded once to make two octavo leaves. It has neither date nor imprint; and the verses are really part of a poem that was published in *Poems and Ballads*, 1866. Mr. Wise (*Bibliography of Swinburne*, I, 133, 134) attributes its production to R. H. Shepherd and dates it March, 1888 (but cf. *Literary Anecdotes*, II, 343, 344; and *The Athenæum*, March 11, 1911).

[6] *Ruskin's Romance*, 1889. This account of Ruskin's marriage purports to have been reprinted from a New England newspaper. It was described as a fictitious account by Mr. Wise in his *Bibliography of Ruskin* in 1892. Its origin has not been explained.

[7] Edmund Yates, *Mr. Thackeray, Mr. Yates and the Garrick Club*, 1859. Undoubtedly a forgery. See pp. 359–60. These fifteen copies appear to have included both states, X and Y.

[8] John Ruskin, *Catalogue of the Turner Sketches in the National Gallery, Part I*, 1857. Edition B. Undoubtedly a forgery. See pp. 230–1.

[9] A. C. Swinburne, *An Appeal to England against the Execution of the Condemned Fenians*, Manchester, 1867. The status of this pamphlet is doubtful. See pp. 291–2.

[10] Matthew Arnold, *St. Brandan*, 1867. This pamphlet is highly suspicious. See pp. 161–2.

[11] John Ruskin, *The Nature and Authority of Miracle*, 1873. This is another highly suspicious pamphlet. See pp. 242–3.

[12] John Ruskin, *The National Gallery*, 1852. This pamphlet is a forgery. See pp. 227–9.

[13] John Ruskin, *Samuel Prout*, Oxford, 1870. The status of this is doubtful. See pp. 240–1.

[14] Charlotte Brontë, *The Adventures of Ernest Alembert*, 1896. This was included in the second volume of *Literary Anecdotes of the Nineteenth Century*. Separate offprints were circulated privately by Mr. Wise.

[15] Anne Brontë, *Self Communion*, 1900. This poem was privately printed for Mr. Wise.

[16] Harry Buxton Forman, *Elizabeth Barrett Browning and her Scarcer Books*, 1896. Issued in the same way as No. 14.

[17] William Morris, *The Two Sides of the River, Hapless Love and the First Foray of Aristomenes*, 1876. The status of this pamphlet is doubtful. See p. 211.

[18] John Ruskin, *Leoni*, 1868. This is a forgery. See pp. 236–7.

[19] Lord Tennyson, *The Lover's Tale*, 1870. According to Mr. Wise this is R. H. Shepherd's first pirated edition. Actually it is a forgery of that edition, and it is very unlikely that Shepherd had anything to do with it. See pp. 307–12.

[20] George Cruikshank, *The Artist and the Author*, 1872. This pamphlet is perfectly genuine. It is the cheapest in the list.

[21] John Ruskin, *The Queen's Gardens*, Manchester, 1864. This is a forgery. See pp. 232–5.

[22] Mr. T. J. Wise was Secretary of the Shelley Society (see p. 65 *n.*). He subsequently returned the six pounds, but allowed Mr. Gorfin to retain the books.

[23] Matthew Arnold, *Geist's Grave*, 1881. The status of this pamphlet is suspect. See pp. 163–4.

[24] *The Religious Opinions of Elizabeth Barrett Browning*, 1896. This was published in *Literary Anecdotes of the Nineteenth Century*, Vol. II, 1896. Separate offprints were also circulated privately by Mr. Wise.

[25] *John Ruskin and F. D. Maurice on "Notes on the Construction of Sheepfolds,"* 1896. The procedure in this case was the same as in No. 24.

[26] Robert Browning, *Gold Hair, A Legend of Pornic*, 1864. The status of this pamphlet is doubtful. See pp. 181–2.

[27] Robert Browning, *The Statue and the Bust*, 1855. This is a forgery. See pp. 179–80.

[28] Robert Browning, *Cleon*, 1855. This is a forgery. See pp. 177–8.

29 R. L. Stevenson, *On the Thermal Influence of Forests*, Edinburgh, 1873. The first edition according to Prideaux. This is a forgery See pp. 247–50.

30 William Morris, *Sir Galahad*, 1858. The first issue according to H. Buxton Forman. This is a forgery. See pp. 207–10.

31 This type facsimile reprint of the first edition of Robert Browning's *Pauline*, 1833, was edited by Mr. Wise for the Browning Society in 1886.

32 Lord Tennyson, *Lucretius*, Cambridge, U.S.A., 1868. This is a forgery. See pp. 305–6.

33 R. L. Stevenson, *Ticonderoga*, Edinburgh, 1887. This pamphlet is perfectly genuine. There is some reason to believe that Mr. Wise was closely connected with those who were responsible for its production. See p. 266.

34 R. L. Stevenson, *Some College Memories*, Edinburgh, 1887. There can be little doubt that this is a fraudulent reprint of an essay that appeared in volume form. See pp. 254–65.

35 Charles Dickens, *To be Read at Dusk*, 1852. This is a forgery. See pp. 185–7.

36 John Ruskin, *The Scythian Guest*, 1849. This is a forgery. See pp. 225–6.

37 Dante Gabriel Rossetti, *Sister Helen*, 1857. This is a forgery. See pp. 215–17.

38 Dante Gabriel Rossetti, *Verses*, 1881. Whether this pamphlet is falsely dated or not, it appears to have been unauthorised. See pp. 218–21.

39 R. L. Stevenson, *The Story of a Lie*, 1882. The status of this pamphlet is very suspicious. See pp. 251–3.

40 A. C. Swinburne, *The Ballad of Bulgarie*, 1893. This was privately printed for Mr. Wise without Swinburne's consent (Wise, *Bibliography of Swinburne*, I. 450).

41 A. C. Swinburne, *Robert Burns*, 1896. This was privately printed for the London Burns Club, of which Mr. Wise was a member.

42 A. C. Swinburne, *A Sequence of Sonnets on the Death of Robert Browning*, 1891. This was printed for Buxton Forman with Swinburne's consent. After Forman's death in 1919 Mr. Gorfin bought from his widow twelve copies of this pamphlet at 36*s*. each.

43 George Eliot, *Agatha*, 1869. The second edition. Its status is a matter of considerable suspicion. See pp. 194–7.

44 George Eliot, *Brother and Sister*, 1869. This is a forgery. See pp. 191–3.

45 Rudyard Kipling, *The White Man's Burden*, 1899. This is correctly dated, but it is proved to be a piracy. See pp. 203–4.

46 Rudyard Kipling, *White Horses*, 1897. This also is correctly dated, but a proved piracy. See pp. 201–2.

This is not a complete list of Mr. Gorfin's purchases from Mr. Wise in these years, but it is the best that he was able give us. He gave us from memory a further list of pamphlets bought for stock, and it is partially confirmed by their occurrence in his catalogues from 1912 to 1932 and by the fact that he still had a quantity of some of them left in 1933.

Mrs. Browning	The Runaway Slave	about 10 copies
D. G. Rossetti	Sister Helen	quantity doubtful
John Ruskin	The Future of England	about 30–40 copies
R. L. Stevenson	Thomas Stevenson	about 6 copies
A. C. Swinburne	Dead Love	about 20 copies
A. C. Swinburne	Laus Veneris	about 15 copies
A. C. Swinburne	Cleopatra	about 6 copies
A. C. Swinburne	Dolores	about 20 copies
Lord Tennyson	Ode for the Opening of the International Exhibition, 1862	1 copy only
Lord Tennyson	The Last Tournament	1 copy only
Lord Tennyson	Ode on the Opening of the Colonial and Indian Exhibition, 1886	about 5 copies
Lord Tennyson	Carmen Sæculare	about 6 copies
Lord Tennyson	Ode on the Death of the Duke of Clarence and Avondale.	quantity doubtful
W. M. Thackeray	An Interesting Event	about 4 copies

In addition to these purchases for his own stock, Mr. Gorfin sold many additional copies of some of the pamphlets here listed as an agent on commission for Mr. Wise. A few further pamphlets which he only handled in this way are set out below.

Mrs. Browning	Sonnets
Lord Tennyson	The Sailor Boy
Lord Tennyson	A Welcome to Alexandrovna
Lord Tennyson	The Falcon
Lord Tennyson	The Cup
Lord Tennyson	The Promise of May
W. M. Thackeray	A Leaf out of a Sketch Book.

Now it is clear from the second and third lists which

we have just given, as well as from the list of Mr. Wise's donations to the Cambridge University Library in 1916, that the first list in this appendix does not exhaust either the range of titles or the number of copies in Mr. Wise's possession in 1910. Nevertheless, it is the most precise document that is available; and it raises an important question. What degree of suspicion attaches to a pamphlet merely from its presence in this list?

To consider this point we will divide the pamphlets in the list into four categories: (*a*) Pamphlets printed for, or under the supervision of Mr. Wise, some of which it would be natural for him to have left over. (*b*) Other genuine pamphlets. (*c*) Those pamphlets on which some suspicion already rests. (*d*) Proved forgeries.

(a) *Privately printed pamphlets.*

Nos. 14[1] (15 copies), 15 (4 copies), 16 (14 copies), 22 (a bundle), 24 (11 copies), 25 (6 copies), 31 (a bundle), 40 (3 copies) and 41 (one copy). This amounts to 52 copies and two bundles, of nine different pamphlets.

(b) *Other genuine pamphlets.*

Nos. 1 (19 copies), 2 (4 copies), 3 (2 copies), 5 (15 copies), 20 (45 copies), 33 (3 copies) and 42 (one copy). The totals of this group would have little significance if the numbers of 1, 5, and 20 did not show that genuine remainders were undoubtedly present in the lot. This group amounts to 89 copies of seven different pamphlets.

(c) *Suspicious pamphlets.*

Nos. 9 (24 copies), 10 (16 copies), 11 (36 copies),

[1] These numbers refer to the list on pp. 373–375.

13 (27 copies), 17 (8 copies), 23 (43 copies), 26 (19 copies), 38 (one copy), 39 (21 copies) and 43 (19 copies). The average number of copies of each pamphlet here is noticeably higher than that in the two preceding groups. Altogether there are 214 copies of ten different pamphlets.

(d) *Proved forgeries.*

Nos. 4 (13 copies), 7 (15 copies), 8 (a bundle), 12 (41 copies), 18 (14 copies), 19 (23 copies), 21 (7 copies), 27 (18 copies), 28 (14 copies), 29 (27 copies), 30 (17 copies), 32 (one copy), 34 (7 copies), 35 (50 copies), 36 (3 copies), 37 (one copy), 44 (24 copies), 45 (30 copies) and 46 (57 copies). This is by far the largest group. The average number present of each pamphlet conforms more to group *c* than to group *a* or *b*. The whole group amounts to 352 copies and one bundle, of nineteen different pamphlets.

The summary of these figures has been given already on p. 151, and the point which concerns us here is the numerical relationship between *c* and the other three groups. Of the nine pamphlets in groups *a* and *b*, of which there were more than half a dozen copies, seven have been satisfactorily explained. Of the twenty-five pamphlets in groups *c* and *d*, of which there were more than half a dozen copies, not one has any explanation for its presence here. Sixteen out of the twenty-five are forgeries, and there are independent points of suspicion against the remaining nine. Their appearance here in quantity suggests rather more than the possibility that they may have come from the same source as their forged fellows.

STOP-PRESS

THE library of the late H. T. Butler was sold at auction by Messrs. Hodgson & Co. on June 13–15 this year, and provided us at the last moment with an opportunity of examining for the first time three pamphlets already mentioned in the present work.

R. L. Stevenson's *Thomas Stevenson*, 1887 (see above, p. 265), has its text printed in the Small Pica modern style which we have scheduled as B on p. 67, and which was used for six proved forgeries and five other suspects. This materially increases the suspicion already aroused by the pamphlet's auction record.

Lord Tennyson's *England and America*, 1872 (see p. 341), has the first line of its title-page set in the same display type as that used for the first line of the title-page of the Shelley Society reprint of *Rosalind and Helen* (see p. 70); and the text is set in Miller and Richard's Long Primer old style which we have classified as C on p. 67. Three forgeries and seven other suspects are printed in this type; so that, although there is some reason for a separate printing of the poem, the present pamphlet must be regarded with suspicion if adequate authentication is not forthcoming.

Lord Tennyson's *Child Songs*, 1880 (see p. 341), has on the title-page the publisher's imprint of Kegan Paul, and at the foot of p. 8 the printer's imprint of Spottiswoode & Co. Its text type is Clay's Long Primer No. 3. We have already shown (p. 65) that this particular type, while not impossible at that date, was peculiar to R. Clay and Sons, and it therefore follows that the printer's imprint is false. *Child Songs*, then, with a false imprint and set up in the same type as that used for sixteen other forgeries, must also be a forgery.

On May 24 this year *The Times Literary Supplement* printed a long letter from Mr. T. J. Wise in which he touched lightly on some of the evidence that has already been considered at length in this book. But on one point his letter contained new information so important that we reprint his exact words:

> "I will now consider the theory of unauthorised printing. With whom could this have originated? One name must be cleared out of the way at once: a name which would never have been brought into the matter but for a mistake of my own. In the introduction to 'A Browning Library,' 1929, writing forty-three years after the event, I told the story of a visit to W. C. Bennett in 1886, and said that I acquired my two copies of the 1847 book from him; and earlier than this, in the first volume of my Ashley Library Catalogue, 1922, I said that my copies came to me from W. C. Bennett. What I actually brought away with me was his own sonnets, 'My Sonnets,' privately printed at Greenwich in 1843. The confusion of two such books may seem incredible, even after thirty-six years. It is to be explained by the subjects of our conversation: his friendship with Mary Russell Mitford, our common interest in the Brownings, Mrs. Browning's association with Miss Mitford and the presence among his poems of two sonnets, one on Robert and the other on E. B. Browning, and the mention of both of them in yet another sonnet. In size and outward appearance the two books are almost identical.
>
> "My two copies came to me not from W. C. Bennett but from Harry Buxton Forman. From whom did he obtain them? Neither I nor his son Mr. Maurice Buxton Forman can tell with any certainty, but how he may have obtained them I hope his son will be able to ascertain from an examination of his father's correspondence."

We have printed in full on pp. 15–16 and pp. 16–17 Mr. Wise's two earlier accounts of his discovery of the Bennett cache. In 1918 Mr. Wise wrote:

"Dr. W. C. Bennett, who had been Miss Mitford's intimate friend . . . disposed of some ten or twelve copies of the *Sonnets* which he had received from her hands. In one of these copies, evidently the one dedicated by Miss Mitford to her own use, was inserted a MS. of *Future and Past*. . . . This copy, with the MS. sonnet inserted, I purchased from Dr. Bennett; it is one of my most valued possessions."

In 1929 the account was more detailed and circumstantial; after describing his purchase of the two copies from Dr. Bennett, Mr. Wise continued:

"Shortly afterwards Dr. Bennett sold the remaining copies. They were bought by Harry Buxton Forman . . . and other friends *to whom I hurried the good news*.[1] Dr. Bennett received £10 for each. All were uncut and without wrappers, but traces of pale buff paper remained upon the spine of each,[2] and told that the wrappers had once been there. The reason why the wrappers had been removed could not be explained by Dr. Bennett, who assured us that the pamphlets were in this condition when they came to him from Miss Mitford's home at Three-Mile Cross, near Reading."

Are we now to understand that all this really refers to Dr. Bennett's *My Sonnets*, Greenwich, 1843?

[1] Our italics.
[2] There is independent confirmation of this. See p. 26.

INDEX

References to books are given under the names of their authors. References to the dossiers are distinguished by bolder type.